WOMEN, EMPLOYMENT AND THE FAMILY
IN THE INTERNATIONAL DIVISION OF LABOUR

In the series
Women in the Political Economy,
edited by Ronnie J. Steinberg

Women, Employment and the Family in the International Division of Labour

Edited by

SHARON STICHTER

Professor and Chair, Department of Sociology
University of Massachusetts at Boston

and

JANE L. PARPART

Associate Professor, Department of History
Dalhousie University, Halifax, Nova Scotia

TEMPLE UNIVERSITY PRESS
Philadelphia

Temple University Press, Philadelphia 19122
Published 1990

© Sharon Stichter and Jane L. Parpart 1990

Printed in Great Britain

Library of Congress Cataloging-in-Publication Data
Women, employment and the family in the international division of
labour/ edited by Sharon Stichter and Jane L. Parpart.
p.   cm.—(Women in the political economy)
Includes bibliographical references.
ISBN 0-87722-739-X
1. Women—Employment.   2. Work and family.   3. Sexual division of labor.
4. International division of labor.   I. Stichter, Sharon.
II. Parpart, Jane L.   III. Series.
HD6053.W6384   1990
306.3'615—dc20   90-31797
                                                              CIP

Contents

Acknowledgements

One incurs many debts in the production of a book of innovative essays. As editors we are particularly grateful to the contributors to this volume for their patience and creative work, and we want to acknowledge the intellectual stimulation and assistance we received from them and from a good many other researchers in this field with whom we have corresponded and exchanged ideas. Special thanks go to Timothy Shaw for his guidance and support throughout this unexpectedly protracted project. We also want to thank our secretaries, Anne Foxx at the University of Massachusetts and Evelyn Flynn at Dalhousie's Centre of African Studies.

List of Figures and Tables

Notes on the Contributors

Marnia Lazreg is Associate Professor of Womens Studies and Sociology at Hunter College, City University of New York. She is finishing a book on women and the contradictions of Islamic socialism in Algeria. She is interested in issues of feminist theory and epistomology, and has published and taught in the areas of women and development and women in the Middle East.

Jane L. Parpart is Associate Professor of History, Dalhousie University, Halifax, Nova Scotia. She is the author of *Labor and Capital on the African Copperbelt* (Temple University Press, 1984) and is the co-editor, with Sharon Stichter, of *Patriarchy and Class: African Women in the Home and the Workforce* (Westview Press, 1988). She is also co-editor, with Kathleen Staudt, of *Women and the State in Africa* (Lynne Rienner Publishers, 1988). She has written extensively on labour and women in Africa, including 'Sexuality and Power on the Zambian Copperbelt, 1926–64', in the Stichter and Parpart volume, and 'Women, Work and Collective Labour Action in Africa', in Roger Southall, (ed.) *Labour and Unions in Asia and Africa: Contemporary Issues* (Macmillan, 1988).

Jean L. Pyle is Assistant Professor of Economics at the University of Lowell, Massachusetts, where she specialises in labour economics, economic development and women in the economy. She has written several articles on the effect of state policies on women in the economy, examining the labour market impact of state-reinforced gender inequality in the household and the effect of discriminatory export-led development policies on the employment of women. Her current research is on the determinants of the female share of the labour force in Western Europe. Jean Pyle holds a PhD from the University of Massachusetts at Amherst and has taught at Smith College and Clark University.

Helen I. Safa is Professor of Anthropology and Director of the Center for Latin American Studies at the University of Florida. She co-edited with June Nash *Sex and Class in Latin America* (1976) and *Women and Change in Latin America* (Bergin and Garvey Publishers, 1985). She has written and edited numerous books and articles in Latin American Studies, including *The Urban Poor of Puerto Rico* (1974); *Migration and Urbanization: Models and Adaptive Strategies* (1975) (with B. DuToit); *Towards a Political Economy of Urbanization* (1976); 'Class Consciousness among Working Class Women in Latin America: A Case Study in Puerto Rico', in R. Cohen, P. Gutkind and P. Brazier (eds), *Peasants and Proletarians* (Monthly Review Press, 1979); and 'Runaway Shops and Female Employment: the Search for Cheap Labor', *Signs*, vol. 7, no. 2, pp. 418–33 (1981).

Constantina Safilios-Rothschild is a sociologist who has published widely in the field of family decision-making. She is currently a Consultant to the Population Council, New York. Her recent articles include 'Female Power, Autonomy and Demographic Change in the Third World', in R. Anker, M. Buvinic and N. Youssef (eds), *Women's Roles and Population Trends in the Third World* (Croom Helm, 1982); and 'Men's and Women's Incomes in Rural Honduras', in Daisy Dwyer and Judith Bruce (eds), *A Home Divided: Women and Income in the Third World* (Stanford University Press, 1989).

Janet W. Salaff is Professor, Department of Sociology, University of Toronto. She is the author of *Working Daughters of Hong Kong: Filial Piety or Power in the Family?* (ASA Monograph Series, Cambridge University Press, 1981); J. Salaff and Aline K. Wong, 'Chinese Women at Work: Work Commitment and Fertility in the Asian Setting', in S. Kupinsky (ed.), *The Fertility of Working Women: A Synthesis of International Research* (Praeger, 1977); J. Salaff and Aline K. Wong, *State and Family in Singapore: Structuring an Industrial Society* (Cornell University Press, forthcoming); M. Sheridan and J. Salaff (eds), *Lives: Chinese Working Women* (forthcoming) and other publications.

Alison MacEwen Scott is Lecturer in Sociology in the Department of Sociology, University of Essex, UK. She has done research in Argentina, Venezuela and Peru on urban and gender issues. Her recent publications include 'Economic Development and Urban Women's Work: the Case of Lima, Peru', in R. Anker and C. Hein (eds), *Sex Inequalities in Urban Employment in the Third World* (Macmillan, 1986); and 'Industrialization, Gender Segregation and Stratification Theory', in R. Crompton and M. Mann (eds), *Gender and Stratification* (Cambridge, 1986). She is shortly to publish a book entitled

Gender, Class and Underdevelopment: An Analysis Based on Peru (Routledge & Kegan Paul).

Ursula Sharma is a social anthropologist who has carried out research on both rural and urban women in North West India. She is the author of *Women, Work and Property in North West India* (Tavistock, 1980); *Women's Work, Class and the Urban Household: A Study of Shimla, North India* (Tavistock, 1986); and other writings on women in India. After obtaining her doctorate from the University of London she taught for two years at the Delhi School of Economics and is currently Senior Lecturer in Sociology and Social Anthropology at the University of Keele.

Sharon Stichter is Professor of Sociology at the University of Massachusetts at Boston. She is co-editor with Jane Parpart of *Patriarchy and Class: African Women in the Home and Workforce* (Westview Press, 1988), and, with M. Hay, of *African Women South of the Sahara* (Longman, 1984). Her other books include *Migrant Laborers*, African Society Today Series (Cambridge University Press, 1985), and *Migrant Labor in Kenya: Capitalism and African Response, 1895–1975* (Longman, 1982). She is presently working on a study of women, employment and the family in Kenya and her recent articles include 'Middle-Class Families in Kenya: Changes in Gender Relations', in the Stichter and Parpart volume, and 'Women and the Family: The Impact of Capitalist Development in Kenya', in M. Schatzberg (ed.), *The Political Economy of Kenya*, (Praeger, 1987).

Introduction

The participation of women in gainful employment has been increasing worldwide since the Second World War, though its distribution among nations has been uneven and its pace has varied according to cycles of the world economy. In industrial societies, particularly the United States, the rise in women's formal labour force participation has been recognised as one of the most profound social changes of the post-war decades. It has prompted extensive research into its causes and consequences, especially its impacts on women's family roles. Among social scientists in all disciplines, research into work-family linkages has assumed increasing interest.

In the Third World, too, the growth in women's paid labour force participation has been recognised as a major social trend, yet we know comparatively little about the impacts of such work on women's personal lives and their position in the household and family. There has been the presumption, for example, that paid employment will lead to a rise in women's status within and outside the household, and to a decrease in fertility, but the first relationship remains controversial, and more evidence is needed as to the conditions under which the second relationship does or does not hold. In addition, it is usually assumed that family demands, that is, women's productive and reproductive roles in the family, limit or condition women's labour force participation. Yet, the correlation of participation rates with age, marital and fertility status is quite variable, and it is precisely this variability which needs explanation and which calls attention to the need to incorporate the variations in family structure into such general formulations.

This book brings together a selection of important recent research on women and work-family linkages in all the major regions of the developing world. It seeks to indicate the importance and complexity of this area of inquiry, and to urge that more attention be paid to it in the development literature.

Much research on linkages between women's employment and the family has been conceived in terms of effects on family structure and women's family roles. Sociologists and demographers, for example, concentrate on the impact of employment on fertility. Historians examine the effect of industrialisation on family structures. Economists argue that wage levels for women workers are the main

1

determinant of women's labour force participation. A number of contributors to this volume, however, view aspects of household organisation, or survival strategies, or fertility levels, as themselves important determinants of the extent and timing of women's labour force participation. Indeed, if one views household and family ties as constituting functioning units of production and reproduction, to which women's labour is crucial, then it would be surprising if there were not systematic effects of women's family roles on their extra-familial employment roles. That household and kin demands for women's productive and reproductive labour tend to limit women's commitment to the formal labour force is an insight which is perhaps even more applicable to the Third World than it is to industrial societies. Yet the question of what weight to give the factors of patriarchal constraint versus those of capitalist demands or capitalist exclusion in explaining women's participation rates and wage levels is still very much unanswered.

In the introductory chapter, Sharon Stichter argues for the independent importance of the household in economic analyses of women's employment. To do so, she critically reviews approaches to conceptualising the household and proposes a detailed categorisation of household-level factors. As part of the argument, she provides a brief description of recent trends in women's employment in the Third World, summarises many of the findings for two-way linkages between households and employment, and indicates how formulations derived from studies of the western nuclear family need modification in the light of world-wide variations in household and kinship relations. Thus this chapter provides the intellectual background to the issues and debates played out in the country-level studies which follow.

In the second chapter, Helen Safa focuses on the impact of paid employment in export manufacturing on women's status in two Caribbean nations, Puerto Rico and the Dominican Republic. She also offers an explanation as to why women have been exploited as a cheap and vulnerable labour force, finding the answer in the enforced specialisation of women in biological reproduction in the home as industrial capitalism moved production largely outside the domestic unit. But even though the family may in this sense be the 'central site' of women's subordination, Safa argues that the labour market and the state are additional and independent sources.

Safa's studies show that in both Puerto Rico and the Dominican Republic family structure and gender ideology in the family are changing under the pressure of new wage-earning opportunities for women. The model of a nuclear family with a dependent wife and a male as the principal breadwinner no longer applies since both single and married women are making major contributions to family income. Surprisingly, the majority of women workers in Safa's samples in export manufacturing in both countries were married or were single heads of households, rather than young, single daughters as in the common pattern in the Far East.

Safa shows how the impact of employment on family decision-making and the division of household labour varies according to the family cycle and the family status of women workers. For example, among older married women in Puerto Rico, long-term employment leads to a greater sense of self-worth, and greater class consciousness, than is true for younger single women. For older women, a small change in the gender division of labour in the household is reported, but more important there was a marked shift in authority patterns, with wives sharing more in household decisions and husbands no longer considering their wives' work as a threat to their authority. Somewhat more patriarchal patterns persist in the Dominican Republic, though even here some renegotiation of husband/wife roles is taking place. The extent of change in women's situation depends a great deal on state policies and the role of unions; in the Dominican Republic lack of unionisation, very low wages, heavy industrial discipline and lack of social services for workers have undermined women's labour force and familial gains, whereas in Puerto Rico unions are more active and the state provides more benefits for workers.

Safa concludes that the effect of industrialisation on women in these cases is contradictory. On the one hand, subordination is reinforced through dead-end jobs, and unions, managers and the state remain resistant to change. On the other hand, traditional familial authority patterns are being challenged and more egalitarian family structures are emerging. This latter change is particularly important for women, since material and ideological pressures still lead women to choose ongoing relationships with a male provider, and women still say they work more for family survival than for personal autonomy.

In an approach somewhat different from Safa's, Janet Salaff employs the concept of family strategies. In this view, families are active, decision-making units which affect the characteristics of the female (and male) labour force. However, they act within the constraints imposed by world capitalism and state development policy, particularly in response to lack of alternative forms of social insurance. Implicit in this approach is Salaff's view, similar to Safa's for the Caribbean, that family goals remain more important for women in Hong Kong, Singapore and Taiwan than do individualistic goals of personal achievement.

Salaff demonstrates how three structural features of the Chinese family are responsible for the predominantly single-peaked age pattern of women's labour force participation in the 1970s and 1980s: the high dependency ratio, the family type, and the division of labour within the family. The effect of each of these factors changes over the family developmental cycle. First, high dependency ratios, the outcome of high post-war fertility, created an overwhelming need to earn money and provided only one means to do so, namely the wage employment of older children. Family fortunes varied directly with the number of members in the labour force. Second, the three concentric family units, the extended patriliny, the residential domestic unit, and the mother-centred uterine family exerted differing pressures on women. The patriliny generated expectations that the wife would drop out of the work force in order to bear sons for the husband's genealogical line, and also biased parents' investments in education toward sons, leaving daughters to constitute the low wage labour force. The often nuclear residential unit coped with sheer survival on a day to day basis; wives needed both to work and to reproduce so that the children could earn money. The uterine family was needed to ensure the mother's old age support; it also motivated daughters to continue supporting their mothers. Finally, the sex division of household labour is strongly maintained, often by elders. It specifies that young girls work for market wages as long as possible (sometimes even postponing marriage), but that after marriage and children, women's domestic work must increase. Women's market wage levels, for several reasons having to do with family, were not high enough, or seen by the family as high enough, to justify any neglect of their homemaking duties. As a result, the great majority of married women with children were forced out of the labour force. Those who did work faced major problems arranging their household tasks, relying heavily on kin and neighbourhood support systems. Thus reproductive responsibilities appear to be the main force depressing married women's labour force participation.

Salaff, like Safa, addresses the consequences of women's waged work. Women received a sense of satisfaction at meeting family obligations, and those who earned more money could achieve widened social contacts and increase individual consumption. But, unlike the Puerto Rican case, such work did not greatly enhance either the single or married women's decision-making role in the family. Nor did it lead to independence from family ties; rather it promoted the interests of the nuclear sub-unit within the extended family. Still, the material and emotional benefits of wage work increased as incomes went up, and as women increased in age.

While in the first two case studies women's labour force participation increased greatly as a result of export-led development, the fourth chapter offers a case in which such development did not lead to much increase. Jean Pyle asks why Irish women were not able to enhance their labour force participation substantially during the 1961–81 period of strong export-led development, when Ireland was experiencing the influx of many multinational corporations which had elsewhere hired women. She argues that in this case unequal gender relations in the household were important in constraining the labour market supply of women, but their efficacy depended on the fact that they were reinforced by strong state policies.

Pyle hypothesises two ways in which social relations in the household could negatively impact female labour supply, first through male dominance in decision-making and second through the constraints of high fertility, as Salaff suggests for East Asia. She finds convincing evidence to support both these relationships, but also attributes importance to a range of state policies which operated to support household patriarchy at a time when it was under considerable pressure. While Safa and Salaff both discuss the role of state policy in setting some key labour market parameters of women's labour force participation, Pyle stresses the state's role in family policy as well. Prohibitions on divorce, lack of protection against wife abuse, limitations on women's ownership rights in family property, and lack of access to contraceptives, in addition to a *de facto* bar against the employment of married women, all contributed to keeping Irish women's labour force participation among the lowest in the Western European OECD countries.

Jane Parpart agrees with Pyle and Salaff that household productive and especially reproductive work may reduce women's formal labour force participation. In the case of southern Nigeria, for example, one important factor is that child bearing has limited women's years of schooling. But Parpart's larger point is that in Nigeria women's employment outside the home has grown, yet has done so with no lessening of heavy domestic responsibilities. These duties limit upward career mobility for many women.

Parpart traces the historical development of educational and employment opportunities for women, drawing on new research to demonstrate that employed women in towns are increasingly experiencing the burdens of the 'double day'. Even in the years of cheap and available household helpers, who were often poor relations, wives still performed a large amount of domestic work, and since the oil boom in 1973 higher minimum wages, alternative employment opportunities, housing shortages and free education for rural children have all combined to reduce the supply of domestic workers and raise their price. The need for commercial day care is great, but it is still scarce and beyond the financial reach of the average urban household. Most working women juggle harried schedules and pressure other family members to take on some of the work, but there are few real solutions except the drastic ones of having fewer children or becoming single, separated or divorced in order to reduce time spent in husband-care.

The paper by Marnia Lazreg considers Algeria where, as in Pyle's case of Ireland, it is women's officially low labour force participation that needs to be explained. Lazreg sees the main causal factors as political-economic, demographic and familial; Islamic religion, she stresses, has much less to do with it than is usually imagined.

She points out first that the reorganisation of the economy along socialist lines between 1962 and 1978 did not result in any measurable increase in women's labour force participation — although all along formal statistics have underestimated women's productive contributions. Second, high population growth rates mean that women are investing a major part of their energies in the production of children, not because of Islamic religious injunctions but because of a deeply rooted pronatalist popular culture. For women, in particular, having children is a source of empowerment in the family in a situation in which there are few economic options outside it. Finally, lack of change in the sex division of labour in the family, plus state reinforcement of family patriarchal authority in the 1984 Family Code, also contributes to women's reluctance to accept outside employment.

Like Pyle, Lazreg sees two aspects of family as undercutting women's employment participation: the pressure to produce children, and women's subordinate position with respect to rights, labour, and decision-making. Lazreg also discusses the state, which in the Algerian political economy both ignores women's work by underestimating it, while at the same time benefiting from women's low-cost labour. Gender ideology, which assumes that the male takes economic responsibility for women, makes it possible for state planners to see their task as creating jobs for men. On the question of whether paid work is liberating for women, Lazreg, like Sharma and to some extent Parpart, believes that this is so only to the extent that women's burden of productive and reproductive labour in the household is lessened.

Like many of our contributors, Alison Scott argues for fuller consideration of family structures, both as a site of gender inequality and as a cause of sex inequality in the labour market. But she argues that in the case of Peru, where female employment is higher than in, say, Algeria, family ideology operates more through the demand for female labour than as a determinant of supply. For the urban popular classes in Peru, Scott stresses the contradiction and variety in the normative patterns of gender ideology, and the disjuncture between ideology and practice. She identifies two levels of contradiction in family ideology, one between the traditional Andean peasant pattern and the urban bourgeois *machista* pattern, the other within each of these two patterns. Thus, effects on women's labour force participation are not easily predicted.

In her sample of working women in Lima, Scott found no marked correlation between labour market participation and marital status, number of children, or stage in the family life cycle. However, other national samples including both working and non-working women do show such correlations. She suggests that in this context family patterns affect working women more directly through the demand side than through supply, that is, through the sex-typing of occupations which reflects the bourgeois gender ideology about women's appropriate roles. In the formal sector, family and gender ideology influences employer discrimination in hiring and promotion and in matching technology to people. In the informal sector, gender differences again appear less in rates of participation than in access to the means and skills of production and to markets. Here, however, family structure would seem to have a more direct impact, unmediated by decisions of employers. In both sectors, patriarchal values did not prevent women from being willing to work at a broad range of jobs, but their job choices were constrained by the limited range of options opened to them.

The chapter by Constantina Safilios-Rothschild focuses on the question of the effects of women's employment on their family status and approaches it in a way that differs from both Safa and Salaff. She pulls together evidence from Greece, Honduras and Kenya to support the argument that whether wives can translate earned income into family decision-making power depends on the class position and economic security of the husband. In general, except in situations of chronic and desperate poverty, the poorer the husband and the less able he is to guarantee family survival, the more likely he is to feel threatened by his wife's income, and to attempt to actively control it even while publicly belittling its importance. When, on the other hand, husbands have a stable and sufficient economic base, they allow their wives more autonomy and income control. These findings seem to apply whether the woman's income is from wages or from the profits of small enterprises or co-operatives.

For example, Safilios-Rothschild reports that wives in the Kikuyu District of Nyeri in Kenya have a higher degree of control over their income from export crops than do Luyia wives in Kakamega District. She interprets this as stemming from the Kikuyu men's higher levels of off-farm income, primarily from wages. The policy implication of these findings, Safilios-Rothschild suggests, is that only development interventions which increase both men's and women's incomes can be successful.

The last chapter, by Ursula Sharma, makes a point not mentioned by any of the other contributors, but which is nonetheless fundamental. She sounds a note of caution about conceptual efforts to distinguish and oppose the non-capitalist domestic sphere to the capitalist market, pointing out that proto-industrial capitalism in many rural areas often builds on and extends family relationships; kin relations in the domestic sphere are often co-opted by capital. Some of the resulting organisation forms, for example, outwork, remain very important even in advanced capitalist societies. In the South Asian context, she reminds us, there is a striking interpenetration of the social relations of gender in the public and the private spheres. Outwork and domestic handicraft work remain very important as sources of income for women; in addition both men and women, but particularly women, must use personal relationships to gain access to labour and product markets.

Looking at those women who do earn wages in the well-organised and relatively impersonal urban labour markets in India, Sharma, unlike Safa, Salaff and Safilios-Rothschild, is sceptical of the proposition that such work will enhance women's family or personal status. An individual's say in household decision-making, she thinks, is still determined by a very large number of different factors. Wage-earning may simply result, as Parpart suggests, in an increase in total labour burden. On the question of independence from the family, Sharma makes the same observation as Salaff for East Asia and Safa for the Caribbean, namely that most women still do not operate as if they had distinct individual interests separate from those of the household, but rather see their destinies as determined by the welfare of the group. This view is reinforced by public ideology, and means that most women say they work 'for their families' rather than 'for themselves'.

The nine papers in this volume elucidate some of the complex ways in which the household and the labour market are intertwined. Covering most major regions of the developing world, they include cases in which women's paid employment has grown rapidly due to export-led development, and cases where it has stagnated. Despite the great variations in national and international context, many of the authors suggest that household factors such as the sexual division of productive and reproductive labour, household structure, income levels, decision-making, and normative conceptions of family roles can all affect the labour market. Most writers also reaffirm that women's position in the labour market is currently affecting her position in the household, finding different effects in diverse cultural and economic contexts. As a group, the papers thus speak to the question of similarities in the position of all women, while also recognising differences. It remains to develop a comprehensive explanation for the many cross-national variations. Thus, these papers suggest both the necessity of further research in this field and the utility of the household perspective.

In a period in which women and development issues are increasingly on the political agenda, it is often simplistically assumed that women have been 'left out', and that the need is for women to be included in development plans and policies. The household perspective suggests, on the other hand, that women have always been integrated into national and global development strategies, but that they have been subordinated and exploited. The task ahead is therefore to raise women's status within the global political economy, and this cannot be accomplished without a recognition of the totality of women's productive and reproductive contributions, and an understanding of the interrelations between them.

1 Women, Employment and the Family: Current Debates

Sharon Stichter

Throughout the 1960s, 1970s and 1980s, the participation of women in gainful employment has grown dramatically, not only in the industrialised nations but also in many parts of the Third World, especially those areas that have experienced increasing investment by multinational manufacturing firms with gender-specific hiring policies. In industrial societies, particularly the United States, the rise in women's labour force participation has been recognised as a major new social trend. In the developing world, the growth in women's employment has been uneven, being most marked in newly industrialising areas with strong export-oriented manufacturing sectors such as Mexico, Brazil, the Caribbean, and East and Southeast Asia. But even in many poorer nations of Africa and Central America, women's labour force participation is increasing, even while their formal, paid employment, and their incomes from such employment, may be stagnating or declining. Between 1985 and 2000, the female labour force is expected to increase faster than the male labour force in the more industrialised parts of Latin America, and to grow at the same rate as the male in East Asia and less industrial Latin America. In Africa, however, the male labour force is expected to increase faster than the female (UNESCO, 1986, p. 13).

National variations in female labour supply, employment levels and employment patterns are influenced to a very great extent by the overall level of world and national development, by the sectoral composition of employment growth or the international division of labour, by commercial cycles in the global economy, and by other national and international demand-side factors. To what extent, however, might these marked variations also be affected by the sex division of productive and reproductive labour in the family? In what ways might household level factors such as fertility demands, sex role socialisation, and patriarchal controls affect women's relation to the labour market? Do they impact mainly on female labour supply, or

11

do they also affect employers' demand for labour?

This chapter will explore this complex question, arguing that household factors are both essential and interesting, and that they directly influence age patterns of participation, time spent in the labour force, earnings, and even aggregate employment levels. The first section will demonstrate the need for a focus on the household in economic analyses of women's employment. The second will critically review approaches to conceptualising the household. The third will propose a categorisation of household-level factors, and review evidence for the two-way linkages between these and female employment.

MARKET AND PRODUCTION FACTORS VERSUS HOUSEHOLD FACTORS IN WOMEN'S EMPLOYMENT

Levels of Employment

In virtually all societies, men have higher labour force participation rates than women, although in a few nations general female rates do approach those of men, notably in the USSR, Eastern Europe, and some Caribbean and African nations (Table 1.1). And, while variations in male labour force participation rates between nations, even between low and high income nations, are small, societal differences in female labour force participation rates are great (Table 1.1; Standing, 1982, 13ff). Similar observations may be made about rates of gainful employment (Table 1.2). Although both the male/female and the inter-country differences are doubtless affected by cultural practices as to the enumeration of women workers and the estimation of their work, it seems unlikely that these factors can account for all of the differentials. Nor can they account for the continuing gap between male and female average wages in most nations of the world (Table 1.3) and the marked segregation in occupations (Anker and Hein, 1986; House, 1986).

Despite the gender gap, female employment in the developing world has shown surprisingly rapid growth in recent years (Table 1.2), particularly in the industrial and service sectors. The overall proportion of women in the industrial labour force in developing countries rose from 21 per cent in 1960 to 26.5 per cent in 1980. (UNESCO, Table 2, p. 70; Joekes, 1987, p. 80). In particular areas growth was even more rapid: the female share of the paid labour force in Singapore, for example, rose from 17.5 per cent in 1957 to

TABLE 1.1   *Total economic activity rates*

	Men	Women	Year
Algeria	33.8	2.4	1983
Argentina	55.3	19.9	1985
Bangladesh	53.5	5.4	1983–84
Barbados	52.2	39.7	1983
Bolivia	48.7	14.6	1986
Botswana	38.1	36.0	1984–85
Brazil	56.6	27.9	1985
Chile	50.2	20.6	1986
China, People's Rep.	57.3	47.0	1982
Costa Rica	53.2	18.5	1985
Cuba	54.0	30.6	1986
Dominican Republic	48.1	19.7	1981
Egypt	49.8	12.5	1983
El Salvador	47.9	23.7	1980
Greece	51.4	27.3	1985
Guatemala	48.1	8.0	1985
Haiti	52.1	36.9	1983
Hong Kong	61.9	39.5	1986
Hungary	51.0	40.9	1987
India	52.7	19.8	1981
Indonesia	50.0	27.9	1985
Iran	47.1	7.2	1982
Ireland	51.7	21.7	1985
Jamaica	49.6	41.1	1985
Korea, South	46.8	30.6	1986
Malawi	52.4	51.7	1983
Malaysia	49.6	25.3	1980
Mauritius	55.8	19.4	1984
Mexico	48.2	18.2	1980
Morocco	47.1	11.6	1982
Nigeria	43.1	20.6	1983
Peru	49.4	34.4	1986
Senegal	55.3	39.1	1985
Singapore	59.8	35.2	1986
South Africa	46.2	22.8	1980
Syria	40.3	6.8	1984
Tanzania	44.4	45.2	1978
Thailand	55.9	50.1	1984
Tunisia	47.4	13.3	1984
United Kingdom	59.5	35.8	1981
United States	57.1	42.5	1986
Venezuela	49.0	18.9	1986
Zambia	46.0	17.4	1984
Zimbabwe	41.1	25.4	1980

SOURCE   International Labour Organisation, *Yearbook of Labour Statistics* 1986, Table I, pp. 13ff; 1987, Table I, pp. 14ff.

33.6 per cent in 1979 (Wong, 1981). And despite the oil price shocks and the world economic recession of the 1970s and early 1980s, of the 32 major developing nations for which data were available, 28 showed increases in the female share of gainful employment between 1977 and the mid-1980s (Table 1.2).

Variations in female employment levels and patterns are affected by complex combinations of economic variables. Recent trends illustrate the effects of two broad categories of factors: firstly, changes in the organisation of production, that is, the growth of the industrial and service sectors and the impact of technological change in industry; and secondly changes in market conditions, particularly in product markets, but also in the availability of male labour. Examination of each of these factors uncovers points at which 'extra-economic' variables must be brought into the analysis.

Between 1960 and 1980, the decline in the number of workers in agriculture and the growth in importance of the industrial and service sectors was a broad sectoral change which had greater impact on women than on men. In these two decades, considering all developing countries as a whole, the total male labour force in agriculture dropped by 12.6 percentage points, but the total female labour force in agriculture dropped by 15.3 points. The percentage of the female labour force in industry doubled — from 8.2 per cent to 16.3 per cent — whereas that of the male labour force rose only from 15.1 per cent to 21.6 per cent. The percentage of the female labour force in services also rose faster than did the male. Sectoral changes affected both men and women, but the change was greater for women. (UNESCO, pp. 72–73, Table 3).

An important reason for the increase in industrial employment in parts of the developing world has been the relocation of industrial production from developed to Third World countries, from whence the goods are re-exported back to developed nations. Relocation first took place in industries of high labour-intensity in which low wage costs were most critical (Safa, 1981). These were mainly textiles, clothing and food processing, in which the employment of large numbers of women was traditional. Often, these industries could utilise local raw materials. Improvements in world transport and communications facilitated the relocation process, as did the streamlining and standardisation of production processes and the increased competitiveness of world markets. Gradually certain types of pharmaceutical production and much production in electronics, in which the full mechanisation of assembly work would have been more

TABLE 1.2   *Female employment as a percentage of total employment,*
1977–86

Country	1977	1978	1979	1980	1981	1982	1983	1984	1985	1986
Algeria	5.9	5.2	5.2	8.2	8.2	7.0	6.8	7.6	8.4	...
Botswana	21.9	21.6	22.0	23.3	21.8	22.9	23.3	23.9	29.1	...
Egypt	6.8	7.9	6.7	7.1	7.8	7.9	...	...	...	...
Kenya	17.1	17.4	17.0	17.6	18.3	18.4	17.8	18.7	19.7	20.4
Malawi	11.4	11.6	11.7	11.4	11.1	11.2	11.5	13.6	13.2	...
Mauritius	24.4	24.5	25.6	26.0	26.6	27.1	27.4	29.8	32.1	33.9
Zimbabwe	...	...	17.1	17.0	16.0	15.1	16.3	16.6	...	...
Barbados	40.7	42.1	42.4	44.2	42.8	43.3	43.3	42.9	43.5	44.3
Bolivia	22.9	23.2	23.4	23.4	24.0	25.1	25.3	25.6	25.6	25.9
Brazil	31.2	31.3	31.7	...	31.2	32.2	33.0	33.0	33.4	...
Colombia	37.8	37.6	38.1	38.2	...	...	...	...	38.2	38.9
Costa Rica	23.0	24.4	25.0	24.3	26.0	25.6	25.3	27.9	25.8	...
Cuba	29.0	29.5	31.2	31.5	33.1	34.5	35.6	36.4	37.2	37.5
Chile	26.1	28.0	28.2	29.5	29.2	30.4	30.8	...	29.6	29.7
Haiti	47.0	47.0	47.0	48.9	49.3	40.3	40.3	...	...	...
Jamaica	39.6	39.5	38.1	39.2	38.9	38.3	38.5	39.9	39.2	40.0
Mexico	24.2	24.4	25.4	26.2	27.2	27.6	28.5	29.3	29.4	30.2
Puerto Rico	34.7	34.7	35.2	35.9	36.3	36.6	37.0	37.2	37.3	38.3
Venezuela	27.7	27.3	27.6	27.9	27.1	27.4	27.6	27.7	27.6	27.7
Hong Kong	...	35.2	34.8	34.8	35.9	36.2	36.4	37.0	36.6	36.6
India	11.9	12.0	11.9	12.1	12.2	12.3	12.5	12.6	12.9	...
Philippines	30.1	35.9	...	35.4	35.5	37.1	38.3	36.5	37.2	...
Singapore	31.8	33.1	33.6	35.0	35.5	35.6	35.5	36.3	36.4	37.4
South Korea	37.1	38.1	38.5	38.2	38.1	39.1	39.2	38.4	38.0	39.8
Sri Lanka	34.6	28.7	32.7	33.7	35.4	36.0	34.9	35.9	...	...
Syria	17.5	13.7	15.8	...	...	...	13.9	13.4	...	...
Thailand	44.4	44.3	43.9	47.3	45.8	...	44.5	45.0	...	...
Ireland	28.0	28.3	28.4	29.2	29.8	30.5	31.2	31.1	31.3	...
Turkey	8.5	7.9	...	8.2	8.9	8.8	9.1	9.3	8.8	...
Trinidad/ Tobago	28.3	...	...	...	...	...	...	...	32.8	...
Panama	26.8	...	...	...	...	...	...	...	29.5	30.1
Indonesia	33.8	...	...	...	...	...	...	...	36.0	...

NOTE   Vertical line indicates break in comparability.
SOURCE   ILO, *Yearbook of Labour Statistics*, 1986, Table III, pp. 325 ff.

TABLE 1.3   *Male-female wage differentials in manufacturing: 1975 and 1982*

	Female wage as a percentage of male wage		
	1975	1982	
Cyprus	45.9	56.2	w
El Salvador	90.4	85.9	h
Greece	69.5	73.1	h
Ireland	60.9	68.5	
Japan	47.9	43.1	m
Kenya	66.1	75.8	m
South Korea	47.4	45.1	m
Tanzania	70.7	78.5*	m

*=1980; w=weekly, h=hourly, m=monthly.
SOURCE International Labour Organisation, *World Labour Report 2*, Geneva 1985, Table 14.5, p. 224.

expensive than the cheap labour solution, were also transferred to 'offshore sources' in the Third World.

The transfer of low-skill manual assembly jobs to developing societies by transnational corporations is a fundamental restructuring of the world economy, and it has been closely associated with the increased role of women in the manufacturing labour force. From the point of view of strategies of Third World development, the older import-substitution approaches, which focused on the establishment of locally-owned industries catering mainly to the domestic market, tended to correlate with a lack of increase in female employment, whereas export-oriented approaches which welcome foreign-owned multinationals have been associated with increases in female employment (Safa, 1981; Chinchilla, 1977; Lim, 1978). Historically, industrial relocation first affected particularly the Caribbean and such Latin American countries as Mexico, Brazil and Colombia. The main relocation areas soon came to be in East and Southeast Asia: Korea, Hong Kong, Singapore, Malaysia, Philippines, Thailand. Some parts of South Asia were moderately affected (India, Pakistan, Sri Lanka), as were a few African nations (Tunisia, Egypt, Morocco, Mauritius and to a small extent, South Africa). For the most part, however, sub-Saharan Africa has not been a favoured site for export-oriented manufacturing. New locations are now being sought instead in China and low-wage areas of Europe. Numerically, the cases of large populous nations such as Brazil, India and China, all of which increased their international trade and the share of industrial goods exported in the 1960s and 1970s, account for a significant part of the total worldwide increase in female industrial employment (Joekes, 1987, p. 94).

It is important to note that the trend toward industrial relocation and employment of women has largely by-passed certain parts of the Third World, notably sub-Saharan Africa. Here, lack of any kind of industrial development, and stagnation in overall employment levels, have entrenched male/female inequities in industrial employment levels. Eleanor Fapohunda (1986) describes this situation in Nigeria, noting that in 1983 the female urban labour force participation rate was 41.9 per cent compared to the male rate of 75.4 per cent, and that the percentage of women in manufacturing declined between 1974 and 1983 (see also di Domenico, 1983). Economic factors play a key part in explaining this situation; the predominant types of industry do not convey any particular productivity advantage to women over men, and in addition there is an oversupply of low-skill, low-wage males in the urban labour market. But also, as described more fully below, African family patterns do not reinforce employer preferences for cheap, single, childless women.

Why have employers in the labour-intensive world market industries, such as garment and footwear assembly and electronics, discriminated positively in favour of women, in hiring if not in promotions or wages? Is it simply that stiff competition in the industry forces them to hire the cheapest labour possible? Elson and Pearson (1981) and others have argued that these hiring practices favouring women do not reflect simply the fact that women's wages are lower than men's, though that is so and is an important fact requiring explanation. It is also the case, they argue, that women are actually more productive than men in certain jobs because of their 'nimble fingers'. Manual dexterity, often cited by employers, represents not a natural advantage, as employers often believe, but a skill derived from prior training in the domestic tasks of sewing, weaving and chopping vegetables. Thus, they conclude, a household skill in which women have a trained productivity advantage has come to have a commercial market (cf. also Lim, 1978, p. 15). This argument deserves further exploration.

Whether women's manual dexterity is learned or is a 'natural endowment', in either case it results in high productivity. Most economic analyses presume that at least in the long run high productivity will be reflected in higher wages. Yet in the world market factories the male/female wage gap runs in the opposite direction. As John Humphrey has noted, there seems in general to be a systematic over-valuation of male attributes and a corresponding under-valuation of female ones; for example, male physical strength commands a wage premium in metal-working industries, but female manual dexterity in the assembly-line industries does not (Humphrey, 1985, p. 223). How long can such a female productivity advantage coexist with lower wages, when from a neo-classical economic point of view it is an inherently unstable situation? Is the origin and persistence of this situation fundamentally dependent on the third factor that Elson and Pearson and many others adduce to explain employers' preference for women, that is, their docility, lack of labour mobility, and lesser likelihood of joining organised labour protests? (Fuentes and Ehrenreich, 1983, p. 12–15; Chapkis and Enloe, 1983). This docility, these writers suggest, is largely the result of subordination to patriarchal controls in the household which are extended into the work place. If this is correct, it is another important example of the effect of household patterns on employment behaviour, as we discuss more fully below.

Another aspect of the changing sectoral composition of the work force which serves to increase women's employment is the growth of the service sector. In Latin American and Caribbean economies today, for example, women constitute 39 per cent of the labour in the service sector, and fully 70 per cent of the entire female labour force is in that sector (Joekes, 1987, p. 107). Services include tourism, much of the informal sector, professional services such as nursing and teaching, domestic service, and transport and communications. As economic development proceeds, this sector is expected to increase and, with it, female employment. But why women? Employer prejudice, and perhaps the workers' own sex role socialisation, both perpetuated through childhood socialisation in the household, seem to be at work in defining such jobs as particularly appropriate for women.

In contrast to those production-related factors which favour women's employment, are those which work against it. A well-documented negative effect on women's employment comes about when more technically advanced, mechanised production methods are introduced in industries which had traditionally employed large numbers of women workers. The textile industry is the classic case in point. In Colombia, for example, as the industry was modernised between 1938 and 1979, more technically skilled labour was needed, and as a result the percentage of women employed fell from 74.3 per cent to 31.7 per cent. Even though the absolute number of women employed in the industry increased during these years, the number of men increased much faster, so the relative position of women suffered (UNESCO, p. 80; Joekes, p. 90). Why? It appears that training in the use of new machinery was not given to women at the same rate as to men. Similarly in Brazil: Saffioti has pointed out that the percentage of women in Brazil's textile industry dropped from 96.2 per cent in 1872 to 65.1 per cent in 1940 to 47.8 per cent in 1970 (1986, p. 110). Indeed, this trend, plus the expansion of other male-dominated industries in the twentieth century, meant that early industrialisation in Brazil led to an actual decline in the female share of total employment between 1872 and 1960 (Saffioti, 1978, p. 184–96). While women's share of employment in secondary industry continued to decline in Brazil between 1940 and 1970, their share in the tertiary sector rose (de Miranda, 1977). In the 1970s, however, the proportion of women employed in manufacturing in Brazil rose markedly, the rise continuing, if slowly, into the 1980s.

Here as elsewhere the rise in women's employment seems correlated with the introduction of the kind of automation which results in 'de-skilling', although, as Susan Joekes (1985) has pointed out, de-skilling does not completely explain employers' sex-selectivity. More particularly, women's employment is correlated with the rise of industries such as electronics in which the labour-intensive assembly-line techniques require high levels of managerial control and supervision to achieve high productivity. Ruth Milkman has suggested that it is actually this importance of discipline and control, arising from the technical nature of production, which is central in explaining why industries such as electrical manufacturing are predisposed toward hiring women (1983, p. 171–3).

The complex of technical and social factors which seems to favour high female employment may ultimately be seen as a particular phase of Third World industrialisation, one which could be undermined by new waves of capital-intensive production. For example, Aline Wong notes that Singapore is now moving to a 'second stage' of export-oriented manufacturing, emphasising high technology, high value-added industries, in order to compete with neighbouring countries which offer even cheaper unskilled labour. She predicts that women will lose out relative to men in the needed upgrading of skills, and thus will bear the brunt of any layoffs (Wong, 1981, p. 443).

In addition to production factors, market factors also have a

critical impact on women's employment, but here, too, the analysis
cannot be divorced from considerations of gender discrimination
deriving from women's position in the household. Prime among
market factors in recent years has been world economic recession and
declines or increased competitiveness in particular product markets.
In the 1970s and early 1980s there was a slowdown in international
trade, and in several countries production stagnated or actually
decreased. In some, particularly in Latin America and the Caribbean, international indebtedness grew to enormous levels, forcing
structural adjustments such as wage reductions, sometimes imposed
by international agencies. The poor, both women and men, suffered
most from price rises and drops in real income.

Recessions have had the effect not of reducing women's labour
force participation, since poverty makes it increasingly difficult to
withdraw from the labour force altogether, but of increasing women's
unemployment, or of shifting them from full-time paid labour into
casual labour, informal sector self-employment, sub-contracting or
home-based outwork or piecework. In a little over half of the countries
shown in Table 1.2, the percentage of women in total unemployment
actually *increased* in the decade between 1976 and 1986. Some of this
may be due to their increasing share in the labour force as a whole,
but the rate of female job loss probably increased faster than that of
men's. In 13 of the 21 countries for which ILO data were available,
women's share of unemployment was greater than their share of
employment in 1984–86; these included Barbados, Chile, Jamaica,
India, Costa Rica, Argentina, Panama, Trinidad and Tobago, Uru-
guay, Philippines, Syria and Thailand. In times of economic downturn, employers often lay off women first. Joekes (1987, p. 96) points
to the cases of Haiti, Venezuela, and Jamaica during the late 1970s,
where, when their manufacturing sectors had difficulty in surviving
international pressures, women had disproportionate job losses; this
was also the case in industry in Sri Lanka and Taiwan. In so far as
these reductions in the demand for female labour are due to gender
discrimination on the part of employers, they would seem to reflect
an ideology which assumes that male incomes are more important
than female incomes, given women's subordinate position in the
household.

In addition to general market factors, conditions in the labour
market can affect female employment. For example, high female
employment rates may come about simply as a result of shortage of

males, due to wars, crises or out-migration. Shortages of male labour due to the war effort seem to be the main reason for the growth of women's labor force participation in Iran in recent years, a somewhat surprising development in view of the strength of the Islamic view that women's role in the family is primary (Moghadem, no date). Similarly, growth in female employment in Egypt is partly due to a shortage of skilled and unskilled male workers (Allam, 1986, p. 42). On the other hand, such an explanation does not appear to weigh heavily in the high employment of women in Mexican border industries, since there male unemployment is high (Fernandez-Kelly, 1983b). Still another pattern was found in Singapore in the 1970s, where high female employment was due to a high demand for labour generally coupled with full employment for males. Conversely, low female employment levels may be due in part to larger numbers of men available in the urban labour markets, a condition which is still found in many parts of sub-Saharan Africa.

Ultimately, however, a broader, more fundamental explanation for labour supply is needed. The availability of both men and women for employment and self-employment in the Third World is determined not simply by population levels but in addition by the degree of self-sufficiency of the rural household economy. Many peasant households and kin groups have traditionally subsisted largely outside the market economy, or only in localised market networks; today many pressures are forcing them to sell their labour or the products of their labour within the circuits of global capitalism. For female labour supply in particular, as argued more fully below, not only its level but also its duration and timing over the life cycle are profoundly influenced by the economic position of the household and by internal sex differences in the allocation of household productive and reproductive work.

This section has suggested that sectoral and technical changes in the organisation of production, as well as various market conditions, all fundamentally affect the levels of women's employment at any given time, and yet are still incomplete explanations. Factors such as women's skills, productivity and work attitudes, derived from sex role socialisation in the household, and also employer prejudices about women's proper productive and reproductive roles, have all been suggested as ways to extend and refine the analysis. These factors can affect not only the demand for women's waged labour but also the levels and patterns of its supply.

Age and Marital Patterns in Women's Employment

In export-oriented areas where female employment is high, the predominant characteristic of the female labour force is that it is young and single. Why? On the one hand, of course, the high turnover[1] and resultant low wages are to the advantage of, and imposed by, employers. Employers have an astonishing array of mechanisms which enforce or encourage women to drop out of employment after a number of years: (a) layoffs, either through temporary or permanent plant closings, are frequent, and when the plant reopens, hiring preference is given to young, unmarried women; (b) the lack of promotion or advancement incentives discourages women from long-term employment; (c) women's health often deteriorates from poor working conditions; (d) employment contracts are often temporary; (e) there are usually no maternity benefits; (f) employers can choose from an oversupply of female labour with the necessary skills. (Lim, 1978, p. 20; Safa, 1981).

Young women are not always cheaper because they are less skilled; sometimes they have higher levels of education and literacy than older women yet are still preferred for assembly jobs. One answer to this problem emerges when one considers the total social costs of reproduction of the labour force. That is, if the employer had to absorb any costs of child bearing and rearing such as maternity leaves, sick pay, frequent absences, higher health care bills, then the cheapness of women over men in the labour market would be undermined. A number of researchers have emphasised these potential costs of maternity and child care as an important factor in employer discrimination against women; Fapohunda (1986) for example, lays great stress on them as an explanation for employer resistance to hiring women in Nigeria (see also Safa, 1984). Considering women's family status, then, it is important to distinguish *daughters* and *childless single women*, on the one hand, from *single or married mothers*, on the other, since the former are the only ones who do not threaten to cost employers more than men.

But are the employer strategies and motivations the sum total of the picture? Are they a sufficient explanation for the prominence of young, single women in employment? Of the border industries in Mexico Maria Patricia Fernandez-Kelly writes:

> Other reasons given by women themselves for leaving their jobs are marriageable, unwed womens' intention to have a child, and

the desire of those who are married to give better attention to children and home. In both cases women, almost without exception, opt for this course of action to respond to the pressures of their male counterparts who urge them to leave their jobs in order to give full time to their homes, that is, to fulfill what is considered their 'normal' or 'proper' role. Such women rarely stay in a job long enough to acquire seniority benefits. (1983b, p. 220)

The larger picture, Fernandez-Kelly believes, is that:

At certain stages of its development, the domestic unit tends to produce and put into circulation young factory workers, that is, *daughters*, who after a few years of work in one or several factories tend to be reabsorbed by newly formed homes as wives, while a new wave of younger women take their place along the assembly lines. (1983b, p. 220)

We should not reject the notion that women's preferences and/or the household constraints of reproduction figure into the analysis simply because this argument is also used by employers to justify their willingness to profit from family strategies. It is striking that the employment of young, single women fits in so well with the needs of families who have become dependent on a high fertility reproductive strategy and multiple wage earning by household members. This strategy comes about in the context of low prevailing wages for men and women, and low skill levels. In her comparison of women garment workers in the United States and Brazil, Helen Safa (1983) found that single women predominated in Brazil, whereas in New Jersey companies had mostly married women workers. In the advanced capitalist society, young women remained in school longer to try to qualify for white-collar jobs; they came from smaller families which could invest in the upward mobility of fewer offspring. The supply of single women for blue-collar work was therefore not sufficient, and married women constituted the cheaper labour pool. In Sao Paulo, in contrast, households were large and were forced into multiple wage earning strategies. The supply of less-educated single women was large enough to meet the demand, and their contributions were needed by their parents' households. Safa reports that today, however, with increasing fertility decline in Brazil, more and more women are continuing in the work force after marriage and pregnancy (personal communication).

We are suggesting that age and marital patterns in the female labour force dramatically reveal the direct (and not just indirect, through employer prejudices) impact of household factors such as fertility and multiple earning strategies. The fact that these patterns have shown marked cross-national variations indicates that differing household structures produce differing effects. One analysis based on data from the 1970s distinguished four main female age patterns: (a) the *central peak* or plateau (for example, Thailand), where there is no drop in labour force participation during child bearing years; (b) the *late peak* (for example, Ghana), in which women enter the labour force mainly after child bearing is completed, some perhaps forced to by widowhood; (c) the *early peak* (for example, Argentina) where the female labour force consists mainly of single or young married women and where participation occurs mainly before child bearing, dropping off steadily during and after it; and (d) the *double peak* (for example, Korea) in which labour force participation drops during child bearing but then rises again after it. (Figure 1.4; Durand, 1975, pp. 38–44).

The early peak pattern has been characteristic of Western Europe and Latin America and the central plateau pattern of the USSR, Eastern Europe and Southeast Asia. Salaff (this volume) reports the early peak pattern for Hong Kong, Taiwan and Singapore. Most of Africa exhibits either the central plateau or the late peak pattern. The most characteristic feature of North Africa and the Middle East remains the lack of peaks and the overall low female labour force participation. The United States has exhibited an early peak pattern with the late peak a little higher. The years since 1945 have seen a conspicuous rise in overall female labour force participation and a rise in the numbers of women with small children entering the labour force, suggesting a move to the central plateau pattern.

The early age peak pattern suggests a situation in which marriage and fertility inhibit labour force participation throughout a woman's lifetime, whereas in the central peak pattern there is obviously no such inhibition, and in the late and double peak patterns, the inhibition occurs for only a certain part of the life cycle. As one might expect from this line of reasoning, marital participation rates, like age rates, show much cross-national variation. It is usually but not always the case that single, widowed and divorced women have higher labour force participation rates than married women. In Brazil in 1970, single women had a rate three times that of married women (de Miranda, 1977, pp. 168, 170). In their 1985 sample of women industrial homeworkers in Mexico City, Lourdes Beneria and Martha

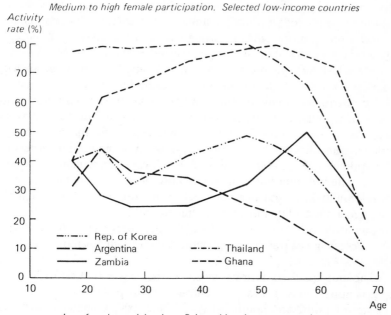

Medium to high female participation. Selected low-income countries

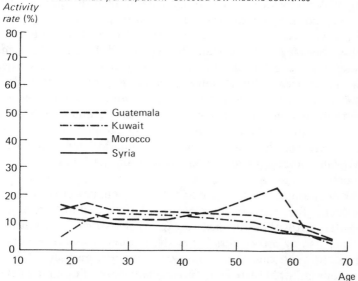

Low female participation. Selected low-income countries

SOURCE G. Standing, *Labour Force Participation and Development*, 2nd edition (copyright, ILO Geneva, 1982) figures 3 and 4, pp. 18–19.

FIGURE 1.4 *Age Patterns in Female Labour Force Participation*

Roldan (1987, p. 90) found that marriage or consensual union meant the interruption of paid work for 80 per cent of the women who had worked when single. On the other hand, Barbara Lewis (1977) found in the Ivory Coast that marriage affected female economic participation only slightly, and that age was a more important predictor; activity increases with age for all marital groups.

No adequate explanation has been offered in the literature as to why marriage and fertility should depress female labour force participation in some cases, but not in others, and only partially in still others. One study by Nadia Youssef (1974) did approach one aspect of this question. She compared female labour force participation rates in the Middle East and Latin America. She argued convincingly that level of economic development alone does not explain the extent of female non-agricultural participation. She linked the low rates of female employment in the Middle East to: (a) the near-universality of marriage; (b) the young age at marriage; and (c) the high fertility levels. By contrast, Latin America has high rates of marital instability especially among non-legalised relationships, postponement of marriage, and non-marriage. Youssef elaborated the argument by referring to the strong code of family honour in the Middle East, which is determined above all by the sexual conduct of the women, their premarital chastity and wifely fidelity. Strong social control thus deters much intermingling of the sexes, even in the job markets. In Latin America, on the other hand, values are similar but much less rigid, and there is a disjuncture between values and behaviour (cf. Scott, this volume). Elsewhere, Youssef (1978) suggests that control over a woman by her agnatic group in the Middle East, together with the economic support the group provides her at all times, perpetuates women's position as economic dependents or home-based workers, and promotes a pro-natalist orientation. The crude birth rate and the child/woman ratio are in fact higher in Muslim societies than in non-Muslim Asia or Central or South America.

Youssef's study indicates that low levels of female employment can be linked with certain features of the marriage and fertility system. More detailed work is needed to explain the variability in age and marital participation patterns over the life cycle, and in general to elucidate the intricate connections between age, marriage, fertility, other household characteristics, and employment/self-employment in the various regions of the world. Some of these interrelations, especially that between fertility and employment, are explored more fully in Section III.

Women's Earnings

One body of literature in which there have been sophisticated attempts to sort out the relative weight of demand as opposed to household supply factors is that which has been concerned to explain the gender gap in earnings. This gap is found world-wide, including in the USSR and other socialist societies. Detailed work on its explanation has occurred with reference to the United States.

The 'household' explanation of the gap comes from the 'new household economics' and human capital theory (see below, Section II). The fact that women invest a large portion of their time and energy in child care and other household work — whether from choice or from family and social constraints — means that they do not invest in developing market skills to the same extent as men. It also means that their market work experience is less, and that when employed they may be constrained in choice of jobs. Each of these labour supply or 'productivity factors' can reduce women's earnings relative to those of men. From this perspective, more years of work experience are expected to increase earnings, in part because a substantial amount of training occurs on the job. In addition to years in the labour force, discontinuous employment is expected to lead to lower pay, since it is associated with a depreciation of skills, and this relationship has received empirical support (Mincer and Ofek, 1982). This explanation runs counter to that which focuses on various kinds of employer discrimination in favour of men, that is, reductions in the 'demand' for female labour.

Various studies in the United States have found that differences in work experience do account for a substantial share of the wage gap, thus lending support to the 'household' explanation. Mincer and Polacheck (1974) argued that approximately 40 per cent of the wage gap could be explained by differences in the amount of time men and women are employed. A large study by Corcoran and Duncan (1979) taking into account a lengthy list of work experience and training measures found that these variables explained 44 per cent of the earnings gap between white women and men. Few such studies have been done in the Third World, but William House's research in Cyprus showed that only 33 per cent of the wage gap could be attributed to training variables, leading to the conclusion that widespread discriminatory practices were at work (House, 1986: 160–2).

An underlying question of interpretation posed by these studies is whether the sex differences in, for example, hours worked and occupation are entirely the result of different individual choices/ household constraints, or are themselves partly the result of differential opportunities in the labour market. For example, it is possible that employers discriminate in not providing as much training to women as to men, so that years of training may not be entirely a supply-side variable. Depending on what weight various researchers attach to this consideration, training and productivity variables have been said to account for anywhere from 20 per cent to 80 per cent of the male/female wage gap (Madden, 1985).

The fact that productivity considerations do not in any study explain all the sex wage differentials lends continued plausibility to the hypothesis that some forms of discrimination are at work. Discriminatory practices can include: (a) direct wage discrimination or unequal pay for equal work; (b) job placement discrimination, in which sex determines which jobs women are hired or promoted to; or (c) devaluation of jobs performed by women *because* they are done by women. One clear research finding is that sex differences in occupations or job titles account for significantly more of the wage differential than do sex differences in pay for workers in the same job (Fuchs, 1971). That is, a large portion of the wage gap results from the concentration of women in lower-paying jobs. However, sex differences in occupations might not result solely from discrimination, but from individual choice, or from the effects of worker socialisation as England and Farkas argue (1986, p. 154).

Probably the best way to approach the question of supply versus demand factors in women's labour force participation and earnings is not as an either/or phenomenon, but as evincing interactive or feedback effects. Some economists have developed a theory of feedback discrimination in which employers' denial of training to women ensures that they will in fact exhibit the characteristics attributed to them. Sociologists England and Farkas, on the other hand, point to households as the source of women's disadvantages, and to feedback effects between the supplying household and the market. They agree with those economists who argue that market forces operate to undercut discrimination, but suggest that working at cross-purposes with these market forces are feedback effects in which household decisions beget new sex differentials in the work force, leading to more discrimination. Discrimination by ascription becomes a self-reinforcing system (1986, pp. 144, 162).

Implicit in this discussion among economists has been the assumption that the effects of the household are limited to the supply side.

However, gender ideologies are transmitted through family socialisation to employers as well as workers, and the ideology prescribes the differential assignment of sexes to household as well as job roles, so that there are at least two senses in which the household could affect employer actions and thus the demand for female labour as well as its supply.

Empirical work on these questions has been done mainly on present-day United States. It is suggestive, but since the structure of both the labour market and households is different in other societies, there is no reason to expect universal applicability. For instance, in the predominantly low-wage labour markets open to women in the Third World, it may not be the case that years of experience, or interruptions in participation, are so closely tied to levels of pay. In fact, if the argument that women are preferred by multinationals because they are specially productive is correct, then their prior training at home is clearly not yielding any pay advantage in the labour market.

We have argued in Section I that many factors deriving from the household can affect the levels and patterns of women's employment and women's wage levels, and that narrowly 'economist' explanations focusing only on the organisation of production and market factors are not satisfying. The organisation of reproduction and non-market production must be taken into account. Household factors can affect the labour market either directly through labour supply, or indirectly through employer demands. As Hannah Papanek has put it, 'the continuous interplay between family households and labor markets determines both female educational and labor force participation through the development of specific family strategies' (1985, p. 322). Accordingly, we now consider basic conceptual approaches to household/labour market relations, and return in Section III to a detailed classification of household factors.

THEORETICAL APPROACHES TO THE HOUSEHOLD

In order to understand the interrelations between the household and the labour market, it is necessary to theorise the household as a socio-economic unit. This problem is currently being addressed within several conceptual frameworks. Among neoclassical economists the 'new household economics' has yielded very important insights. In this approach, the household is located within a market economy yet performs both productive and reproductive functions, according to some division of labour. Reproduction is the outcome of the 'demand' for a certain quantity of children, or for a given 'child quality' (for example, college educated), and there are quantity/ quality tradeoffs, since children pose costs and household resources are limited. (T.P. Schultz, 1981; T.W. Schultz, 1974). Families produce some goods within the home and purchase others in the market with income from earnings. These activities require investments in specific skills which have both direct costs and opportunity costs resulting from time foregone in a job or other market or non-market activity. Since incomes are pooled, the whole family gains when individual members practise their specific skills (Becker, 1981).

This theory provides two fundamental explanations for the division of labour by sex, that is, for the empirical fact of specialisation of women in household production and men in market production. One explanation is that women have an inherent comparative advantage in reproductive labour, and are for that reason at a disadvantage to men in market labour. Becker cites both this biological determinant and secondly efficiency, arguing that a division of labour between employment and home is more efficient than sharing such roles. Feminists, while conceding that in the past biology may have determined that women would bear the greater labour and risks of child production, have strongly criticised the assumption that a natural sex differential persists today, noting that in industrial societies child-spacing, infant-formula feeding, and advances in child health care which lower the total number of births, have all reduced the total time that women must spend in child care. Thus, technology is rapidly narrowing the male-female gap in reproductive work. A second point made by critics is that the importance of reproductive skills is not categorical but is determined by the level of demand for their use. Women's labour market participation should vary according to number of children, and childless women should show no labour market differentials from men. Since the latter is patently not the case, the theory is not adequate. Nevertheless, household reproductive regimes need to be more fully conceptualised. For example, the household demand for children may well depend on the relationship of the husband and other household members to the labour market, not simply the woman's, and there may be a need to sell children's labour.

A different line of approach comes from economists with a human capital orientation who have argued that the question of female labour force participation is reducible to the fact that, at a given level of need, the family will send out first whichever member possesses the greatest marketable skills. As need increases, the family may also send out less-skilled members. This, too, is plausible, but it does not explain why family investments in child training and schooling vary by sex, that is, why males tend to possess more marketable skills than women. Inequities of skills and training are one of a number of intra-household inequalities by sex and age which the 'new household economics' does not address (Folbre, 1982; 1986). With reference to the child training issue, some sociologists have attempted to broaden the economic approach to include the concept of differential sex role socialisation, stemming from learned psychological attitudes and society-wide values (England and Farkas, 1986).

The tendency among neoclassical economists has been to take reproductive labour for granted as a cause of female disadvantage in the labour market, and the task of feminists has been to argue that female specialisation in child rearing and domestic labour is not 'natural' but socially constructed and hence susceptible to change. The tendency among marxist economists has been almost the reverse: to downplay the feminine reproductive role as a cause for labour market participation and wage differentials, to argue that working-class women are exploited by capitalists in the same way as are working class men, and that women's liberation will emerge from fuller incorporation into working class struggles. Only recently have marxists begun to emphasise women's role in reproduction as much as their role in production.

Like neoclassicists, marxists and marxist-feminists have approached the household as the basic unit of biological and social reproduction, but most particularly as a unit within which 'domestic labour' or other production is organised in non-capitalist ways, producing either commodities or use values. The relation between household production and the market economy was addressed in the 'domestic labour debate', which sought to determine whether domestic work was commensurate with wage work, whether one could speak of a separate 'domestic mode of production' articulating with the capitalist mode, or whether domestic work is more directly part of, and useful to, capitalism (Seccombe, 1974; Gardiner, 1975; Himmelweit and Mohun, 1977; Bennholdt-Thomson, 1981). In the view of many, the confinement of women to domestic work and the lower levels of the labour force — the 'sex division of labour' — was the outcome of, or at least functional for, capitalist development (for example, Deere, 1976; Beechey, 1977). But as Michele Barrett (1980) pointed out, this still did not explain why *women*, in particular, were the ones subordinated.

The 'sex division of labour' is obviously an omnibus term; within the household it does not distinguish household production from reproduction. Recently, attention has shifted to the problem of the status of human reproduction as part of the larger process of 'reproduction of the mode of production'. Early writers pointed to the importance of distinguishing the two kinds of reproduction, biological and social (Edholm, Harris and Young, 1977); others called attention to human reproduction as still part of social reproduction (Beneria, 1979); still others saw reproduction as determined by the mode of production (Seccombe, 1983). Some feminist writers shifted to a view of human reproduction as *the* fundamental determinant of women's social status, within the household and without (Ryan 1981; Barrett, 1980). In this vein, the call to analyse a 'mode of human reproduction' separately from the mode of production has gained currency (Bryceson and Vuorela, 1984) while others have argued for an emphasis on social and technical relations of reproduction analysed in tandem with the social and technical relations of production (Stichter and Parpart, 1988).

Neither the neoclassical nor the marxist economic approaches to the household have given adequate weight to intra-household inequities in labour, property, incomes and decision-making power. The neoclassical model incorporates assumptions about 'joint utility functions' and 'altruistic income pooling' which have been widely criticised by feminists as unrealistic. Traditional marxism, in giving much greater role to production than reproduction, virtually ignored the household as a unit mediating between the individual and the forces of the capitalist market, and determining differential male/female access to productive means.

A number of historians and anthropologists have contributed greatly to our understanding of the family/economy interface by conceptualising the household as having various kinds of subsistence strategies, survival strategies, migration strategies, or social mobility strategies (Wood, 1981; Schmink, 1984; Tilly and Scott, 1978; Papanek, 1985). Economically these strategies may include home production for use or sale; labour exchanges, petty entrepreneurship, migration, and wage labour, as well as human reproduction, in which case one might refer to a 'reproductive strategy'. The household is seen as operating within the dominant economic system, which provides both opportunities and constraints, and it intervenes between these larger structures and a myriad of individual decisions (Schmink, 1984). Patterns of household decisions are affected not only by the national and global context, but also by internal forces, the household retaining a variable degree of autonomy from the dominant economy. The concept of strategies is a useful metaphor, calling attention to an important level of analysis, yet it obviously begs a number of questions.

To say that the household has a 'strategy' is a loose way of saying that it has an economic dynamic. A more precise conceptualisation of this principle is one of the great needs of the economic theory of the household. Such a conception is not new in the theorising of peasant households; Chayanov (1966), for example, saw the dynamic as variable depending on the ratio of producers to consumers, but as different from the logic of profit maximisation. Others, focusing on the internal allocation of labour and consumption among members, see the dynamic as one of accumulation by peasant patriarchs (Henn, 1988). Both these conceptions see household work as involving a combination of productive and reproductive labour.

Two important and related questions remain matters of debate. One has to do with how much relative independence or autonomy the household may be said to have within the larger economy; the other is whether household work is quantifiable in such a way as to be commensurate with wage employment, so that comparisons may be made. In the neoclassical household analysis, the household does not have much autonomy. The implicit model of the household is drawn from the dependent family within advanced industrial societies, and therefore focuses on family as provider of market labour and on family consumption. It does, however, see child rearing decisions as 'investments' in child quality from which parents presumably expect to see some return. All these household decisions could be seen as determined by some internal household economic strategy, but instead they are seen as responses to external changes in prices.

Within the marxian framework, the question of household independence from capital has occasioned sharp disagreement. Views range from those of Bennholdt-Thomson (1981, p. 19), who argues that theoretically 'it would be wrong to consider the production of use-values as being outside the capitalist mode of production, even though at first sight it may not seem to be integrated into generalised exchange relations', to those of Norman Long, who suggests from a more descriptive point of view that 'if one concentrates on subsumption one is likely to miss the important ways in which non-wage, non-capitalist forms . . . resist the penetration of commodity relations or transform them in some way in accordance with existing non-capitalist principles' (1984, p. 11; see also other articles in this collection). The view that capital has been unable to dissolve or supplant non-capitalist modes based on the household has been widespread; in this vein, for example, Nash and Fernandez-Kelly (1983, p. 93) write that 'from the early years of the Industrial Revolution in England to the present in developing countries, the household unit has resisted dependency on factory employment by clinging to a semisubsistence strategy'. If this view is correct, then we need to know more about the internal logic through which such resistance is achieved.

Whether household work and wage work are quantifiable in the same terms is not a problem for neo-classical economics, since prices and wages can be imputed from market valuations using several different approaches, such as market-price equivalents for labour or goods and services produced, or opportunity costs (Goldschmidt-Clermont, 1982). Some marxists have argued, however, that it does not make sense to impute capitalist valuations into a non-capitalist system, and that the labour theory of value is not applicable to the household either, since neither socially necessary labour time for a given task nor an efficient organisation of production can be defined (Himmelweit and Mohun, 1977). Others have taken the view that analysis in terms of labour times and returns to labour, and even the notions of surplus and value, can be applied to a non-capitalist household within a socially equilibrated production system, and that comparison with wage incomes is possible. Thus, both exploitation within the household (Folbre, 1982), and household accumulation (Henn, 1988) can be defined.

Complementing the economic approach to work/family interactions are the insights drawn from sociological role theory, in which individual behaviours and psychological states are structured by roles, clusters of norms which make up social institutions. Major role sets for individuals are occupational roles and family roles, making up what Joseph Pleck (1977) calls the 'work-family role system'. The term 'sex roles' is commonly used to refer to the sex differences in the work-family role system, but in fact the term poses real conceptual problems: many have argued convincingly that it is about as meaningful in the literal sense as the terms 'class role' or 'race role' would be (Lopata and Thorne, 1978). Rather, we need to begin from a concept of productive and reproductive roles and allocation of the sexes to them. Using this approach, Pleck (1977) for example, argues that the boundaries between work roles and family roles are asymmetrically permeable for men and women. For women, the demands of the family role are permitted to constrict their work role more than vice versa, whereas for men the demands of the work role are permitted to intrude upon family time. A husband is expected to manage his family so that their needs do not interfere with his work efficiency. Nevertheless to a certain extent all persons who are gainfully employed must manage the competing demands of work and family, and two significant modes of doing so are role sequencing, and differential role allocations between family members (Voydanoff, 1987; Bailyn, 1978).

In peasant and pre-industrial contexts, much of this analysis would not be applicable, since it, like the neo-classical economic approach, assumes an incompatibility between work and family roles. But for non-home-based wage work in a factory setting, the assumption of time and role demand conflicts seems reasonable. Even so, work-family role links remain strong; so strong that some would like to use the term 'worker-earner role' to emphasise that from the family point of view the worker role is simultaneously an earner role, which should be seen as in itself an important contribution to the family system (Rodman and Safilios-Rothschild, 1983).

Sociological and social-psychological approaches direct attention to an important range of issues, particularly how characteristics of work roles affect men's and women's performance of family roles, and vice versa. For example, high levels of job stress affect marital happiness and the quality of parent-child interactions; demands of 'greedy' occupations require individuals to restrict family roles; unemployment levels affect the level of family violence and the divorce rate. Family effects of husbands' employment will differ from the effects of mother's or daughter's employment. Recent research in the United States has focused on effects of wife's employment on marital satisfaction (no effect when chosen freely), on marital power (increases wife's marital power), and on children's psychological well-being (no clear positive or negative effect) (Hoffman and Nye, 1974; Nieva, 1985). However, full-time employment of the mother does appear to weaken traditional sex role stereotypes among children, having positive effects on daughters' feelings of confidence and self-worth, but less positive effects on sons' self-confidence and ambition. Other interesting findings are that unemployment of the husband causes less stress in families with less traditional sex role conceptions, and that dual-career families have less stress if there are flexible role conceptions. At present such research has been confined largely to industrial societies; there is a fertile field for more such research in areas of the Third World where paid employment for both women and men is growing.

Another important concept from the sociological and anthropological literature is that of the family developmental cycle. Most fundamentally, the family cycle denotes the spacing out over time of the household's reproductive work. The pioneering anthropological work of Fortes (1949) among the Tallensi and Ashanti in Ghana established the general usefulness of the concept, as has the more recent work of Goody (1958; 1972). Both of them identify phases based on marriage, birth of first and last child, and departure of children. The expansion phase ends with birth of last child and is followed by a period of stability and then a contraction phase beginning with departure of first child.

As applied in the United States, the divisions into stages of the family cycle can be numerous and variable, depending on the interests and hypotheses of the researcher (for example, Hill, 1964; Aldous, 1978). A common set of divisions results in six general stages: (a) establishment: pre-child phase; (b) pre-school phase: youngest child under six; (c) school-age family: youngest child six through 12; (d) adolescent family: youngest child 13 through 18; (e) family as launching centre: youngest child 18–22; (f) post-parental family: all children departed from household and/or joined labour force. While divisions such as these may make sense in the contemporary American context, they are clearly time, class, and culture-bound. The rationale for such divisions involves numerous unstated assumptions about unspecified institutional or cost influences, for example, that marriage comes before parenthood, that school becomes an important socialiser at age six, that adolescent children do not bring in income but rather pose greater cost and/or disciplinary demands, and that the 'launch phase' will be expensive since it involves college education. Also assumed is a stable nuclear family, although recent work is attempting to identify stages for divorced, remarried, single parent and childless families.

Little wonder that this particular model has proved to have limited usefulness even in the study of the larger families of nineteenth-century America (Elder, 1978, p. 45; Hareven, 1978, p. 4–5). Both Hareven and Elder point out that the greater fertility and lower life expectancy at that time meant that child-bearing stretched out over a larger number of years, and that the post-parental phase was reduced if not eliminated (Hareven, 1977). Similar considerations would be relevant in the Third World today. Elder seeks to subsume the family cycle approach into the individual 'life course' framework, which uses age and age cohort not only as an index of typical work or family career stage, but also of historical location and of exposure to larger socio-economic events. (Elder, 1974; 1978). We suggest, however, that the family cycle approach remains a useful way to map the household reproductive strategy, and that for differing family systems and economic settings throughout the Third World, new sets of appropriate phases or stages should be defined.

If the family cycle stage is combined with the trajectories of each member's productive work, the key determinants of the household's economic situation can be plotted. With longitudinal data, stages in the work careers of household members can be combined with stages in their family careers (Voydanoff, 1987, p. 87). An important concept here is the dependency ratio, or the ratio of net producers to net consumers. This in fact is only approximated by age measures, since in many contexts one cannot assume that anyone under 15 or over 55 makes no net contribution to family. The family cycle concept points to the fact that dependency ratios vary over time, so for example investments in children at one phase may pay off for parents at a later stage.

The combination of the household's reproductive and work cycles may result in certain periods of economic pressure which have been termed 'life cycle squeezes'. This occurs when, given costs, consumption needs/aspirations exceed incomes. Valerie Oppenheimer (1982) has identified two common life cycle squeezes in American families, one is early adulthood, just after marriage, when couples are establishing households and bearing children while husbands' earnings are still low, and the other is later adulthood, when childrearing expenses of adolescence and college education are not matched by sufficient increases in husbands' earnings (see also Moen and Moorehouse, 1983). The severity of the squeeze varies by class position. Such squeezes may be a factor predicting when married women's labour force participation will increase.

There has been relatively little research done on family/work cycles in the Third World or other non-western societies. One exception is the work of Janet Salaff (1981; this volume), who has documented the way in which the balance between earners and consumers varies over the family cycle among Hong Kong workers, and affects women's labour force participation. As in the United States, families experience the 'squeeze' of high dependency ratios when children are small, although most mothers do not work unless they can find substitute care. As children become adolescents, though, they bring in income, and families with working sons and daughters are comparatively well off. Parents often attempt to stretch this period, discouraging daughters, especially, from marrying, since this usually means she will move out and cease to contribute her earnings. On the other hand, the patriarchal desire for descendants pushes elders to allow sons to marry, and this will usually, by contrast, improve the family's economic position if the son's wife moves in and contributes her earnings. But as son's wives begin to bear children, and as daughters finally leave to marry, the family is back to high dependency ratios again.

All of the theoretical approaches discussed in this section are built on the abstract category of 'household' as the basic unit of analysis, and they present household models which are implicitly drawn from the nuclear family in western cultures. However, anthropologists have long pointed out that the term 'household' lumps together a number of family functions in a way that is inappropriate for many cultures (Yanagisako, 1979; Oppong, 1982; Guyer, 1981). Pittin, (1987) for example, decries its usefulness for the Hausa of northern Nigeria, and Oppong (1980) presents an alternative emphasis on various parental, conjugal, and domestic roles of women as counter to the household focus.

We believe, however, that productive and reproductive relations at the 'household' — family, kin, domestic — level are so critical a determinant of the quality of women's lives that they must be conceptualised and understood as a system with an internal dynamic. At the same time, in many non-western cultures the effective units of co-residence, production (including property-ownership), consumption (including income pooling), and reproduction (sexual relations, child rearing and socially defined kinship) do not in fact coincide (cf. Goody, 1972). They are not reducible to the residence unit as the term household implies. The appropriate course in these cases is to conceptually distinguish the various kinds of domestic units, and to analyse separately the implications of each for women's employment. Some examples of this strategy are given below under 'household structure'. Notions of family cycle, sex division of labour, and family roles must be similarly recast in order to pinpoint the relevant domestic unit. In general, the term 'household' should be recognised as no more than a convenient shorthand referring to the complex of domestic systems in which women are enmeshed.

HOUSEHOLD EFFECTS ON EMPLOYMENT

Having established the need to consider household impacts on the patterns of Third World women's employment, and reviewed theoretical approaches to the household from this perspective, we now turn to a more detailed examination of household/employment linkages.

I propose that the following aspects of the social relations of household production and reproduction can be expected to have an impact on women's employment patterns:

1. *Reproductive work*
   (a) Amount of reproductive work: level of completed or expected fertility in the household
   (b) Allocation of reproductive work: particularly the sex division of childbirth and child rearing, but also the distribution of such work among other household members
   (c) Ability to transfer such work to others outside the household
2. *Productive work*
   (a) Amount of productive work: varies according to how much the household produces for itself and for the market economy, and how much it purchases from the market economy. Also includes shopping, entertaining, 'housework'
   (b) Allocation of productive work: sex and age divisions of work; allocations among all household members
   (c) Ability to transfer such work to others outside the household
3. *Household structure*
   Size, age/sex composition and persistence of the household unit. Important sub-types include single households and female-headed families.
4. *Income and resources*
   (a) Total level of household income; total value of productive resources
   (b) Distribution of income and resources among all household members. Includes immediate distribution as well as inheritance patterns

5. *Decision-making and power relations among members*
   Particularly husband-wife relations but also parents' decisions
   about daughters, their schooling, training and employment.

Subsequent discussion in this chapter will examine each of these
factors in turn.

From the vantage point of the labour market these are all supply-
side factors, affecting which household members will offer for outside
employment. I hypothesise that these factors will affect: (a) the
aggregate supply of labour; (b) the age and sex composition of the
labour force and patterns of participation by age and sex; and (c) the
supply price and thus wage levels for various categories of workers.
Although these factors are expected to impact the labour market
primarily through labour supply, other family variables may affect
the market through the demand side, via employer discrimination.
Ideological conceptions about normative family structure and division of labour is the aspect that is usually considered to affect
employers' decisions (cf. Scott, this volume). Other demand factors
will also affect the final outcome, and there will be interactive or
feedback effects. Contextual factors, such as the price and availability
of non-familial child care, of domestic servants, and of other com-
moditised alternatives to domestic work, and the cost of schooling
and health care for children, will also affect the results.

Reproductive Work

Most research in this area has focused on the effect of employment on
fertility, rather than vice versa. The widely presumed inverse relationship between fertility and women's labour force participation is
frequently theorised in neoclassical economic terms, in which the
opportunity costs of time use determine the allocation of time by
women between labour force activities, and fertility, childcare, and
other domestic work. In fact, the empirical implications of this theory
are somewhat unclear, since two separate relationships are predicted.
First, holding household income constant, it is predicted that fertility
will vary according to the woman's opportunity wage, so that for
women commanding low wages in the market the opportunity cost of
economic inactivity will be low, leading to high fertility, but where
women command high wages, fertility will drop. (Similarly, where
there is a large gap between female and male opportunity wages,

females will tend to specialise in housework.) Second, however, there is the income effect, whereby rising family incomes, perhaps due precisely to women's labour force participation, should lead to an increased demand for children and could allow purchase of alternative forms of child care. In spite of the income effect, it is usually assumed that the first effect will predominate. Thus the theory implies that in situations where female wage work can lead to family upward mobility, or among educated white-collar women, female wage work is more likely to reduce fertility than among low wage groups (Standing, 1982, pp. 165–72).

Examining the reverse effects, of household on employment, the theory usually assumes that the number and ages of children, that is, the timing of the reproductive cycle, affects the female labour supply curve, since the greater the number and the lower the ages of the children, the greater the demand for child care time as opposed to employment. A possible counter effect, however, is that the number of children should increase the need for income, thus tending to raise the cost of non-participation in the labour market. Some studies in rural areas of the Third World have found a positive relationship between number of children and female labour force participation; however, in industrial societies number of children is correlated with an increase in the hours worked by men, but not by women.

All of these hypothesised relationships are critically dependent upon a number of unexamined assumptions — assumptions which become much less tenable when the theory is applied to less industrialised and non-western societies. The resultant qualifications severely restrict its applicability to these cases.

First, because the analysis was developed with reference to industrial societies, it assumes that households, and in particular women, have no other sources of income except market labour, and that subsistence production, cash crops, and other domestic labour for use or exchange does not produce income. This is obviously not the case for peasant and other semi-proletarianised households in the Third World. For them, an analysis is needed which distinguishes between wage work, self-employed work outside the household, work done within family labour relations which yields market income, and non-market household work for subsistence. In order to determine how a woman would allocate her time among these four options, her income or imputed wage from each would have to be calculated, and total family income would have to be measured so as to include income from domestic work. If, for example, a peasant woman could increase family income through non-market production, she might well choose that over wage employment; she might do this either in response to the needs of an already existing large number of children, or increased income might lead to an increase in her demand for children. In this more complex and refined analysis a woman with children is faced with a four-way trade-off between various kinds of productive work. The next question that must be examined is the time/effort compatibility of each type of work with reproductive work.

Assuming that non-market domestic work might affect fertility, Nadia Youssef has suggested two ways the relationship might work. First, fertility may be a response to the woman's perceived value of children as helpmates in performing the amount of household work allocated to her. High domestic workloads for women would be expected to lead to high preference for children where children are perceived to lessen the burden of women's tasks. This relationship would be independent of the husband's interest in having children, and the actual household outcome might then be further contingent on the division of decision-making power in the household. Second, Youssef hypothesises that women who lose access to the productive processes within the household, or whose role in them is limited, will have higher fertility rates. She notes that the shift from communal land ownership with women's usufruct guarantee to private ownership has led to women's loss of access to productive means, and to higher fertility, and that women in the upper and middle strata of peasantries who have fewer household productive functions have higher fertility than those in the landless peasant and wage labour classes. In these cases, a woman's incentive for children may be rooted in her need to gain power in the domestic arena via reproductivity, since the sex division of labour constrains her access to production. Attempts to control men through sexual attractiveness, and through children, and attempts to control children, are part of this strategy (Youssef, 1982).

The second major problem with the neoclassical economic theory is that it is built fundamentally on the assumption of incompatibility between work and fertility. But whether productive and reproductive work are in fact incompatible depends directly on a number of factors, mainly type of employment, type of child rearing, and structure of the household. It is well established that the more employment is home-based or has flexible hours, the less will be the negative effect on fertility (Jaffe and Azumi, 1960; Stycos and Weller,

1967). Subsistence work is even less likely to be incompatible. Type of child-rearing expected, on the other hand, is a variable which has not been much examined cross-culturally. What human capital theorists refer to as the 'quality' of child care ought clearly to affect the degree to which it acts as a constraint on women's labour force participation (Standing, 1982, p. 169). A more accurate and value-neutral term for this factor would be 'time-intensity of child care by biological mother'. This avoids the projection of western middle class prejudices about the need for mothers to spend large amounts of time with their children.

A major reason why child care may not be incompatible with mother's employment in non-western cultures is the prevalence of extended families in which grandmothers, older siblings, co-wives, or other adults substitute for the mother in caring for the children. The neo-classical model, by contrast, assumes the western nuclear family. The extended family has been cited in accounting for why presence of children does not seem to reduce female employment in the consanguineal households in urban Africa, Latin America, and the Caribbean (Nieves, 1979; Lewis, 1982; Bolles, 1986; Peek, 1978). Extended kin are especially important as caretakers in female-headed families. Christine Oppong (1982, pp. 142–5) reminds us that non-parental child care is a significant norm in most non-western societies, and cites the practices of pawning, fostering, housemaids, wardship and apprenticeship. In these cases, the 'cost' of rearing children is obviously not affected by the price of the mother's time in the marketplace, even if the mother is educated.

However, the extent to which extended kin are actually available as child-care substitutes in urban areas of the Third World today may be overstated. In assessing the situation in Nigeria, Eleanor Fapohunda reports that this support system is breaking down, since aged parents are reluctant to stay in cramped, strange urban environments when they have more comfortable options in the villages, and since co-wives usually live in separate houses and have their own outside employment. Only to a limited extent do urban families send their children to be raised by rural relations; also declining is the reverse migration in which poorer relatives are sent to help with child care in the urban kin's homes. Even when there are housemaids, sick children remain the mother's responsibility, and often the mother of small children is forced to spend long hours away from her job sitting in line in overcrowded public health clinics (Fapohunda, 1986, p. 109; 1982; Parpart, this volume). The growing urban child-care dilemma has led to the demand for commercial day care in Lagos (see also di Domenico, 1983, 1987; and for Ghana, Oppong, 1977).

Two further qualifications to the neoclassical model of household-employment linkages are important, both having to do with the context within which the household functions. First is the extent of child labour in the society; the model assumes that it is not important. But if children can bring in a wage or other forms of income, this will tend both to reduce the market demand for adult female labour and to increase family incentives toward childbearing. This consideration underscores the necessity of examining *family* tradeoffs in the choice of which members enter employment and which do not, not simply husband-wife tradeoffs. Wives' labour force participation has been shown to depend on husband's employment status and his wage level, and clearly will also depend on whether children are employable. Whether and when children enter the labour market will also depend on the amount of investment in schooling that is required to make them marketable — the cost of children. A final qualification to the model is the availability and cost of alternative non-family forms of child care, since these too will greatly reduce the presumed incompatibility between working and motherhood.

In explaining fertility decline, other considerations, both family and attitudinal, have been proposed as intervening mechanisms between employment and fertility. For example, widespread opportunities for non-domestic employment for women may very well raise the average age at marriage, and age at first pregnancy, and also the proportion of women who do not marry. These factors may in turn be more directly responsible for fertility declines than employment itself. Another strand of argument focuses on attitudes. Safilios-Rothschild's research suggests that work commitment, rather than the work itself, may be the most important factor. She found in urban Greece that women with a high work commitment had fewer children than those with a low work commitment, but working women with a low work commitment had about as many children as housewives (Safilios-Rothschild, 1972). Still other considerations are women's level of education, and their decision-making status in the household, especially in cases where the wife may desire fewer children but the husband does not.

The limitations of the neoclassical model may help explain the fact that the inverse relationship between fertility and female labour force participation does not hold as well in the Third World as it does in industrial societies, although the model would explain this as resulting from the fact that low-wage jobs for women do not pose high opportunity costs for child bearing and from the income effect (Standing, 1982, pp. 176–81; Youssef, 1982, pp. 179–80). Some studies have found the expected negative relationship, especially when they focus on non-domestic or non-agricultural employment rather than total economic activity.

In general, many studies leave the direction of the causal relationship unclear; for example, the correlation of present labour market activity status and past fertility suggests that fertility depresses labour force participation rather than the reverse. On the whole, studies of fertility and women's employment need to become much more sophisticated, taking into account the multiplicity of factors we have mentioned, and clarifying the direction of causality and possible feedback effects.

Women's Productive Work in the Household

The emphasis on the sex division of labour in the household as a factor limiting female waged labour participation has been especially prominent in marxist work. The neoclassical approach to this problem is the same as that just discussed for fertility, that is, that the choice is determined by the opportunity wage, so that women commanding low market wages would be more likely to choose domestic work, and the reverse. There is also the income effect, in which rising household incomes may lead to increased demand for domestic work. This analysis is subject to many of the same limitations described above in relation to fertility.

The marxist analysis begins with the concept of proletarianisation; the concept is widely applied to women as well as to men (for example, Deere and de Leal, 1981; Tilly, 1981). It is argued that women, like men, become more available for employment the less their access to independent productive resources such as land. Proletarianisation is not, as is sometimes implied, synonymous with wage employment levels; dependence on wage labour is shown by levels of employment plus unemployment. Some analysts also include petty self-employment.

I would argue that the concept of proletarianisation should not be applied directly to women in this way, because for the majority of the world's women access to productive means is not direct, not defined individually, but is structured through kin and marital relationships, that is, through the household. Actually, such access for men is also structured through the household, but this is less easily perceived, since men are often in charge of distribution of household resources, and since legally adult men are defined as free-acting individuals. But even where women are also legally free to enter into contracts and own property, their *de facto* situation is often different.

The sex division of labour within the household may indeed cut a woman off from active use of the land, yet she may still not be proletarianised, because she is supported by the household. This is largely the case in all male-farming systems in the rural Third World, particularly those where customs such as *purdah* physically confine women to the house. Even in female dominated farming systems, such as those common in Africa, a woman usually has only use rights to the land, and these are directly contingent upon her marital status. A single, widowed or divorced woman usually has great difficulty achieving and maintaining access to the land, and it is precisely these women who are more likely to migrate to towns in search of wage or self-employment (cf. the discussion in Stichter, 1985). For African men, as well, status within the household affects the decision to offer oneself on the labour market; for example, junior males often migrate to work sites because fathers or older brothers retain control of family lands.

Specific to women is the fact that specialisation in reproductive work, bearing and rearing children and housework, may provide an alternative source of income, buffering them from proletarianisation, providing they can find males to support them. This specialisation generally has the cost of submission to male control. In discussing proletarianisation, Marx refers not only to the lack of access to the means of production, but to what he called pre-capitalist constraints on the disposition of labour, the legal and socio-political position of labour. Workers, he said, had to be free in a double sense — in that the means of production do not belong to them, and in that they themselves are not owned as part of the means of production, like serfs or slaves. Applied to women's reproductive labour, this observation strikes at the heart of the female dilemma. In many societies, women's reproductive labour is effectively owned and controlled by men through the marriage system, upheld by law and cultural values. Marriage payments such as bridewealth and dowry establish male rights of paternity to children, and institutions of seclusion reinforce male control over female labour. Only in female-headed and matrifocal families do we find a lessening of such control, but usually at the price of a loss of male financial support. Where heavy patriarchal controls on women's labour obtain, it is more accurate to refer to women as 'semi-proletarianised', as do a number of authors (Safa, 1975; Beechey, 1977).

The way in which the sex division of non-reproductive labour in the household may affect the composition of the labour force is illustrated by an example first put forward by Boserup. In colonial Africa, the pre-existing sex division of labour led to junior males being the primary component of the labour force, since women had key responsibilities in agricultural food production. In striking contrast, in parts of east, southeast and south Asia women's paid labour force participation did grow during the colonial era. In these areas too impoverishment on the land led to pressure on households to send out workers, but since the traditional farming system required the input of both men and women, capitalists had to 'face the fact' that neither the women nor the men could be left behind alone to support themselves. In contrast to Africa, the 'whole family', including children, had to be employed for wages, on plantations in Ceylon, Vietnam and Malaysia (Boserup, 1970, p. 78). In both cases, capital managed to avoid paying a 'family wage' to each worker, but capital could and did accommodate to a differing composition of the labour force resulting from differing forms of rural household organisation. The result for women's employment differed dramatically in the two cases.

Aside from the simple question of access to productive resources, proletarianisation may also come about when households are faced with market processes which undermine the value of domestic production, whether it is for use or is petty commodity production for sale. A key process is that in which competition from cheap factory-made consumption goods devalues the time spent on subsistence work relative to any wage-generating work. Capitalism invades and transforms housework, changing it from a complete and independent production process to a simple bit of end-stage processing, such as heating a can of pre-cooked beans.

Again, this process has to be seen as mediated through the household division of labour by sex and age. Whose household work is affected may determine who is sent out for wage work. An illustrative study is that by Kate Young showing how young girls in rural Oaxaca, Mexico, came to be 'selected out' for labour migration (Young, 1983). Here women were largely excluded from agricultural work; their primary role was domestic production. The introduction of cheap factory-produced goods such as domestic utensils, ready-made clothes, and prepared foodstuffs such as biscuits, pastas, rice, corn-meal, and soft drinks, all greatly reduced the time necessary to maintain the standard of living. Households could afford these goods because of the sale of the coffee crop, grown by men. New tools such as the hand mill, and later a diesel-powered corn mill, drastically reduced the amount of female labour time needed to grind corn, and whereas surpluses of corn used to be marketed locally, now there was no such market. Provision of running water saved countless domestic hours. Since mothers were still needed to care for children, young unmarried daughters came to have a particularly high rate of out-migration. Young writes:

> Although a mother might protest her daughter's being sent away on ground that she needed her help in the house and with child care, her arguments could easily be overruled . . . In sharp contrast . . . sons were discouraged, if not prevented, from mi-grating. Often a father would refuse to give one son permission to go until the next was of an age to help in the fields. Daughters themselves, not surprisingly, were often eager to go.

Elizabeth Jelin has proposed that it would be useful to classify women according to their participation in household domestic work (1982, p. 247). Broadly, there are four categories: (a) those without major domestic responsibilities, for example, single women and daughters; (b) those who are devoted solely to domestic work; (c) those who can find or afford to hire substitutes; and (d) those forced to take wage employment anyway but who cannot find or pay for substitutes. In cases (a) and (c), there is much less conflict between wage and domestic work. Women may be in different categories at differing points in their lives.

There is widespread agreement that a household division of labour assigning a heavy burden of domestic work to women will probably constrain participation in the market labour force. It is important to note, however, that housework is much less incompatible with petty commodity production than it is with paid employment. In northern Nigeria, Islamic seclusion of wives does not prevent the home-based production of goods for sale, though it does constrain open market sale and the purchase of supplies. But as for employment, Fapo-hunda points to the case of one company which employed 364 women in its Lagos plant, and no women in its Zaria plant in the North (1986, p. 102).

The recent emphasis on domestic work has given rise to several attempts to extend the conceptualisation of it, as a way of underscoring its importance. Hanna Papanek (1979) has coined the term 'family status production', while Ursula Sharma (1986) refers instead to 'household service work'. Both wish to highlight the function of certain types of domestic work in raising or lowering the family's class or status, of producing or reproducing status. The kind of work referred to by these terms is largely social: entertaining, making marriage arrangements for children, keeping up ties of mutual aid with neighbours and extended kin. There is no need, however, to create a special category of domestic work to encompass these activities. If all domestic work is seen as contributing to household income, then *all* of it produces or reproduces status.

Household Structure and Women's Employment

Family and kin structures vary enormously; so does the age/sex composition of a typical co-resident household unit in various cultures. Often there are several concentric sub-units, like nested boxes, such as conjugal families embedded within extended families, or there may be parallel sub-units, such as mother-child units within polygynous families. In such cases, notions of household strategies, sex divisions of labour or reproductive cycles must be broken down by sub-unit. In addition, households of different structures may have quite different effects on women's employment. Three different examples will be discussed here: the nested extended family, the polygynous family, and the female-headed household.

Janet Salaff (this volume) identifies three relevant units within complex urban Chinese families: (a) the extended patriliny; (b) the residential domestic unit; and (c) the mother-centred 'uterine family'. The extended patriliny exists mostly as an ideal today, but continues to generate pressure on women to produce children, especially sons. The domestic unit, on the other hand, is focused on present-day economic survival, and depends on daughters' and mothers' incomes as well as those of sons and husbands. It motivates both husband and wife to offer themselves for wage employment as well as to have children. The uterine family, based on ties between a woman and her children, also motivates women to marry and bear children to ensure their own old-age support. It helps ensure a single daughter's continued willingness to contribute to her family of origin, despite her eventual exclusion from family inheritance. Even married daughters continue to retain ties to their natal kin, especially their mother, partly in order to receive help with combining child care and employment. As can be seen, the different domestic units exert differing pressures on women in the choice between child bearing and employment. The upshot is that most women work both before and after child bearing, but sacrifice some years of wage income to child bearing.

In the African context, Eleanor Fapohunda (1986) has similarly called attention to the contradictory effects of polygynous extended family relations and conjugal relations on the motivation of Nigerian women to participate in the industrial labour force. Noting, as have others, that the power and prosperity of extended families in rural and even in urban areas increases with the number of male members, she too observes that this system encourages high fertility and discourages female wage employment. (She also notes that high fertility may increase employer discrimination against women.) At the same time, characteristics of the Nigerian conjugal relationship work to promote women's labour force attachment, especially polygyny, marital instability, and the presumption that wives are to a great extent responsible for their own and their children's welfare. She explains that

> Polygamous Nigerian marriages encourage women to work outside the home as the husbands income is shared among several wives and their progeny. Support payments may also be small and irregular. . . . In urban areas, an elite man may have a wife married under the imported British legal system and a second wife married under native law and custom. The monogamous urban wife, living with the potential instability of her marital arrangement and fearing that her spouse's financial commitments might change, values her economic independence and seeks continuous employment. (1986, p. 103)

One major variation in family structure which has not been incorporated in most theories of the household is the mother-child or female-headed family. This form is distinct from the mother-child residential arrangement which exists as a sub-unit within extended, often polygynous, African families. Blumberg and Garcia (1977) argue that from an evolutionary point of view both kinds of mother-child units, within and without larger kin structures, tend to emerge in situations where women as individuals have economic options comparable to those of males of their class; that is, (a) where women have independent access to viable subsistence opportunities; (b) where women contribute a great deal to subsistence, so that the minimum family unit does not require a male to be present; and (c) where women can reconcile subsistence work with child care responsibilities. These conditions are most often approximated in precapitalist horticultural farming systems. Thus Blumberg and Garcia trace the origin of this form to the distribution of productive resources between men and women, but they also argue that for the form to persist in the modern world it must remain functional to the capitalist political economy.

The prevalence of female-headed families in the African-influenced areas of the Caribbean, and North, Central and South America leaves no doubt that structural terms derived from the Eurasian 'conjugal estate' systems are not appropriate (R.T. Smith, 1956; M.G. Smith, 1962). Much comment has focused on the relative instability of marital ties, but more salient perhaps is the persistent strength of loosely defined extended kin ties through women. Constance Sutton writes of Barbados that 'although the system is in principle bilateral, kinship connections through women figure more prominently in defining the sets of people considered to be "family" to each other. The strong sense of family based on these connections counterbalances the relative instability of conjugal unions' (1977, p. 308). For example, women tend to be the main recipients of the important economic assistance provided by adult sons and daughters.

In terms of impact on women's labour force participation, it is useful to distinguish three types of marital relations: stable co-resident unions, whether legalised or not; visiting unions; and single women. The residential arrangements of the latter two are particularly likely to include extended family members who share domestic work (Bolles, 1986). For example, Standing (1978) found for urban Jamaica that the relation between number of children and labour force participation depended on type of marriage — the constraining effect of children was less among women in common-law marriages and visiting unions.

Employer hiring policies can either promote the continued existence of such families by providing female employment, or can undermine them. Sutton and Makiesky-Barrow point out that historically in the Caribbean the first form of capitalist development was the slave plantation, which surprisingly did not favour male economic participation at the expense of females (1977, p. 293). By contrast, the case of Curacao provides evidence that matrilocal families may decline as a result of the impact of industrial development favouring men. Eve Abraham-Van der Mark (1983) reports that a Shell refinery which opened there in 1918 provided employment only for men. In the 1940s, the company, supported by the Catholic Church, increased benefits such as medical care and pensions to legally married couples only. As a result, nuclear families with a single male wage earner became common. Until its closing in the 1950s, the refinery provided only a few white-collar jobs for women.

Isabel Nieves (1979) suggests that in a context of good employment opportunities for women, female centred families in fact facilitate women's employment. She found in San Salvador a number of consanguineal household groups, often consisting of two generations of female adults and perhaps adult male kin, for example, two or more adult sisters and their elderly mother, and perhaps her spouse. Other men visited the women, and perhaps fathered their children, but were not considered members of the residential group. She argues that these units are adaptive for women's employment, since members can share domestic work and child care. Similarly, the prevalence of female-headed consanguineal households in the Caribbean area probably goes far toward explaining that area's distinctive age patterns of female employment in which participation is actually highest among women of child-bearing years.

After finding that 21 per cent of urban households in Morocco in 1971 were female-headed, Susan Joekes argued that this type of structure, disconnected from the extended family, tended to depress the general female labour supply price, and thus the wage rate, since women in such households are in a weak bargaining position and are forced to work (1985, pp. 204–7). However, the position of these women in no way differs from that of poor male household heads whose wives do not work. Both are heavily dependent on the labour market. In fact it is daughters, or members of multi-wage households generally who, because they have access to some subsistence from other household members, might be less likely to hold out for higher wages.

It is important to realise that family structure is not always a given, but may change in response to employment opportunities. Two particular aspects of household structure have been thought to be especially affected by women's waged employment: divorce rates and women's marriageability. Helen Safa (1981, pp. 427–8) has contrasted the situation in the border area of Mexico, where there seems to be a high rate of household break-up as well as high female employment, with that in Jamaica, where high female employment has not led to any increase in the already high number of female headed families. Wong and Ko report that the rate of divorce in Singapore, while still low, has been rising during the 1970s (1984, p. 33), and in east and west Africa, an increase in voluntary singlehood, desertion, divorce and unhappy marriages is reported for women white-collar workers in urban areas (Dinan, 1983; Schuster, 1979).

Safa suggests that two factors condition whether female employment is associated with marital break-up: the level of male unemployment, and the extent of patriarchal attitudes. The high level of household instability noted among families of Mexican border industry workers may be due more to high male unemployment, which forces men to leave for illegal immigration to the United States, than to female employment. Among female assembly workers in Cuidad Juarez interviewed by Fernandez-Kelly in 1978–79, the majority of men in their households were underemployed. Almost one-third of the women who worked in the textile and garment manufacturing industries were heads of households and the sole providers of income for their offspring (1983, pp. 217–9). The pinpointing of male unemployment is consistent with findings in the United States that whereas male unemployment often leads to family violence and break-up, female unemployment does not. An important factor is the existence of patriarchal attitudes in which men perceive failure to perform the earner role as undercutting their masculine identity, and see wives' employment as a threat to their authority. In Jamaica, significantly, there is also high male unemployment, but the less patriarchal attitudes mean that it does not pose such a threat to men's family roles.

Does employment for young, single women adversely affect their marriageability? This is an important question, since fear of such adverse consequences for daughters is one of the chief reasons for patriarchal opposition to their employment. Here there is a good deal of cultural variability and change, and more research is needed. In addition norms often vary by class, employment being more acceptable for upper-class and for very low-class women, but not for those in between. Writing of Egypt in the 1970s, Smock and Youssef (1977, p. 45) were pessimistic about the degree of attitude change in this highly patriarchal culture: except among the tiny westernised elite, 'The mere fact that a girl is highly educated or employed often jeopardises her chances of a good match' since she is thought more likely to be loose, immoral or promiscuous. Perhaps in reaction, parents maintained tight control over working daughters: even professional women were expected to live with their parents until marriage, to contribute their earnings to the family budget, to have a restricted social life, and to submit to parents' wishes as to whom they should marry. Indications are, however, that such attitudes are beginning to change. A 1980 study by Barbara Ibrahim reports approval by families of women working in factories, and continued or even enhanced marriageability for these workers (cited in Papanek, 1985, p. 327; for Mauritius, see Hein, 1986, pp. 288–9).

Hanna Papanek cites the persistence of localised marriage patterns in explaining why in Bangladesh rural areas it is still perceived that allowing an unmarried girl to attend secondary school away from the village would seriously threaten her marriage chances, whereas for an upwardly mobile urban family, a secondary education for a woman, and even a job, is perceived to increase her marriage chances (1985, p. 339). In Bangladesh in 1974, less than 5 per cent of rural women between 15 and 19 years were attending school, compared to 27 per cent of urban women.

Such differing views of the education, employment and marriageability nexus appear to prevail in Northern India as well, and Sharma describes the coexistence of two quite separate marriage markets, one for girls who are already employed or are in training, and one for girls who do not expect to do wage work. Matrimonial advertisements in newspapers are explicit on this point (1986, pp. 140–1). Sharma describes the strategy of providing a daughter with secondary or university education, in expectation of reciprocity later, as common among upwardly mobile or recently arrived urban Indian families (1986, pp. 130–1). But there appears to be a price in the marriage market: first, in the existence of a dual market — that is some educated men do not want or need an educated wife — and then in the nature of their sub-market. Often it is men of uncertain means who want a wife whose employment they can count on. An educated woman of modest class background may have to accept a husband of slightly less status or less reliable income prospects.

The marriage of daughters remains strongly tied to the distribution of family power. Only in cases where parents no longer control the marriage arrangements can one ask whether employment for women affects the woman's actual choice between marriage and singlehood, or timing of marriage. Growth in women's employment does seem to be correlated with rising age at marriage for women, for example in Singapore (Wong, 1981, p. 450) and in Ireland (Pyle, this volume). But whether this reflects the daughters' or the parents' choice must still be demonstrated, since parents often have a motivation to prolong the period when they benefit from a daughter's income.

Household Income and Resources

All relationships between household factors and women's employment can probably be shown to vary according to the household's class or income level. Among peasants, lack of productive resources such as land, when refracted through the household sex division of labour, may mean lack of resources for women and create tendencies toward women's proletarianisation. Among urban wage-earning households, low incomes force more members of the household, including women, to seek employment. Put another way, low incomes make it more likely that patriarchal cultural norms prohibiting women from working outside the home will be disregarded. On the other hand, higher household incomes and resources can make possible the observance of these norms.

Rising income levels will also, according to neoclassical theory, increase the demand for children but also make possible the purchase of alternative child-care options, each of these relationships having opposite effects on women's labour force participation. Income levels presumably also affect the demand for other domestic services in like fashion. Income also affects ability to afford education, and if equally allocated by sex this should increase women's level of marketable skills and their success in the job market. Perhaps because of its association with western education, income has also been shown to be positively correlated with egalitarian decision-making patterns between husband and wife, another factor which might tend to increase women's employment.

In assessing the reasons why women seek and accept employment, one must be wary of the response that 'economic need' is the only relevant factor. For example, one study of female textile workers in Egypt reported that every worker interviewed, whether married, single or divorced, stated that the sole reason for seeking employment at the factory was the economic insolvency of her household.

They reported that it would be nearly impossible for the family to survive without her earnings (Hammam, 1979). However, given the strong religious and social norms that factory work is demeaning for women, it is likely that economic pressures were seen as the only socially acceptable reason for their participation in such work. In the similar case of Morocco, Joekes (1982, pp. 41–2) points out that even though commerce and factory work are strongly condemned by theologians as unsuitable for women, women are in fact working at these occupations. They then seek to excuse, if not fully justify, their behaviour by reference to economic necessity. Their shame at working may persist, however; one was cited as saying 'I am not a good woman because I work'. Their behaviour has changed, but their religious values have not — a not uncommon human foible.

Theory would predict that the lower the household income, the greater the availability of women for economic participation. However, when actual employment, and sometimes even official labour force participation are examined, it appears that rates are disproportionately high among educated women and women from high-income families. Lustig and Rendon show for Mexico in 1968 that employment of women (as opposed to availability for employment) was much greater among high-income strata where the male head was employed than among similar low-income strata (1979, p. 147). De Miranda showed that for Brazil in 1970, rates of labour force participation increased with the level of schooling for both single and married women. For married women with a husband present, women from higher status households were much more likely to participate than women from low status households; however, for single women living with parents, there was little relationship between household socio-economic status and labour force participation (1977, pp. 270 and 272). Papanek shows for Egypt in 1976 that the proportion of the labour force accounted for by secondary educated women was increasing, while the proportion accounted for by illiterate women was decreasing (1985, pp. 323–5). Both Papanek and Miranda see the increasing demand for educated women in the market as seriously diminishing the earning chances of less-educated women. Stronger employer demand for educated female labour may be in a sense calling forth an increased supply from middle-class households; however these households may also be more willing to have wives work, since in comparison to the working class they may have more egalitarian sex role definitions. Some studies do show the reverse, however; Chaudhury (1979) reports for Dacca, Bangladesh, that the higher the husband's income, education and occupational level, the less likely the wife is to be employed. More studies on the relations between household income, demand for various types of labour, and levels of women's employment are obviously needed, especially those which distinguish more clearly between supply of labour and its actual employment, and which document female unemployment more adequately.

Household Decision-Making and Women's Employment

Household power and decision-making patterns ought to be considered as a relatively independent and autonomous factor affecting the supply of women to the labour market. Even if power and decision-making is an aspect of family life which is in some ultimate sense derived from the division of productive and reproductive work or from the distribution of income and resources, still, power in the family is not reducible to those material bases and its relation to them is not necessarily immediate or direct. Changes in resources may lead to changes in power only after considerable time lag.

Constantina Safilios-Rothschild (1982) has noted that women's power in the family can have a number of bases. She points particularly to reproductive power, of which there are two kinds: power based on number of children or sons, and power based on unequal love or sexual attraction of husband for wife. Second, there is power based on women's income or resources, or on her husband's or father's resources. There is also power based on women's own productive contributions to the household, and even power based on age. Safilios-Rothschild argues that in highly patriarchal societies all these various resources can be translated into power *only if men allow it*, that is, that there is residual power based on sex alone. Reproductive power is usually heavily dependent on men, since unless a woman also has independent productive resources she cannot support children herself. A man must recognise the child as legitimately 'his' and agree to support it. Too, there are many societies in which the productive contribution of women to the household is equal to or greater than that of men, but where men are still in control. Patriarchal ideology giving power to men can therefore arguably be said to have an independent effect.

Ann Whitehead (1981) also argues against the notion that power in the household depends directly or simply on relative incomes or labour inputs, drawing on material from both northeast Ghana and industrial Britain. In the British working class, where there is a single male breadwinner, the wage is not divided equally between husband and wife. Men generally reserve or receive a sum for individual consumption, and the rest of the wage goes for household expenses. The woman is expected to merge her personal interests and needs with those of the family, and any personal expenditure has to be taken out of the 'housekeeping money'. In the case where both husband and wife have jobs, their incomes are distinguished within the household, rather than simply pooled. The wife's, being looked upon as less stable, is used for 'extras', or discretionary spending, whereas the husband's is used for necessities. Thus male and female money wages become unequally 'gendered' when they enter the household, and the wife loses some control over her wage. In both cases, 'the conjugal contract, including the ideology of maternal altruism, effectively creates barriers to women disposing of their income freely on the market' (1981, p. 107). Whitehead implies that a rise in the wife's wage would not lead to a change in the household allocation system via an increase in the woman's power, but no concrete evidence to this effect is presented. Similarly, Beneria and Roldan find that wives in Mexican working-class families do not earn enough from home work to be able to significantly renegotiate any of the husband's strongly patriarchal prerogatives (1987, pp. 113–36).

Much more common, however, is the assumption that wives' employment, and resultant increase in their incomes, will be translated into increased decision-making influence for her in the household. This view sees the labour market as having a positive effect on women's status under some conditions. For Singapore, Wong and Ko report 'an increasingly egalitarian relationship between husbands and wives' (1984, p. 31), and that working wives had more say in household decisions than did non-working wives (1984, p. 33). Wives spend some of their salaries without consulting their husbands, although they often 'make little practical distinction between what they spend for the family and what they spend or save for their own use' (1984, p. 21). Stichter (1988) reports similar results for middle-income wives in Kenya, the move toward joint decision-making increasing with increases in household income. Acharya and Bennett's research on Nepalese families shows that women's employment outside the village significantly increased their domestic decision-making role (1982, p. 37). (See also Safa and Salaff this volume; Chaudhury, 1979; Pessar, 1984). Similar findings are largely accepted for the

United States (Blood and Wolfe, 1960). Some other studies, how-ever, have not found such a relationship, for example various studies in India (Mukherjee, 1974; H. Standing, 1985; Sharma, this volume). Safilios-Rothschild argues that the relation between relative incomes and decision-making will vary by class. Her findings from Greece indicate that in the upper middle and middle classes, the wife's income equality or superiority made for a more egalitarian relation-ship, but in the working and low-income class, the wife's equal or superior income threatened the husband's masculinity and actually led to a more patriarchal and oppressive relationship (Safilios-Rothschild and Dijkers, 1978; Safilios-Rothschild, this volume). In addition the relationship will vary by household structure; in the Caribbean, where female independence is already high, female wage employment does not seem to confer any *additional* family decision-making status on women (Moses, 1977).

For daughters, as opposed to wives, the effect of wage employment on family power seems to be much less, suggesting that parental patriarchal prerogatives may crumble more slowly than marital patri-archy. Salaff's classic work (1981) reports that daughters have been able to expand consumption levels and gain short-term freedoms in social life, but that most of their earnings are received and controlled by parents, and working daughters do not significantly expand their input into family decision-making. Nor does their low wage enable them to transcend their economic dependence on the family. Most continue to marry, and to cease employment when child-bearing commences. Kung's (1976, 1983) work on Taiwan, and Fernandez-Kelly's (1983a) on the Mexican border area, come to similar conclu-sions. Arizpe and Aranda's (1981, p. 471) study in the Zamora area of rural Mexico reports that half of the daughters employed in strawberry-packing plants turned over the greater part of their earn-ings to their parents and have only slightly improved their personal consumption. They do have more say in who they will marry, although they are still closely restricted and supervised by factory personnel, recruiters, and union leaders. As their job experience increased many women at the packing plants had increased their desire for education, and many complained bitterly that their fathers would not allow them to finish primary school or go on to secondary school. '. . . our parents say it does not pay for itself because we then go and get married, and it has only been a waste' (1981, p. 463).

The converse effects of household decision-making on women's employment can perhaps be seen most clearly when it comes to permitting wives and daughters to enter the labour force, or compelling them to leave it. If wives or daughters lose out in the distribution of family income, if family income is low, or if wives are given the responsibility of providing for children without adequate resources to do so, women will very likely have individual reasons for wanting to seek employment. Yet often they can exercise this option only if the husband or father gives permission. To take account of this common fact, we need to move beyond the neo-classical assumptions of individual preferences or joint utility functions, and to acknowledge that some people's preferences within the household are likely to prevail over other people's.

In their study of industrial homeworkers in Mexico, Beneria and Roldan found that 40 per cent of the husbands in the sample opposed their wives' desire to work outside the home. Accepting piecework at home was a compromise, enabling the wives still to care for their home, children, and husband properly, and to show 'respect' for their husbands (1987, p. 146). Pyle (this volume) reports for Ireland that husband's approval was the largest single factor affecting whether wives worked, and Hein (1986) reports similar findings for Mauritius.

In a ceramics factory in rural Brazil, Neuma Aguiar (1975, p. 84) found that women workers did not make the decision as to whether they should work there. One worker said that her father had given her a sound beating when he found out that she and her sister wanted to work there. While most fathers had relented after a few years, husbands and fiancés continued to disapprove. A typical woman said that her fiancé expected her to quit work after marriage. 'I would prefer to stay', she said, 'but he says that he does not want me to. I think that two people earning makes life easier'. In strawberry packing plants in rural Mexico, Arizpe and Aranda found similar attitudes, fathers initially fearing that their daughters would become sexually loose and become pregnant. The local priests were also initially opposed; one thundered every Sunday from the pulpit that women would go to hell if they sinned by working in the factories. It was said that after the owners of the plant spoke with the priest and offered to pay for the cost of a new altar, he changed his view and began exalting the dignity of work (1981, p. 466).

The situation described by Arizpe and Aranda illustrates the ability of household-level decisions to affect the female labour supply and thus wages. In the areas around the factories, there is a large population of young women who have very few alternatives for work, a local crowding of the labour market, which drives down female wages. This is because fathers have now permitted daughters to work locally, but still forbid them to migrate to towns or to the United States border, whereas a majority of the young men do engage in outmigration in search of employment (1981, p. 470). Families are able to opt for restricting outmigration to males and still survive economically. In this way the family itself, in addition to employer discrimination, creates and sustains the dual labour market through patriarchal prohibitions on young women.

Where employment for daughters has persisted for a longer time, and involves more women, especially married women, the feedback effects on the household may be greater (for example, Safa, this volume). Already in the rural Brazil and Mexico cases just cited, fathers have moved from absolute prohibition of daughters' employment to conditional acceptance. Young single workers in electronics factories in Singapore have a good deal of freedom today: although they contribute about half of their incomes to help support their families, they often live in company flats, have active social lives, date men, choose their own marriage partners, and choose to delay marriage. The Malaysian girls in the sample reported that although they had initially migrated to Singapore against their parents' wishes, their families 'treat us better now that we are sending more money home' (Wong and Ko, 1984, pp. 10–13). Still, habits of obedience to patriarchal authority at home may persist, and may contribute to hesitancy by women workers to undertake strikes and other direct labour protests while at work (Elson and Pearson, 1981).

Research focusing on fertility has usually taken account of husband/wife decision-making as a critical variable. The classical hypothesis is that the more egalitarian, companionate, and communicative the husband-wife relationship, the lower the fertility and the higher the likelihood of effective contraceptive use. This hypothesis might hold for a number of reasons, but the more persuasive one is that one of the main obstacles to the limiting of fertility stems from the opposition or indifference of men. If this is the case, then if employment for wives in traditional societies leads to their greater input into household decision-making, it might in this way lead to fertility decline. Nadia Youssef cautions, however, that mere high female power or female participation in fertility decision-making might not automatically lead to lower fertility if other conditions do not favour it; it might not be a sufficient condition (1982, pp. 193–5). As Safilios-Rothschild puts it, where women's power is based strongly on their reproductive capacities, they will not have the motivation to reduce fertility even if they have the power. Only when women have satisfactory alternative power bases do they wish to lower fertility via birth control (1982, p. 121).

Family power must be examined in more detail for various kinds of extended families, and for matrilocal families; most research thus far has examined only nuclear or conjugal units. Likewise, most research has focused solely on the husband-wife relationship; ways must be found to assess the relative power of various members of complex households: children, siblings, grandparents, co-wives and others. Another persistent problem in the conceptualisation of power involves the confusion of the jointness/separateness (autonomous) dimension with the power dimension. These are patently not the same; jointness cannot be equated with equal power, nor can autonomy. Ways must be found to assess relative power in situations of clearly separated husband-wife domains of decision-making, such as are found, for example, in many African families. Despite the sophistication achieved in the study of family power in the United States, similar studies in the Third World pose a new range of unanticipated challenges.

CONCLUSION

This overview has concentrated on fertility, domestic work, structure, income and decision-making as the household factors having the most important impacts on female employment. Inevitably, a range of other aspects of family relations has been neglected. In particular there are the bio-social-psychological dimensions, such as adult physical and mental health, stress, marital happiness, and children's self-esteem, social adjustment, and school performance. A particularly fertile new field of research lies in assessing the effects of maternal employment on these factors. Increasingly, work and family are coming to be recognised as closely interacting structures, perhaps the two social systems that most profoundly impact individuals' lives.

One aim of this review has been to suggest that research on the linkages between family/household and women's gainful employment is increasingly needed and relevant to the situation of Third World women. The changing international division of labour is resulting in the shift of more and more production jobs to certain areas of the Third World, and a large number of these jobs are going to women. What effect is this major global economic change having on the quality of women's lives? What changes are taking place in the relation between work and family systems, between women's productive and reproductive roles? To answer such questions concepts drawn from the study of nuclear families in industrial settings cannot be mechanically applied. As this review has attempted to illustrate, world-wide variations in household and kinship structures pose challenges for the western-based economic theory of the household, yet the challenges are not insurmountable. In addition, we have attempted to show that household and kinship variations do affect female labour force participation in systematic and demonstrable ways. Existing research has provided a great deal of insight into these relations, yet in many ways it has barely scratched the surface. More research is needed, not only to understand women's lives, but to help them change them for the better.

Note

1. This refers to turnover between employment and non-employment over the life cycle, not to job turnover. Several writers, for example Joekes (1985) for Morocco and Humphrey (1985) for Brazil, point out that because of lack of promotion ladders and fewer job options, women actually have lower job turnover rates than men.

References

Abraham-Van der Mark, Eve E. (1983) 'The Impact of Industrialization on Women: A Caribbean Case', in J. Nash and M. Fernandez-Kelly, 1983, pp. 374–86.

Acharya, Meena and Lynn Bennett (1982) 'Women and the subsistence sector: economic participation and household decision making in Nepal', World Bank Staff Working Paper, no. 526.

Afshar, Haleh (ed.) (1985) *Women, Work and Ideology in the Third World* (London: Tavistock).

Aguiar, Neuma (1975) 'Impact of Industrialization on Women's Work Roles in Northeast Brazil', *Studies in Comparative International Development*, vol. X, no. 2, pp. 78–94.

Aldous, Joan (1978) *Family Careers: Developmental Change in Families* (New York: John Wiley).

Allam, Etimad Mohammad (1986) 'Egypt: Islam, Women's Industrial Work Patterns and Male Labour Shortages', in United Nations Economic Commission for Africa, African Training and Research Centre for Women, *Women and the Industrial Development Decade in Africa*, pp. 23–58.

Anker, Richard and Catherine Hein (1986), 'Sex Inequalities in Third World Employment: Statistical Evidence', in R. Anker and C. Hein (eds), *Sex Inequalities in Urban Employment in the Third World* (London: Macmillan) pp. 63–115.

Arizpe, Lourdes and Josefina Aranda (1981) 'The "Comparative Advantages" of Women's Disadvantages: Women Workers in the Strawberry Export Agribusiness in Mexico', *Signs*, vol. 7, no. 2, pp. 453–73.

Bailyn, Lotte (1978) 'Accommodation of Work to Family', in R. and R. Rapoport (eds) *Working Couples* (New York: Harper) pp. 159–74.

Barrett, Michele (1980) *Women's Oppression Today* (London: Verso).

Becker, Gary S. (1981) *A Treatise on the Family* (Cambridge, Massachusetts: Harvard University Press).

Beechey, Veronica (1977) 'Female Wage Labour in Capitalist Production', in *Capital and Class*, 3, pp. 45–66.

Beneria, Lourdes (1979) 'Reproduction, Production and the Sexual Division of Labour', *Cambridge Journal of Economics*, vol. 3, no. 3, pp. 203–25.

Beneria, Lourdes (1981) 'Conceptualizing the Labor Force: The underestimation of women's economic activities', in Nelson N. (ed.), *African Women in the Development Process*, pp. 10–28. London: Frank Cass.

Beneria, Lourdes (1982) 'Accounting for women's work', in Beneria, L. (ed.), *Women and Development: The Sexual Division of Labor in Rural Societies* (New York: Praeger).

Beneria, Lourdes, and Martha Roldan (1987) *The Crossroads of Class and Gender* (University of Chicago Press).

Bennholdt-Thomson, Veronika (1981) 'Subsistence Production and Extended Reproduction', in K. Young, C. Wolkowitz and R. McCullagh (eds), *Of Marriage and the Market* (London: CSE Books) pp. 16–29.

Blood, R.O. and D.M. Wolfe (1960) *Husbands and Wives: The Dynamics of Married Living* (Glencoe, Illinois: Free Press).

Blumberg, Rae Lesser, and Maria Pilar Garcia (1977) 'The Political Economy of the Mother-Child Family: A Cross Societal View', in L. Lenero-Otero (ed.), *Beyond the Nuclear Family Model: Cross-Cultural Perspectives* (Beverly Hills, California: Sage) pp. 99–163.

Bolles, A. Lynn (1986) 'Economic Crisis and Female-Headed Households in Urban Jamaica', in J. Nash and H. Safa, *Women and Change in Latin America* (South Hadley, Massachusetts: Bergin and Garvey) pp. 65–83.

Boserup, Ester (1970) *Women's Role in Economic Development* (London: Allen and Unwin).

Bryceson, Deborah and V. Vuorela (1984) 'Outside the Domestic Labor Debate: Towards a Theory of Modes of Human Reproduction', *Review of Radical Political Economics* vol. 16, nos. 2 and 3, pp. 137–66.

Chapkis, Wendy and Cynthia Enloe (1983) *Of Common Cloth* (Washington DC: Transnational Institute).

Chayanov, A.V. (1966) in D. Thorner, B. Kerblay, R.E. F. Smith (eds), *On The Theory of Peasant Economy* (Homewood, Illinois: American Economic Assn.).

Chaudhury, Rafiqul H. (1979) 'Marriage, Urban Women and the Labour Force: The Bangladesh Case', *Signs*, vol. 5, no. 1, pp. 154–63.

Chinchilla, Norma (1977) 'Industrialisation, Monopoly Capitalism and Women's

Work in Guatemala', in Wellesley Editorial Committee, *Women and National Development* (University of Chicago Press) pp. 38–56.

Corcoran, M. and G.J. Duncan (1979) 'Work History, Labor Force Attachment and Earnings: Differences between races and sexes', *Journal of Human Resources*, 14, pp. 3–20.

Deere, Carmen Diana (1976) 'Rural Women's Subsistence Production in the Capitalist Periphery', *Review of Radical Political Economics*, vol. 8, no. 1, pp. 9–17.

Deere, Carmen Diana and Magdalena Leon de Leal (1981) 'Peasant Production, Proletarianization and the Sexual Division of Labor in the Andes', *Signs* (Winter) vol. 7, no. 2, pp. 338–60.

Deere, Carmen Diana (1983) 'The Allocation of Familial Labor and the Formation of Peasant Household Income in the Peruvian Sierra', in M. Buvinic, M. Lycette and W. McGreevey (eds), *Women and Poverty in the Third World* (Baltimore and London: Johns Hopkins University Press) pp. 104–29.

di Domenico, Catherine (1983) 'Male and Female Factory Workers in Ibadan', in C. Oppong (ed.) *Female and Male in West Africa* (London: Allen and Unwin) pp. 256–65.

di Domenico, Catherine, de Cola, L. and Leishman, J. (1987) 'Urban Yoruba Mothers: At Home and At Work', in C. Oppong (ed.) *Sex Roles, Population and Development in West Africa* (London: James Currey) pp. 118–32.

Dinan, Carmel (1983) 'Sugar Daddies and Gold-Diggers: The White Collar Single Women in Accra', in C. Oppong (ed.), *Female and Male in West Africa* (London: Allen and Unwin) pp. 344–66.

Durand, J.D. (1975) *The Labor Force in Economic Development: An International Comparison of Census Statistics* (Princeton University Press).

Edholm, F., O. Harris, and K. Young (1977) 'Conceptualising Women', *Critique of Anthropology*, 3, 9 and 10, pp. 101–30.

Elder, Glen H. Jr. (1974) *Children of the Great Depression* (University of Chicago Press).

Elder, Glen H. Jr. (1978) 'Family History and the Life Course', in Tamara K. Hareven (ed.), *Transitions: The Family and the Life Course in Historical Perspective* (New York: Academic Press) pp. 17–64.

Elson, Diane and Pearson, Ruth (1981) '"Nimble Fingers make Cheap Workers": An Analysis of Women's Employment in Third World Export Manufacturing', *Feminist Review*, 7, pp. 87–107. Also appeared as 'The Subordination of Women and the Internationalisation of Factory Production', in K. Young, C. Wolkowitz and R. McCullagh, *Of Marriage and the Market* (London: CSE Books, 1981) pp. 144–66.

England, Paula and Farkas, George (1986) *Households, Employment, and Gender: A Social, Economic and Demographic View* (New York: Aldine).

Fapohunda, Eleanor (1986) 'Nigeria: Women and Industrialization in Anglophone West Africa', in UN Economic Commission for Africa, African Training and Research Centre for Women, *Women and the Industrial Development Decade in Africa*, pp. 87–147.

Fapohunda, Eleanor (1983) 'Female and Male Work Profiles', in C. Oppong (ed.), *Female and Male in West Africa* (London: Allen and Unwin).

Fapohunda, Eleanor (1982) 'The Child-Care Dilemma of Working Mothers in African Cities: The Case of Lagos, Nigeria', in Edna G. Bay (ed.), *Women and Work in Africa* (Boulder, Colorado: Westview Press) pp. 277–88.

Fernandez-Kelly, Maria Patricia (1983a) *For We Are Sold, I and My People* (Albany, New York: SUNY Press).

Fernandez-Kelly, Maria Patricia (1983b) 'Mexican Border Industrialization, Female Labor Force Participation and Migration', in J. Nash and M. Fernandez-Kelly, 1983, pp. 205–23.

Folbre, Nancy (1982) 'Exploitation comes home: a critique of the Marxian theory of labour power', *Cambridge Journal of Economics*, vol. 6, no. 4 (December) pp. 318–29.

Folbre, Nancy (1986) 'Cleaning House: New Perspectives on Households and Economic Development', *World Development*, January.

Fortes, Meyer (1949) *The Web of Kinship among the Tallensi* (Oxford University Press).

Fuchs, V. (1971) 'Recent trends and long-range prospects for female earnings', *American Economic Review*, 64.

Fuentes, Annette and Barbara Ehrenreich (1983) *Women in the Global Factory* (Boston: South End Press).

Gardiner, Jean (1975) 'Women's Domestic Labour', *New Left Review* 89, pp. 47–58.

Goldschmidt-Clermont, Luisella (1982) *Unpaid Work in the Household* (Geneva: International Labour Office).

Goody, Jack (1958) (ed.) *The Developmental Cycle in Domestic Groups* (Cambridge University Press).

Goody, Jack (1972) *Domestic Groups* (New York: Addison Wesley).

Guyer, Jane I. (1981) 'Household and Community in African Studies', *The African Studies Review* vol. 24, nos. 2/3, pp. 87–137.

Guyer, Jane I. and Pauline Peters (eds) (1984) *Conceptualizing the Household: Issues of Theory, Method and Application*, proceedings of a conference held at Harvard University, November 1984 (Charlottesville, Virginia: Teleprint Publishing. Social Science Research Council).

Hammam, M. (1979) 'Egypt's working Women: Textile workers of Chuba el-Kheima', *MERIP Reports* 82, November.

Hareven, Tamara K. (1977) 'Family Time and Historical Time', *Daedalus*, 106, Spring.

Hareven, Tamara K. (ed.) (1978) *Transitions: The Family and the Life Course in Historical Perspective* (New York: Academic Press).

Hein, Catherine (1986), 'The Feminisation of Industrial Employment in Mauritius: A Case of Sex Segregation', in R. Anker and C. Hein (eds), *Sex Inequalities in Urban Employment in the Third World* (London: Macmillan) pp. 277–311.

Henn, Jeanne (1988) 'The Material Basis of Sexism: A Mode of Production Analysis', in S. Stichter and J. Parpart (eds), *Patriarchy and Class: African Women in the Home and Workforce* (Boulder, Colorado: Westview) pp. 27–59.

Hill, Reuben (1964) 'Methodological Issues in Family Development Research', *Family Process*, 3, pp. 186–206.

Himmelweit, Susan and Simon Mohun (1977) 'Domestic Labour and Capital', *Cambridge Journal of Economics*, 1, pp. 15–31.

Hoffman, Lois W. and F. Ivan Nye (eds) (1974) *Working Mothers* (San Francisco: Jossey-Bass).

House, William J. (1986), 'The Status and Pay of Women in the Cyprus Labour Market', in R. Anker and C. Hein (eds), *Sex Inequalities in Urban Employment in the Third World* (London: Macmillan) pp. 117–69.

Humphrey, John (1985) 'Gender, pay, and skill: manual workers in Brazilian industry', in H. Afshar, 1985, pp. 214–31.

Jaffe, A.J. and Azumi, K. (1960) 'The birth rate and cottage industries in underdeveloped countries', *Economic Development and Cultural Change* 9, 1 (October) pp. 52–63.

Jelin, Elizabeth (1982) 'Women and the Urban Labour Market', in R. Anker, M. Buvinic and N. Youssef (eds), *Women's Roles and Population Trends in the Third World* (London: Croom Helm) pp. 239–67.

Joekes, Susan (1982) 'Female-led Industrialisation: Women's Jobs in Third World Export Manufacturing: the case of the Moroccan clothing industry', IDS Research Report no. 15, Sussex University.

Joekes, Susan (1985) 'Working for lipstick? Male and female labour in the clothing industry in Morocco', in H. Afshar, 1985, pp. 183–213.

Joekes, Susan (1987) *Women in the World Economy: An INSTRAW Study* (New York: Oxford University Press).

Kung, Lydia (1976) 'Factory Work and Women in Taiwan: Changes in Self-Image and Status', *Signs*, vol. 2, no. 1, pp. 35–58.

Kung, Lydia (1983) *Factory Women in Taiwan* (Ann Arbor, Michigan: UMI Research Press).

Kupinsky, Stanley (ed.) (1977) *The Fertility of Working Women: A Synthesis of International Research* (New York: Praeger).

Lewis, Barbara (1977) 'Economic Activity and Marriage among Ivoirian urban women', in A. Schlegel (ed.), *Sexual Stratification: A Cross-Cultural View* (New York: Columbia University Press) pp. 161–91.

Lewis, Barbara (1982) 'Fertility and Employment: An Assessment of Role Incompatibility among African Urban Women', in E. Bay (ed.), *Women and Work in Africa* (Boulder, Colorado: Westview Press) pp. 249–76.

Lim, Linda (1978) 'Women Workers in Multinational Corporations: The Case of the Electronics Industry in Malaysia and Singapore', Michigan Occasional Paper no. 9, Fall, University of Michigan.

Lim, Linda (1983) 'Capitalism, Imperialism, and Patriarchy: The Dilemma of Third-World Women Workers in Multinational Factories', in J. Nash and M. Fernandez-Kelly, 1983, pp. 70–91.

Long, Norman (1984) *Family and Work in Rural Societies: Perspectives on Non-Wage Labour* (London: Tavistock).

Lopata, Helena Z. and Barrie Thorne (1978) 'On the Term "Sex Roles"', *Signs* vol. 3, no. 3 (Spring), pp. 718–21.

Lustig, Nora and Teresa Rendon (1979) 'Female Employment, Occupational Status, and Socioeconomic Characteristics of the Family in Mexico', *Signs* vol. 5, no. 1, pp. 143–53.

Madden, Janice (1985) 'The Persistence of Pay Differentials: The Economics of Sex Discrimination', in L. Larwood, A. Stromber and B. Gutek (eds),

Women and Work: An Annual Review, vol. 1, (Beverly Hills, California: Sage) pp. 76–114.

Milkman, Ruth (1983) 'Female Factory Labor and Industrial Structure: Control and Conflict over "Women's Place" in Auto and Electrical Manufacturing', *Politics and Society*, vol. 12, no. 2.

Mincer, J. and H. Ofek (1982) 'Interrupted work careers: Depreciation and restoration of human capital', *Journal of Human Resources*, vol. 17, no. 1, pp. 3–24.

Mincer, J. and S. Polachek (1974) 'Family investments in human capital: Earnings of Women', *Journal of Political Economy*, 82, S76–S108.

de Miranda, Glaura Vasques (1977) 'Women's Labor Force Participation in a Developing Society: The Case of Brazil', in Wellesley Editorial Committee, *Women and National Development: The Complexities of Change* (University of Chicago Press) pp. 261–74.

Moen, Phyllis and Martha Moorehouse (1983) 'Overtime over the Life Cycle: A Test of the Life Cycle Squeeze Hypothesis', in H. Lopata and J. Pleck (eds), *Research in the Interweave of Social Roles: Jobs and Families*, vol. 3 (Greenwich, Connecticut: JAI Press) pp. 201–18.

Moghadem, Val, (no date) 'Women, Work and Ideology in the Islamic Republic', unpublished paper.

Moses, Yolanda T. (1977) 'Female Status, the Family and Male Dominance in a West Indian Community', in Wellesley Editorial Committee, *Women and National Development: The Complexities of Change* (University of Chicago Press) pp. 142–53.

Mukherjee, B.N. (1974) 'The status of married women in Haryana, Tamil Nadu and Meghalaya', *Social Change*, vol. 4, no. 1.

Nash, June and Maria Patricia Fernandez-Kelly (eds) (1983) *Women, Men and the International Division of Labor* (Albany, New York: SUNY Press).

Nash, June, and H. Safa (eds) (1986) *Women and Change in Latin America* (South Hadley, Massachusetts: Bergin and Garvey).

Nieva, Veronica F. (1985) 'Work and Family Linkages', in L. Larwood, A. Stromberg and B. Gutek (eds), *Women and Work: An Annual Review*, vol. 1 (Beverly Hills, California: Sage Publications) pp. 162–90.

Nieves, Isabel (1979) 'Household Arrangements and Multiple Jobs in San Salvador', *Signs* vol. 5, no. 1, pp. 134–42.

O'Neill, June (1985) 'Role Differentiation and the Gender Gap in Wage Rates' in L. Larwood, A. Stromberg and B. Gutek (eds) *Women and Work: An Annual Review*, vol. 1 (Beverly Hills, California: Sage Publications) pp. 50–75.

Oppenheimer, Valerie K. (1982) *Work and the Family: A Study in Social Demography* (New York: Academic Press).

Oppong, Christine (1977) 'The crumbling of high fertility supports: Data from a Study of Ghanaian Primary School Teachers', in J. Caldwell (ed.), *The Persistence of High Fertility* (Canberra: Australian National University Press) pp. 331–61.

Oppong, Christine (1980) 'A synopsis of seven roles and statuses of women: An outline of a conceptual and methodological approach', Geneva: ILO World Employment Programme working paper.

Oppong, Christine (1982) 'Family Structure and Women's Reproductive and

Productive Roles: Some Conceptual and Methodological Issues', in R. Anker, M. Buvinic and N. Youssef (eds), *Women's Roles and Population Trends in the Third World*. (London: Croom Helm) pp. 133–50.

Papanek, Hanna (1979) 'Family Status Production: the "Work" and "Non-Work" of women', *Signs*, vol. 4, no. 4, pp. 775–81.

Papanek, Hanna (1985) 'Class and Gender in Education-Employment Linkages', *Comparative Education Review*, vol. 29, no. 3, pp. 317–46.

Peek, Peter (1978) 'Family composition and married female employment: The case of Chile', in G. Standing and G. Sheehan (eds), *Labour Force Participation in Low-Income Countries* (Geneva: ILO) pp. 51–74.

Pessar, Patricia (1984) 'The Linkage between the Household and Workplace in the Experience of Dominican Immigrant Women in the United States', *International Migration Review*, vol. 18, no. 4 (Winter), pp. 1118–1211.

Pittin, Renée (1987) 'Documentation of Women's Work in Nigeria: Problems and Solutions', in C. Oppong (ed.), *Sex Roles, Population and Development in West Africa* (London: James Currey) pp. 25–44.

Pleck, Joseph (1977) 'The work-family role system', *Social Problems*, 24, pp. 417–28. Reprinted in R. Kahn-Hut, A. Kaplan Daniels and R. Colvard (eds), *Women and Work: Problems and Perspectives* (New York: Oxford University Press).

Rodman, Hyman and Constantina Safilios-Rothschild (1983) 'Weak Links in Men's Worker-earner Roles: A Descriptive Model', in H. Lopata and J. Pleck (eds), *Research in the Interweave of Social Roles: Jobs and Families*, vol. 3, (Greenwich, Connecticut: JAI Press) pp. 219–38.

Rothstein, Frances (1986) 'Capitalist Industrialization and the Increasing Cost of Children', in J. Nash and H. Safa, 1986, pp. 37–49.

Ryan, Mary (1981) *The Politics of Reproduction* (London: Routledge and Kegan Paul).

Safa, Helen I. (1975) 'Class Consciousness Among Working Class Women in Latin America: A Case Study in Puerto Rico', *Politics and Society*, vol. 5, no. 3, pp. 377–94.

Safa, Helen I. (1981) 'Runaway Shops and Female Employment: The Search for Cheap Labor', *Signs*, vol. 7, no. 2 (Winter), pp. 418–33.

Safa, Helen I. (1983) 'Women, Production, and Reproduction in Industrial Capitalism: A Comparison of Brazilian and US Factory Workers', in J. Nash and M. Fernandez-Kelly, 1983, pp. 95–116.

Safa, Helen I. (1984) 'Female Employment and the Social Reproduction of the Puerto Rican working Class', *International Migration Review*, vol. 18, no. 4 (Winter), pp. 1168–87.

Saffioti, Heleieth I.B. (1978) *Women in Class Society* (New York: Monthly Review Press).

Saffioti, Heleieth I.B. (1986) 'Technological Change in Brazil: Its Effect on Men and Women in Two Firms', in J. Nash and H. Safa, 1986, pp. 109–35.

Safilios-Rothschild, Constantina (1972) 'The Relationship between Work Commitment and Fertility', *International Journal of Sociology of the Family* 2, pp. 64–71.

Safilios-Rothschild, Constantina (1977) 'The Relationship between Women's Work and Fertility: Some Methodological and Theoretical Issues', in S. Kupinsky, 1977, pp. 355–69.

Safilios-Rothschild, Constantina (1982) 'Female Power, Autonomy and Demographic Change in the Third World', in R. Anker, M. Buvinic and N. Youssef (eds), *Women's Roles and Population Trends in the Third World* (London: Croom Helm) pp. 117–32.

Safilios-Rothschild, Constantina and Dijkers, M. (1978) 'Handling unconventional asymmetries' in R. Rapoport and R. Rapoport (eds), *Working Couples* (London: Routledge and Kegan Paul; New York: Harper Colophon) pp. 62–73.

Salaff, Janet W. (1981) *Working Daughters of Hong Kong* (Cambridge University Press; ASA Rose Monograph Series).

Schmink, Marianne (1984) 'Household Economic Strategies: Review and Research Agenda', *Latin American Research Review*, vol. 29, no. 3, pp. 87–101.

Schmink, Marianne (1986) 'Women and Urban Industrial Development in Brazil', in J. Nash and H. Safa, 1986, pp. 136–64.

Schultz, T. Paul (1981) *The Economics of Population* (Reading, Massachusetts: Addison-Wesley).

Schultz, T.W. (1974) *Economics of the Family: Marriage, Children and Human Capital* (University of Chicago Press).

Schuster, Ilse (1979) *New Women of Lusaka* (Palo Alto, California: Mayfield Publishing).

Seccombe, Wally (1974) 'The Housewife and her Labour under Capitalism', *New Left Review*, 83, (Jan.–Feb.), pp. 3–24.

Seccombe, Wally (1983) 'Marxism and Demography', *New Left Review*, 137, (Jan.–Feb.), pp. 22–47.

Sharma, Ursula (1980) *Women, Work and Property in North-West India* (London: Tavistock).

Sharma, Ursula (1986) *Women's Work, Class and the Urban Household: A Study of Shimla, North India* (London: Tavistock).

Smith, M.G. (1962) *West Indian Family Structure* (Seattle: Washington University Press).

Smith, R.T. (1956) *The Negro Family in British Guiana* (London: Routledge and Kegan Paul).

Smock, Audrey and Nadia Youssef (1977) 'Egypt: From Seclusion to Limited Participation', in J. Giele and A. Smock (eds), *Women: Roles and Status in Eight Countries* (New York: John Wiley) pp. 33–80.

Standing, Guy (1978) 'Female labour supply in an urbanising economy', in G. Standing and G. Sheehan (eds), *Labour Force Participation in Low-Income Countries* (Geneva: International Labour Office) pp. 87–122.

Standing, Guy (1982) *Labour Force Participation and Development*, 2nd edition (Geneva: International Labour Office).

Standing, H. (1985) 'Women's Employment and the Household: Some Findings from Calcutta', *Economic and Political Weekly*, vol. 20, no. 17 (April 27) pp. 23–38.

Stichter, Sharon (1985) *Migrant Laborers* (Cambridge University Press).

Stichter, Sharon (1988) 'The Middle Class Family in Kenya: Changes in Gender Relations', in S. Stichter and J. Parpart (eds), *Patriarchy and Class: African Women in the Home and Workforce* (Boulder, Colorado: Westview Press) pp. 177–203.

Stichter, Sharon and Jane Parpart (1988) 'Introduction: Towards a Materialist Perspective on African women', in S. Stichter and J. Parpart (eds), *Patriarchy and Class: African Women in the Home and Workforce* (Boulder, Colorado: Westview Press) pp. 1–26.

Stycos, J. and R.H. Weller (1967) 'Female working roles and fertility', *Demography*, vol. 4, no. 1, pp. 210–17.

Sutton, Constance and Susan Makiesky-Barrow (1977) 'Social Inequality and Sexual Status in Barbados', in A. Schlegel (ed.), *Sexual Stratification: A Cross-Cultural View* (New York: Columbia University Press) pp. 292–325.

Tilly, Louise A. (1981) 'Paths of Proletarianization: Organization of Production, Sexual Division of Labor, and Women's Collective Action', *Signs* vol. 7, no. 2, pp. 400–17.

Tilly, Louise A. and Joan W. Scott (1978) *Women, Work, and Family* (New York: Holt, Rinehart and Winston).

UNESCO (1986) *World Survey On The Role of Women in Development* (New York: United Nations).

Voydanoff, Patricia (1987) *Work and Family Life* (Beverly Hills, California: Sage).

Whitehead, Ann (1981) '"I'm hungry, mum": The Politics of Domestic Budgeting', in K. Young, C. Wolkowitz and R. McCullagh (eds), *Of Marriage and the Market: Women's Subordination in International Perspective* (London: CSE Books) pp. 88–111.

Wong, Aline K. (1981) 'Planned Development, Social Stratification, and the Sexual Division of Labor in Singapore', *Signs*, vol. 7, no. 2, pp. 434–52.

Wong, Aline K. and Yiu-Chung Ko (1984) 'Women's Work and Family Life: The Case of Electronics Workers in Singapore', Michigan State University, WID Working Paper no. 64, September.

Wood, Charles H. (1981) 'Structural Changes and Household Strategies: A Conceptual Framework for the Study of Rural Migration', *Human Organisation*, vol. 40, no. 4, pp. 338–43.

Yanagisako, Sylvia J. (1979) 'Family and Household: The Analysis of Domestic Groups', *Annual Review of Anthropology*, vol. 8, pp. 161–205.

Young, Kate (1983) 'The Creation of a Relative Surplus Population: A Case Study from Mexico', in L. Beneria (ed.), *Women and Development: The Sexual Division of Labor in Rural Societies* (New York: Praeger) pp. 149–78.

Youssef, Nadia H. (1974) *Women and Work in Developing Societies* (Westport, Connecticut: Greenwood Press).

Youssef, Nadia H. (1978) 'The Status and Fertility Patterns of Muslim Women', in L. Beck and N. Keddie (eds), *Women in the Muslim World* (Cambridge Massachusetts: Harvard University Press) pp. 70–85.

Youssef, Nadia H. (1982) 'The Interrelationship Between the Division of Labour in the Household, Women's Roles and their Impact on Fertility', in R. Anker, M. Buvinic and N. Youssef (eds), *Women's Roles and Population Trends in the Third World* (London: Croom Helm) pp. 173–201.

2 Women and Industrialisation in the Caribbean[1]
Helen I. Safa

Export-led development strategies have become increasingly popular in Latin America and the Caribbean in the past decade, especially in the manufacturing sector. Although the Border Industrialisation Programme in Mexico is the best known and most important in terms of exports to the United States, other countries also have turned to export as a way of earning foreign currency and alleviating the current debt crisis, sometimes spurred on by the neo-liberal policies of the International Monetary Fund.

In the smaller countries of Central America and the Caribbean, exports have long been the primary development strategy, ever since their incorporation into the world economy in colonial times. However, starting in the 1960s, in addition to traditional agricultural exports such as sugar, coffee and bananas, there was an increase in manufacturing, following the 'industrialisation by invitation' strategy initiated by Puerto Rico a decade earlier. Import substitution industrialisation, which was designed in the post-war period to stimulate domestic industry in the rest of Latin America, never achieved great success in the Caribbean, due to the lack of capital and technology in these countries (even more acute than in the larger countries). The small size of these countries combined with their low purchasing power also limited the possibilities of developing a viable internal market, which is critical for import substitution. In order to gain access to foreign markets, capital, and technology, Caribbean countries are forced to sell through multinational corporations.

In recent years, spurred on by the debt crisis and growing unemployment, the competition among Latin American and Caribbean countries for foreign investment in export manufacturing has been intense. Governments attempt to encourage foreign investment by lifting trade barriers and by offering tax holidays, subsidised credit, export subsidies and freedom from import duties on raw materials and machinery needed for production. Special export processing zones are constructed at public expense for export manufacturing plants, complete with water, electricity and roads. Thus the state has played a major role in fostering export manufacturing, often aided by the United States Agency for International Development, which has recently made this a key development strategy throughout Latin America (Joekes, 1987b, p. 5).

United States government support for export manufacturing is also reflected in the 1983 enactment of President Reagan's Caribbean Basin Initiative or CBI. The CBI enables qualified Caribbean Basin countries to acquire one-way duty-free access to United States markets for certain exports for a twelve-year period. This expands the market for export growth, and obviates the need to develop an internal market required under import substitution. The market for export manufacturing is entirely external, and therefore demands the maximum reduction of production costs, principally wages, in order to compete effectively on the international level. In fact, the availability of cheap labour appears to be the prime determining factor for investment; hence, most of the jobs generated through export manufacturing are for women, who previously represented a small percentage of the industrial labour force under import substitution. It has been estimated that there are approximately one million jobs in export processing zones in developing countries, about one quarter of them in Central and South America and the Caribbean (Joekes, 1987b, p. 10). International Labour Organisation surveys indicate that employment in multinational enterprises in developing countries has increased very rapidly since the 1960s and that employment opportunities for women have increased roughly parallel to those for men (ILO, 1985, p. 11).

This paper will examine the impact of paid employment in export manufacturing on the status of women in two Caribbean countries, Puerto Rico and the Dominican Republic. Although it has never been publicly stated, Puerto Rico's Operation Bootstrap has served as a model for export-oriented industrial development under the CBI, as well as earlier strategies of 'industrialisation by invitation' (Pantojas-Garcia, 1985). Thus, Puerto Rico can offer important lessons for the rest of the Caribbean on the limitations of this model. The Dominican Republic, on the other hand, is a classic case of recently initiated export manufacturing, with three well-developed free trade zones employing a total of 16 000 persons in 1979. Between 1975 and 1980 the revenues generated by the export processing zones increased five-fold, while exports grew from 27 million to 116 million in the same period (Duarte and Corten, 1981, p. 6). In 1986 there were a total of 30 000 women working in export processing zones, employing between one-fifth and one-third of the national female labour force in manufacturing (Joekes, 1987a, pp. 67–8). In addition to a small fourth zone opened in Puerto Plata in 1983, two new sites were in an advanced stage of preparation in 1986, and several other sites have been designated as zones in various parts of the country (ibid, p. 33). Clearly export manufacturing is a key component of Dominican development strategy, and now constitutes a principal source of female industrial employment.

In this study, we shall focus on the garment industry, which along with electronics, has been the area of greatest growth in export manufacturing in the Caribbean Basin. Although textiles and garments have been excluded from the CBI, due to opposition from United States labour and manufacturers, they continue to benefit from special import quotas assigned by the United States to certain Caribbean countries (ibid, p. 40). The Puerto Rican data consists of a survey conducted in 1980 among 157 women workers in three branch plants of the same United States garment manufacturer, all of which were located in the western part of the island. While the interviews were done by a research assistant, I also interviewed plant managers and collected secondary information, and in 1986 followed up with in-depth interviews with a sub-sample of 15 women. For the Dominican Republic, I was fortunate to be able to utilise survey data collected by CIPAF (Centro de Investigacion para la Accion Femenina), a private Dominican women's research centre, which in 1981 conducted a survey of 529 women workers in both domestic industries and in the three major export processing zones then operating in the country. In this paper, I have analysed only the data on the 231 women workers in export processing zones. In 1986 together with a research assistant, I conducted similar in-depth interviews with a sub-sample of 18 women, all working in the garment industry in La Romana, the largest of the export processing zones. This paper focuses largely on the results of the sample survey, but the insights gained from the in-depth interviews enabled me to go beyond the survey data and obtain a better understanding of the impact of paid employment on the lives of these women workers, as I shall try to outline below.

GENDER SUBORDINATION AND INDUSTRIALISATION

There is now an intense debate in policy as well as academic circles regarding the benefits of export manufacturing for women workers (Tiano, 1986). Some argue that export manufacturing 'integrates women into development' by providing them with badly needed jobs, while others maintain that this form of industrialisation only intensifies women's exploitation because the jobs are unskilled, poorly paid, and offer no possibility of upward mobility. In reality, these positions are not mutually exclusive, since women, like other marginal groups, may be integrated into exploitative jobs. Thus, in this paper we wish to go beyond this debate and explain what permits women to be taken advantage of as a cheap and vulnerable labour force. The essential question then becomes: what makes women more vulnerable as workers than men? Why have they become the preferred labour force for export manufacturing?

Clearly there are historical precedents for the use of women in labour-intensive industries such as export manufacturing. Historical studies show that women have always constituted a source of cheap labour for industrial capitalism, since the early days of the Industrial Revolution in England, France and other western European countries (Tilly and Scott, 1978). In the United States as well, there was a constant search for cheap labour, with industries moving from the employment of the daughters of native farm families, to immigrant women, to overseas production through export manufacturing as the cost of domestic labour became too high (Safa, 1981). But what made women cheaper to employ than men?

The answer lies in the sexual division of labour brought about by industrial capitalism. With the movement of production outside the home into the factory, the family ceased to function as a productive unit and became dependent on wages earned outside the home. Although production became increasingly public, reproduction remained within the private sphere of the family, though many reproductive functions such as education were also taken over by the larger society. Men became the primary breadwinners and women were relegated largely to the domestic sphere, because of their child-rearing responsibilities. In this way, the new sexual division of labour forced most women to become dependent on men as wage earners, and the family lost much of its economic autonomy.

Marxist feminists have emphasised the separation of women's productive and reproductive roles resulting from industrial capitalism as a primary source of women's subordination. Paid employment is seen as one way of breaking down women's isolation and dependence on men. Paid employment is expected to give women greater economic autonomy, to increase their authority in the household, and to develop their class consciousness as workers. However, there are many obstacles to achieving such goals, including the segregation of women into poorly paid, unstable jobs (such as export manufacturing), their double burden of paid employment and domestic labour, and a gender ideology which continues to portray women as 'supplementary' workers even when they are fully employed (Hartman, 1981).

In short, women's dual productive/reproductive role weakens the effects of paid employment on women's status. Women are a more vulnerable labour force than men because they are still primarily defined in terms of their domestic role, and therefore not given full legitimacy as workers. This has led feminist scholars like Barrett (1980, p. 211) to argue that the family is 'the central site of the oppression of women'. Barrett maintains that gender ideology is formed principally within the family through a woman's dependence on a male wage and is reflected at other levels of society such as the workplace and the state.

However, I would argue that there are various levels of women's subordination, within the family, within the workplace, and within the state, and that these different levels need to be kept analytically separate. It is true that the social construction of gender takes place largely within the family and is reflected at other levels of society. However, this does not eliminate the labour market or the state as independent sources of women's subordination, as I shall try to show here. In short, I do not dismiss the family as a source of women's oppression, but I think its importance needs to be examined in relationship to these other two areas.

Our data also demonstrate that paid employment has an impact on gender ideology, which is neither as static or uniform as Barrett depicts. Her model of a nuclear family with a principal male wage earner and dependent housewife does not apply to our Puerto Rican and Dominican households, where women are making a major contribution to the household economy. As we shall see, this has had a major impact on gender ideology in the family, but it has not affected women's status as subsidiary workers in the workplace and in the eyes of the state. We shall examine the status of Puerto Rican and Dominican women workers in the workplace, at home, and at the level of the national state in the following pages.

WAGES AND WORKING CONDITIONS

Between 1970 and 1980 the female industrial labour force in developing countries increased by 56 per cent. In 1980, 28 per cent of industrial workers in developing countries were women, led by Asia, and followed by Latin America and Africa. (ILO, 1985, p. 7). The continued search for cheap labour helps to explain this increase. The ILO (ibid, p. 39) reports that wages for women workers in multinational industrial enterprises in developing countries typically range from a minimum of 5 to 25 per cent of wages for similar jobs and workers in their western industrialised home countries. These wages are usually at or above the legal minimum wage, and compare favourably with women's wages in domestic industries and alternative low-skill occupations, such as farming, domestic service, and most service sector jobs. Still these wages are 25 to 50 per cent lower than those of comparable male workers, and are usually not sufficient to support a family (ibid, pp. 42–3).

Low wages in export manufacturing reflects the common misconception that women's wages are only a supplement to the family income and therefore need not be adequate to support their dependents. This tends to confirm Barrett's argument that men are seen as primary wage earners, which legitimises the payment of lower wages to women. It is reinforced by the fact that most women workers in export manufacturing worldwide are young and single and it is assumed that they are only responsible for their own expenses and may even be supported by their families. However, our data from Puerto Rico and the Dominican Republic show that even young, single women are making a major contribution to the family income. This is especially true for single women who live at home and may be one of several contributors to the family income. For example, in our sample of Puerto Rican women workers in the garment industry, a woman's salary never represents less than 40 per cent of the total family income, while among female-headed households, most women are the sole source of support for their families (Safa, 1985, pp. 91–2).

Management prefers to hire young women because they are supposed to be more efficient, have lower rates of absenteeism, and cost less in terms of maternity benefits. In line with traditional gender ideology, many managers also believe that married women belong in the home. This helps to explain the overwhelming predominance of young, single women in export manufacturing, where 85 per cent of women workers worldwide are under the age of 25 (ILO, 1985, p. 31). Both in Puerto Rico and the Dominican Republic, however, in a departure from the global pattern, the majority of women workers in export manufacturing are married, while there is also a considerable percentage of women who head their own households. In fact, employers in the Dominican Republic indicate a preference for women with children because they feel their need to work ensures greater job commitment (Joekes, 1987a, p. 59). Their economic need is shown by the fact that, in the CIPAF study of women workers in the three principal free trade zones, nearly three-quarters of the female heads of households and nearly half of the married women claim that they are the principal breadwinner for the family (Ricourt, 1986, p. 49). It is clear that these women are not dependent on a male wage in the way that Barrett suggests. However, the preference for women with children has not led employers to improve their wages, which have actually been reduced through devaluation. With the exchange rates prevailing in August 1986, the monthly average wage for these women was approximately $90 (Joekes, 1987a, p. 55).

Wages are much higher in Puerto Rico than in other areas, and in our sample most women earned between $120 and $129 weekly in 1980, or more than five times as much as in the Dominican Republic. Most women are paid on a piecework basis, and can increase their wage considerably with more experience and greater productivity. In Puerto Rico, despite a concerted effort to diversify industrial employment, the garment industry is still the largest industrial source of employment on the island, representing one-quarter of all manufacturing employment. The average hourly wage of $3.39 an hour in 1980 was the lowest industrial wage on the island, but still much higher than neighbouring Caribbean countries such as Haiti, Barbados, or the Dominican Republic. This competition from other areas has led to a severe decline in industrial employment in Puerto Rico, including the garment industry, where employment fell from 40 300 workers in 1973 to 33 900 workers in 1980 (Departamento del Trabajo, 1981, Table 1). Competition from other areas is likely to be increased by the CBI, unless Puerto Rico is able to establish a twin plant syndrome, similar to that along the Mexican border. Several twin plants have already been set up in the Dominican Republic and other Caribbean islands.

Competition from other areas also helps account for the high unemployment rates in Puerto Rico, despite continuing outmigration to the United States. Unemployment rates for men have risen more rapidly than for women, and in 1980 stood at 19.6 per cent and 12.3 per cent respectively. Ninety per cent of our Puerto Rican sample say it is easier for a women to find a job than for a man, again emphasising that these women no longer look to men as primary wage earners. This reflects the shift from an agrarian to an industrial economy since 1940, with occupational changes tending to favour female employment over male. More than half the new jobs created between 1960 and 1980 went to women, and in 1980 their participation in the manufacturing sector was approximately equal (ibid, pp. 2–3). By 1980, labour force participation rates for women had increased to 27.8 per cent, while those for men declined from 80 per cent to 60 per cent in 1975 (Safa, 1985, p. 85). Some men withdrew from the labour force, while others migrated to the United States in search of employment.

Export manufacturing tends to seek out areas of labour surplus, since high unemployment (for men as well as women) often forces women into paid employment as an alternative. In the Dominican Republic, for example, open unemployment in 1980 stood at 19 per cent, and was still higher for women (25 per cent) than for men (16.5 per cent), many of whom are still employed in the agricultural sector. However, there were signs that, like in Puerto Rico, women were taking on increasing responsibility for the maintenance of their families. As in Puerto Rico, male labour force participation rates have been declining since 1960, while female rates have increased nearly fourfold over the same period, to 38 per cent among women aged 15 years or more in 1980 or 20 per cent for the entire female population (Joekes, 1987a, p. 5). Thus, in both Puerto Rico and the Dominican Republic, high male unemployment combined with job opportunities for women increases the burden on women to support their families, and further diminishes the myth of the male breadwinner.

The severe economic crisis in the Dominican Republic since 1980 has reinforced the need to incorporate additional wage earners into the family for survival. The crisis was brought on by declining terms of trade, rates of investment and growth in GDP (0.6 per cent in 1984), engendering a severe external debt and public sector deficits. The Dominican government appealed to the International Monetary Fund, which imposed an austerity programme resulting in devaluation, a decline in real earnings, growing unemployment and rampant inflation. Open unemployment stood at 27 per cent of the economically active population in 1986, while inflation rose to 38 per cent in 1985 (ibid., p. 9). Under pressure from industrialists in the export processing zones, the Dominican government granted them access to the parallel market, which enabled them to buy Dominican currency at a far more favourable rate. This resulted in a drastic lowering of operating costs, including labour (ibid., p. 39). Although wages were eventually adjusted to reflect devaluation, they have not kept up with the continuing decline of the Dominican peso. This new exchange rate policy is the main reason for the rapid growth of export manufacturing in the last three years. As one Dominican government official proudly told me: 'We have the lowest wages in the Caribbean — even lower than Haiti!'

Why don't workers protest? An abundance of surplus unskilled labour, ready to take even these low-paying jobs, and the constant threat of companies to relocate elsewhere weakens the possibility of labour solidarity among women workers in export manufacturing. There is little investment in machinery or physical plant, so these labour-intensive firms can move to a new location at no great cost. Labour turnover is very high, due both to the footloose nature of these plants, and to some questionable labour practices. In the Dominican Republic, one-third of the sample working in free trade zones had been employed by the same plant for less than a year (Reyes, 1987, p. 43). Workers are forced to serve an apprenticeship, which can last as long as three months, during which they receive only half the regular wage and can be discharged for any reason. Many workers cannot withstand the intense competition of piecework and the pressure of high production quotas. The normal work week is 44 hours, but many plants require employees to work overtime, whether they wish to or not, which puts a particular strain on women with young children. Export manufacturing plants generally lack transport, proper eating facilities, medical services or child care. Discontent is expressed in absenteeism and eventual withdrawal, rather than through unions, which do not operate in the export processing zones of the Dominican Republic, although not legally prohibited (Joekes, 1987, p. 46). Workers are fired and blacklisted with other plants if any union activity is detected.

Turnover in export manufacturing has also been attributed to the nature of the labour force recruited. Since the great majority of women workers in export manufacturing are young and single, it is assumed that many of these women are only working for a few years until they marry and/or have children, thereby reinforcing a traditional sexual division of labour and dependence on a male wage. However, most of the single women we interviewed in the Dominican Republic and Puerto Rico plan to continue working after they marry and/or have children, which again suggests that gender ideology is changing. In fact, in our Puerto Rican sample, a higher percentage of single women feel that married women with children should work than married women or female heads of household, which probably reflects their age difference. Given the high rates of unemployment and cost of living in both countries, women realise they cannot depend solely on a male wage to support a family.

In Puerto Rico, where all the plants studied are unionised, working conditions are considerably better, with shorter work weeks, comprehensive medical insurance, paid vacations, and other fringe benefits provided both by the government and the union contract. However, workers still lack public transport and child care facilities, though the majority of women workers see the latter as a need and would be willing to pay for it. The relative stability of employment helps to explain the high proportion of long-term employees, many of whom had worked in the same plant for 20 to 30 years, although there was no increase in salary with seniority. The greatest problem facing these women is the possible loss of employment due to production cutbacks and possible plant closings. In fact, one plant did close down in the process of our fieldwork, but because of union regulations, workers were given the opportunity to relocate to another branch plant of the same firm in a nearby town. All of the plants have been plagued with production cutbacks, which has brought about periodic loss of employment for 85 per cent of the women in our sample. Because of the many years they have been working in the garment industry, the older workers do not feel capable of starting a new job, and are not likely to be hired over younger workers. Thus, the lack of job alternatives also restricts labour unrest among women workers in export manufacturing.

In the Dominican Republic, the job alternatives open to women are even more limited. In 1980, one-quarter of Dominican women were still employed in domestic service (Joekes, 1987a, p. 21), while others tried to eke out a living in the informal economy as self-employed vendors or artisans. In fact, many Dominican factory workers try to supplement their meagre incomes with a *san* or rotating credit association and other informal economic activities. Advancement on the job is also limited because there are relatively few technical or supervisory personnel, most of whom are men and often foreigners (ILO, 1985, p. 56).

Thus many factors contribute to the lack of class consciousness and worker solidarity in these new industrial plants, including the youth and constant turnover among workers, their recency of entry into industrial employment, low wages, high unemployment, lack of job alternatives, the fear of plant closures, and restrictive labour legislation which prohibits unions, strikes, and other forms of protest. All of these are class-related factors which could apply as well to men. In fact, we have seen that these women are entering the labour force in increasing numbers in part because of the difficulties men face in finding a decent job. Still women suffer from certain gender-specific disadvantages in the labour market which are rooted in their position in the household. Barrett (1981, p. 157) is correct in maintaining that women's primary role in the family prevents them from achieving full legitimacy as workers, and increases their possibilities of exploitation in the workplace. Women's increasing importance as wage earners has not yet been recognised, and makes management, unions and the state regard them as subsidiary workers. However, the women themselves recognise the importance of their paid employment, and it has had a significant impact on household authority patterns, as we shall see in the next section.

THE FAMILY, LIFE CYCLE AND HOUSEHOLD COMPOSITION

While Barrett underlines the importance of the family in understanding women's subordination, she fails to take into account all the structural as well as ideological factors that influence the impact of paid employment on gender roles in the family. In particular, the impact is likely to vary considerably for single women, married women, and female heads of household. These households vary considerably in size and composition, which in turn affects the sexual division of labour and authority patterns. At the same time, these different stages in the life cycle also affect women's attitudes toward work and their identification as workers.

For example, hiring young, single women is less disruptive of traditional authority patterns, since, as a daughter, a woman worker does not directly challenge the male role of economic provider in the same way a wife may (cf. Lamphere, 1986, p. 127). A daughter continues to defer to her father, even if he is not working, especially if he owns the house in which the family lives. Most of the young, single Puerto Rican women in our Puerto Rican sample are members of large rural households, where there are usually two and often three to five persons working. The effects of this multiple wage-earning strategy can be seen in the relatively high family incomes among these single women, where over 40 per cent of the households have annual incomes over $14 000 (Safa, 1985, p. 90). However, these relatively high incomes represent a particular stage in the family's life cycle, when they have a maximum number of wage earners contributing to the family income, which will be lost as children marry and set up households of their own. No households reported income from children no longer living at home.

These large rural Puerto Rican households tend to maintain strong patriarchal traditions and to follow a strict sexual division of labour, which is supported by the extended family setting. Men are not expected to participate in housework or childcare as long as there are other women around to carry out these chores. Mothers, on the other hand, often take over household responsibilities like cooking and cleaning for their working daughters. In this way, daughters are relieved of the double burden of paid employment and household responsibilities which wives face, and feel less conscious of the need to challenge traditional gender ideology.

These rural Puerto Rican households are part of a tightly knit network of kin and neighbours, who help each other out in child care, house building and shopping. Nearly all of the younger women in our sample have relatives living nearby, and over 60 per cent have relatives working in the same factory, and often travel to work together. Though there is a strong sense of sharing and solidarity, it is not so much with fellow workers, as with female kin and neighbours, who constitute for these young women their most important reference group.

There is little evidence of class consciousness among these young, single Puerto Rican women. They have not been working very long, and are generally satisfied with their jobs. Though they are aware of problems on the job and in the larger society, such as inflation and the movement of industry to other areas, they do not identify with these issues. If they lost this job, most of these young women would look for another job rather than staying home, because they need the money. Younger women are quite confident that they can find another job if they should be laid off, even in a better paying pharmaceutical or electronics firm. Nearly 80 per cent have a high school diploma, which gives them an advantage over older, less educated women. Most of them plan to continue working after marriage, and are already saving to buy or build their own home (still a tradition in the rural area). They are concerned with getting ahead, finding a husband and having a family, all matters which do not challenge the existing gender ideology or system of class inequality.

Older Puerto Rican women are less optimistic and some are also more isolated and alienated. This is particularly true of female-headed households, who tend to live in the city in smaller households of one to three persons. They have fewer kin living nearby, and tend to socialise infrequently, even with neighbours or fellow workers with whom they may have been working for many years. Small family size limits the number of wage earners per family, and many of the female-headed households depend entirely on their own salary for a living. Not surprisingly, over half of these female-headed households have the lowest incomes of $5000 to $8000 annually.

However, older married Puerto Rican women whose husbands also contribute to the family often enjoy incomes as high as $12 000 to over $14 000 annually. Despite the lack of male employment in the area, some of these men make over $175 a week, and may be employed as managers or other lower level professionals. Most men, however, earn between $100 and $175 a week, working in a factory, for the government, or in their own business such as carpentry or driving *públicos* (cabs that follow standard routes and take several passengers). Very few husbands are unemployed, and over half have been employed at the same job for the last five years, suggesting most of these men have stable jobs. Still married women generally contribute from 40 to 60 per cent of the household income.

Older Puerto Rican women are more likely to question management's authority and to argue for their rights than the younger, rural women. This helps explain why management prefers young workers, who are not considered as 'troublesome'. Many of the older workers have worked in the plant for 20 to 30 years and, unlike younger women, have little opportunity of obtaining another job outside the garment industry. They are very concerned with job stability, and feel extremely threatened by production slowdowns and possible closure, as happened with one plant. This is particularly true of female-headed households, whose entire livelihood often depends upon their continued employment, and who may even be cut off from union pensions if they are let go before age 62. While this could tend to make them more docile, it would appear that long-term paid employment has contributed to a sense of self-worth and independence among these older women, while urbanisation and isolation from kin has weakened the patriarchal tradition still prevalent in the rural area. Thus, older women may identify more strongly with the workplace than younger women, but they lack the cohesion necessary to develop a sense of collective action and to promote class solidarity.

Paid employment has had a greater impact on the sexual division of labour in the households of married than single women. Married women tend to live in nuclear families, and cannot count on the assistance of other household members as much as single women do. The husband is forced to help out more with household chores, although primary responsibility still rests with the wife. Age also makes a difference, with a slightly higher percentage of younger married women saying their husband helps out, reflecting generational changes in gender roles.

Authority patterns have shown a more decisive shift than the sexual division of labour, although most married women claim that paid employment has not given them more authority in the household. Nevertheless, the majority of married women now maintain that they share household decisions with their husbands. Since both are working, earnings are usually pooled for household expenses and husbands no longer have exclusive budgetary control, as was common when the man was the sole breadwinner. Most importantly, most Puerto Rican men now expect their wives to work and no longer consider it a threat to their authority. It is interesting that none of the divorced or separated women, most of whom are over 45, blamed the breakdown of their marriage on their working outside the home. Marital breakdown was generally blamed on the man's personal behaviour, such as drinking, other women or jealousy. Most men were employed at the time of the breakdown, suggesting that unemployment and the inability of the man to carry out his role as economic provider was also not a major problem. According to the women, their husbands were not threatened by their working. It would appear that paid employment, while not precipitating marital breakdown, at least enables the woman to leave an unsatisfactory marriage by providing her with an alternative source of income.

In the Dominican Republic, the industrialisation programme is much more recent than in Puerto Rico and nearly half the women workers in the CIPAF sample have been employed less than two years. These women are also much younger than the Puerto Rican sample, with most being under 30 years of age. Nevertheless, over one-half of the Dominican women workers are married and one-quarter are female heads of household. Most of the married women are in consensual unions, which are far more prevalent than in Puerto

Rico, where almost all of the married women in our sample have been married in a church or civil ceremony. Fertility levels are also higher, with almost half of the Dominican women with children having three or more children (Catanzaro, 1986) compared to a mean in our Puerto Rican sample of under two. Educational levels, however, are roughly comparable, and in both cases 39 per cent of the sample have completed high school. Although the general educational level is higher in Puerto Rico, it must be remembered that most of the women in the Dominican sample are much younger, and many of them continue to study at night or on weekends as they work.

As in Puerto Rico, life cycle has a profound impact on the way in which women regard their earnings and their contribution to the household economy. While 38 per cent of Dominican women workers consider themselves the principal economic provider, the figure is much lower for single and married women, and much higher for female heads of households, most of whom are divorced (Catanzaro, 1986, Tables 3–14). Among married women, husbands are generally considered the principal economic provider, and are chiefly responsible for basic items like food and housing. However, the great majority of single and married women also maintain that their families could not survive without their wages, suggesting that their wages are not supplementary but are making an essential contribution to the family income.

At the time of this study, the unemployment rate among the husbands of these Dominican workers was lower than the national average (11 per cent versus 16.5 per cent) and a number of them held fairly good jobs in factories or other skilled employment. The importance of the man's wages in the household economy of Dominican women workers may help explain the persistence of strong patriarchal authority patterns among the sample. Eighty per cent of the married women consider their husband to be the head of the household, and he tends to dominate financial decisions, such as making major purchases or paying the bills. On the other hand, couples have begun to share decisions on matters such as the number of children to have and the children's education, while the majority of married women make their own decisions on matters such as the use of contraceptives, and what organisations to join.

Women in consensual unions have a greater tendency to make their own decisions regarding finances and childrearing than women who are legally married, suggesting that the former may be less subordinate to men, and less dependent on them economically (cf. Brown, 1975). However, the reverse is true when women were asked their opinions about women's rights at home and in the workplace. Women were asked what they thought about matters such as the sharing of household tasks, whether women should work outside the home, whether domestic concerns should be left entirely to women, and whether men and women should enjoy equal access to education and to equal rights at work. In almost all these cases, women in consensual unions consistently favoured less autonomy for women than women who are legally married, though the majority of women in all cases were in favour of more egalitarian relationships. In part, this may be explained by the higher educational level of legally married women, among whom 49 per cent have completed high school as compared to 23 per cent of women in consensual unions. Higher educational level and legal marriage also implies that these women may come from a higher class background. However, the greater receptivity of women in consensual unions to patriarchal norms also suggests that these women may want the relative economic security and high status that is supposed to accompany legal marriage. It suggests that while women in consensual union may enjoy greater autonomy than those in a conjugal relationship, they also must carry a greater burden of responsibility for maintaining the family than women who are legally married. In order to oblige a man to assume this responsibility, a woman cannot directly challenge his role as head of the household and thus she is forced to support the maintenance of patriarchal authority patterns. This strong indication of the persistence of traditional gender ideology reflects the constraints women feel in raising a family on their own.

The extreme poverty which most female-headed households suffer helps explain the continued dependence upon the man as a provider. Even in Puerto Rico, female heads of households are very poor, since they are largely dependent on their low wages for survival. However, in our Puerto Rican study, most female heads of households are older and living alone or with other adults, so they can manage on their low wage, particularly if they own their own home. If they have young children, they are also eligible for AFDC and other forms of welfare assistance for survival.

No such transfer payments exist for female heads of household in the Dominican Republic, however, and many female heads of household have young children to support, which makes their situation far more precarious. In 1980, employed female heads of households in the urban areas of the Dominican Republic earned only slightly more than half as much as male heads from their principal occupation (Baez, 1985). Due to the shortage of housing and child care, as well as for economic reasons, unmarried mothers often leave their children with their mother or other relatives in the rural area, and visit them only once a week or less. Female heads of household often result from unstable consensual unions, and women may have to support children from more than one union. Therefore it is not surprising that they would prefer to have a man share this responsibility.

We cannot assume that paid employment is the only factor explaining the change in gender ideology that has taken place in some Dominican and Puerto Rican households. In our study, we have also noted the importance of other factors such as age, household composition, the life cycle, rural versus urban residence, the level of education and length of employment. It is clear that paid employment has a greater impact on wives than on daughters, because of the critical role that wives play in the household division of labour. It is also clear that changes in gender ideology have been more extensive in Puerto Rico than in the Dominican Republic, where most married women still regard the husband as the principal economic provider and head of household. Undoubtedly, many other factors need to be taken into account in explaining the wider acceptance of female paid employment and more egalitarian authority patterns that have developed in Puerto Rican working class households, including migration and greater exposure to the women's movement in the United States, the level of education, as well as the virtual total transformation from an agrarian to an urban industrial society, which is far less complete in the Dominican Republic. But in both areas, we can begin to see the erosion of patriarchal authority patterns as women become essential contributors to the household economy.

ROLE OF THE STATE

The final factor to be taken into account in examining the impact of paid employment on the status of women workers in export manufacturing is the role of the state. In order for countries to remain competitive in the international market, governments must assure export manufacturers a cheap and reliable labour force, and may institute restrictive legislation prohibiting unions, strikes and other forms of labour unrest. Governments fear that labour unrest and higher wages will induce export manufacturing industries to move elsewhere, as happened in Jamaica under the Manley government (Bolles, 1983) and in Puerto Rico with the extension of the federal minimum wage law to the island. Nevertheless, the ILO (1985, p. 62) claims that 'there appears to be no correlation between restrictive labour legislation or unionisation and attractiveness for foreign investment'. The ILO maintains that there are great differences in unionisation rates by country and by industry, and that multinational enterprises (not only those employing mainly women) are more likely to be unionised than national enterprises.

The CIPAF data from the Dominican Republic contradict the ILO assertions regarding the level of unionisation in multinationals and national enterprises. There are no labour unions in the export processing zones of the Dominican Republic, although 70 per cent of the women interviewed in the CIPAF survey indicated they were in favour of unionisation. Unions are not legally prohibited in the free trade zones, and in fact, workers' right to organise is supposedly required under the United States General System of Preferences and the Caribbean Basin Initiative, both of which have been extended to the Dominican Republic (Joekes, 1987, p. 46). In the CIPAF study, comparative data was drawn from women working in national manufacturing industries, and it was found that one-quarter of these women are unionised compared to none in the free trade zones. In addition, among women working in national manufacturing industries, wages were generally higher than in the free trade zones and daily working hours were shorter (Ricourt, 1986, p. 55). Part of the wage differential may be explained by the fact the 65 per cent of the women in national industries had received salary raises, compared to 46 per cent in the free trade zones, who have generally been working for less time (ibid., pp. 55–6).

Nevertheless, wages in the export processing zones fall well below the mean level of women's earnings in the Dominican Republic, and since they are tied to the minimum wage, they are unlikely to be raised without government support (Joekes, 1987a, p. 71). As we noted previously, labour costs have actually been lowered by the government granting industrialists in the export processing zones access to the parallel market, which gives them a far better exchange value for the dollar. Although wages were raised after the devaluation of the Dominican peso, there was a 17 per cent reduction in the actual average real wage in manufacturing industries between

1981–84 (ibid., pp. 54–5). At the same time, worker productivity in the Dominican Republic is estimated at 70 per cent of United States levels, which is higher than in almost all Caribbean and Central American countries (ibid., pp. 47–8), so employers could clearly afford to pay higher wages.

Several studies have noted that the discipline in the Dominican export manufacturing plants is brutal, with women not being allowed to talk to anyone or to go to the bathroom, while some women are forced to stand for hours (Duarte and Corten, 1981; Catanzaro, 1986; Ricourt, 1986, Reyes, 1987). Sexual harassment and favouritism has also been reported. Workers have lost their jobs for attempting to organise unions or other pro-labour activity, and are then blacklisted by other firms in the zone as well. Women who have tried to take complaints of mistreatment or unjust dismissal to the government Labour Office have generally been rejected in favour of management. It is not surprising, then, that in the CIPAF survey, less than 20 per cent of the women had ever presented complaints to the Labour Office (Catanzaro, 1986).

State services for workers are sorely inadequate. There is no public transportation to the zones, so women are forced to use private minibuses which are costly, hazardous and far from many of their residences. Some women are forced to take two buses, so the trip can last over an hour. Child care is also a severe problem, and housing is very expensive, so that many women decide to leave their children behind in the rural area. The lack of state health services is a major cause of absenteeism and reduced productivity for women workers, to the extent that some industrialists have begun to offer health facilities to workers directly. Not only are the state health services very slow, but there is an appalling lack of personnel and supplies, and services are not extended to workers' families, causing secondary absenteeism among women with children (Joekes, 1987a, pp. 49–50).

In Puerto Rico, working conditions in unionised plants are much better. The majority of our Puerto Rican respondents feel that unions have brought about improvement, particularly fringe benefits such as medical insurance plans and vacation and retirement pay. However, the most important concerns of workers are higher wages and more job stability, and unions in Puerto Rico have been rather ineffective in promoting either. Unions realise that industry has been leaving the island because of the competition of lower wages elsewhere, including the Dominican Republic, where the firm studied already has a twin plant which does the initial processing. Therefore, they try to offer workers compensation in the form of fringe benefits rather than higher wages. However, even here unions are in a difficult position because the Puerto Rican government already offers an array of worker benefits, such as medical care, unemployment insurance and social security. The majority of the population receive food stamps, which enables them to buy food at cheap prices. About one-quarter of our Puerto Rican sample received food stamps, chiefly in the large, rural households or among female household heads (Safa, 1985, p. 91).

Ostensibly a subsidy to workers, these transfer programmes, all of which are supported by the Federal government, actually enable marginal industries such as garment manufacturing, to continue paying low wages, and to weather fluctuations in demand by temporary layoffs. Transfer payments thus have become a device for holding low-wage, labour intensive industries on the island. Plant managers complain that these transfer payments have reduced the work ethic of the Puerto Rican worker, causing absenteeism and withdrawal from the labour force. However, in our sample, nearly 90 per cent of our respondents indicated that they expected to stay on the job indefinitely, and 85 per cent indicated they would look for another job if they were laid off, indicating a strong work commitment. In addition, over half of our respondents have never stopped working for prolonged periods, even for illness or pregnancy, particularly among female heads of household. Clearly there is a difference between this group and the large number of Puerto Rican female heads of household who are dependent on welfare payments for survival. It would appear from our data that in Puerto Rico, welfare payments are a more important factor in the formation of female-headed households than female paid employment.

Puerto Rico is not able to adopt the harsh, coercive anti-labour measures of the Dominican Republic because its workers are better organised and have more options, principally transfer payments and migration. Jobs have tended to hold more women than men on the island (Monk, 1981), and about one-fifth of our sample has worked in the United States, while over 60 per cent of the husbands of married women have migrated for a year or more. These workers also bring back principles of labour organisation learned in the United States, and are likely to be more knowledgeable about worker rights. Although Dominican migration to the United States has increased considerably during the past two decades, it still has not reached the proportions of Puerto Rico.

Both coercion in the Dominican Republic and co-optation in

Puerto Rico have produced a relatively docile labour force. The major threat to Puerto Rican workers is the fear the plants will move elsewhere, and unions and the government seem unable to stop the exodus. In the Dominican Republic, export manufacturing plants have also experienced a considerable attrition rate, with one-third of the plants leaving between 1970 and 1982 (Joekes, 1987a, p. 69). However, the continued influx of new plants and the growing importance of export manufacturing as a development strategy suggest that the government will do little to deter foreign investment in the near future, which means little improvement in wages, working conditions, or even state services. It could be argued that the government has little choice, given its staggering debt and poor terms of trade. Nevertheless, workers are being exploited in the process, and the fact that most are women may contribute to the state's apparent indifference to their plight.

CONCLUSIONS

While export manufacturing has served to integrate women into development by offering them a new source of industrial employment, its impact on their status in the family and in the larger society is contradictory. By taking advantage of women's inferior position in the labour market, export manufacturing may reinforce their subordination through poorly paid, dead-end jobs. On the other hand, women's increased ability to contribute to the family income may challenge traditional patriarchal authority patterns and lead to more egalitarian family structures. This is particularly true where, as in Puerto Rico and the Dominican Republic, women have become critical contributors to the household economy.

The data presented here on Puerto Rican and Dominican women workers enabled us to discern several factors which condition the level of contribution women make to the household economy. We have seen that the impact differs according to wages, working conditions and other job-related factors; the structure of the household economy and in particular, the nature of male employment patterns; the life cycle of the women employed, which partly determines the degree of dependence on their wages; alternative income sources for women including not only jobs, but transfer payments and the possibility of migration; and the role of the state and unions in supporting women's demands and workers' rights generally. In each of these areas, Puerto Rican women workers generally fare better than their Dominican counterparts, suggesting that they are in a better position to make a substantial contribution to the household economy, and therefore should have more leverage in family decisions.

The results appear to confirm this hypothesis. It would seem that with the increased incorporation of Puerto Rican women into paid employment, there has been a fundamental change in authority patterns and in the sexual division of labour in the household. Even in the Dominican Republic, the absolute authority of men in the household is being increasingly challenged, although men are still considered the head of the household. In place of the patriarchy of the past, a more egalitarian pattern is emerging in which women and men share responsibility for the maintenance of the household as well as sharing decisions and household tasks. This pattern is the result of a gradual process of negotiation, in which women use their earnings and the family's increased dependence on them to bargain for increased authority and sharing of reponsibilities within the household (cf. Roldan, 1985, p. 275).

Among female-headed households, paid employment is often critical to the family's survival and income levels are much lower. This is particularly true in the Dominican Republic, where women do not have recourse to transfer payments as in Puerto Rico. However, our data suggest that these female heads of household feel even more vulnerable than other women workers and have not lost their ideological dependence on a male provider. In fact, we have seen that women in consensual unions in the Dominican Republic remain committed to patriarchal norms, at least at the ideological level. It would seem that women prefer to bargain for more authority and respect in the household than to live alone with their children and fend for themselves. Why?

The evidence presented here suggests that women, even if they are working and major contributors to the household economy, prefer a stable conjugal relationship, though they are aware that it subjects them to male dominance. As Stolcke (1984, p. 292) notes, there are material as well as ideological pressures which continue to reinforce the nuclear family among the working class. The extreme poverty of female headed households makes all women realise how difficult it is to get along without a male provider. Women may be disillusioned with men as providers, but they are also aware of the severe disadvantages they face in the labour market. Women's ideological commitment to the family is more difficult to explain. As Stolcke (ibid., p. 286) notes, the family provides women with a social identity as wives and mothers which proletarianisation as wage workers has not diminished. This is evident among the women workers studied here, who continue to identify primarily as wives and mothers, despite their increasing importance as wage earners. In fact, most of these women now consider paid employment part of their domestic role, because they are working to contribute to the family's survival rather than for their own self-esteem or personal autonomy.

Thus, the family provides women with a social identity at the same time that it is a source of their subordination. Barrett fails to recognise the benefits the family provides for women, and stresses only its negative aspects. It may be that the social role of wife and mother is more highly valued and less alienated in Latin American culture than in the English middle class families upon which Barrett's theory is based. Class differences are also apparent, because middle-class women can obtain greater gratification from their employment than the working class women studied here. It seems to me that these Dominican and Puerto Rican women are aware of the contradictory nature of the family. But they are attempting to resolve this contradiction by trying to establish a more egalitarian relationship with their husbands, while retaining the family as a source of emotional and material support and social identity.

At least the women studied here have been more successful in negotiating change at the household level than in the public world of work. It is clear from the data presented here that in the Dominican Republic, women workers are subject to extraordinary exploitation by management, and receive little or no support from the government in their efforts to achieve better wages and working conditions. Puerto Rican women workers are much better off, but they too are limited by a paternalistic union which refuses to recognise many of their needs, and a government very dependent on foreign investment. Here the fault lies more with the lack of support women workers receive from government, political parties and unions than with the women themselves. At present these women workers have no adequate vehicles to express their grievances or to transform their sense of exploitation (which is very real) into greater class consciousness. Until women workers are given the same legitimacy as men, and not regarded as subsidiary or supplementary, they will be more vulnerable as a source of cheap labour.

Women's increasing importance as wage earners should enable

them to achieve greater recognition and higher levels of class consciousness as workers in their struggle with unions, management and the state. It would appear from our data that these institutions have proven more resistant to change than the family, and are still governed by a traditional gender ideology which the women themselves have begun to abandon. Dominican and Puerto Rican women workers have effected considerable change at the household level, which is one domain over which they still have some control. Their exploitation and vulnerability at the extra-household level may explain their reluctance to abandon the family, and their continued primary identification as wives and mothers.

Note

1. I wish to acknowledge the financial support of the National Institute of Mental Health for collection of the Puerto Rican survey data, and the Wenner Gren Foundation for collection and analysis of the in-depth interviews in both Puerto Rico and the Dominican Republic. Several institutions and individuals assisted me in this endeavour. Foremost thanks go to Magaly Pineda, Director, and the other staff members of CIPAF, who supplied me with the data on Dominican women workers that they had collected. I am grateful to Francis Pou, who assisted me in conducting the in-depth interviews in the Dominican Republic, and to Lorraine Catanzaro, Quintina Reyes and Milagros Ricourt, whose analysis of the survey data in their MA theses greatly facilitated my own study. Susan Joekes' data on the export processing zones in the Dominican Republic and her general paper on women and export manufacturing provided me with valuable insights. I also wish to thank Carmen Perez who conducted the survey on the Puerto Rican women in 1980, and Clifford Depin and his staff of the Puerto Rican office of the International Ladies Garment Workers' Union, who facilitated access to the factories and data from their own files. Finally, my appreciation goes to Lourdes Beneria, Carmen Diana Deere and June Nash, for their critique of an earlier draft and for their constant support and encouragement.

References

Baez, C. (1985) *La Subordinación Social de la Mujer Dominicana en Cifras* (Santo Domingo: Dirrección General de Promoción de la Mujer/ INSTRAW).

Barrett, Michele (1980) *Women's Oppression Today* (London: Verso).

Bolles, Lynn, (1983) 'Kitchens Hit by Priorities: Employed Working-Class Jamaican Women Confront the IMF', in J. Nash and M.P. Fernandez

Kelly (eds), *Women, Men and the International Division of Labor* (Albany: State University of New York Press).

Brown, Susan (1975) 'Love Unites Them and Hunger Separates Them: Poor Women in the Dominican Republic', in R. Reiter (ed.), *Toward an Anthropology of Women* (New York: Monthly Review Press).

Catanzaro, Lorraine (1986) 'Women, Work and Consciousness: Export Processing in the Dominican Republic', masters thesis, Centre for Latin American Studies, University of Florida.

Departamento del Trabajo y Recursos Humanos, Estado Libre Asociado de Puerto Rico (1981) *La Participación de la Mujer en la Fuerza Laboral* (Informe Especial E-27).

Duarte, Isis and Andre Corten (1981) 'Proceso de Proletarización de Mujeres: Las Trabajadoras de Industrias de Ensamblaje en la República Dominicana', in I. Duarte with A. Corten and F. Pou, *Trabajadores Urbanos: Ensayos sobre Fuerza Laboral en República Dominicana* (Santo Domingo: Editora Universitaria, Universidad Autónoma de Santo Domingo).

Hartman, Heidi (1981) 'The Family as the Locus of Gender, Class and Political Struggle: The Example of Housework', *Signs*, vol. 6, no. 3, pp. 366–94.

International Labour Organisation (ILO/United Nations Centre on Transnational Corporations) (1985) *Women Workers in Multinational Enterprises in Developing Countries* (Geneva: ILO).

Joekes, Susan (1987a) *Employment in Industrial Free Trade Zones in the Dominican Republic*, prepared for USAID/Dominican Republic (Washington DC: International Centre for Research on Women).

Joekes, Susan with Roxana Moayedi (1987b) *Women and Export Manufacturing: A Review of the Issues and AID Policy*, prepared for the Office of Women in Development, USAID (Washington DC: International Centre for Research on Women).

Lamphere, Louise (1986) 'From Working Daughters to Working Mothers: Production and Reproduction in an Industrial Community', *American Ethnologist*, vol. 13, no. 1., pp. 118–30.

Monk, Janice (1981) 'Social Change and Sexual Differences in Puerto Rican Rural Migration', in *Papers in Latin American Geography in Honor of Lucia C. Harrison* (Muncie, Indiana: Conference of Latin Americanist Geographers).

Pantojas-Garcia, Emilio (1985) 'The US Caribbean Basin Initiative and the Puerto Rican Experience: Some Parallels and Lessons', *Latin American Perspectives*, vol. 12, no. 4., pp. 105–28.

Reyes, Quintina (1987) 'Comparative Study of Dominican Women Workers in Domestic and Free Trade Zone Industries', masters thesis, Center for Latin American Studies, University of Florida.

Ricourt, Milagros (1986) *Free Trade Zones, Development and Female Labor Force in the Dominican Republic*, masters thesis, Center for Latin American Studies, University of Florida.

Roldan, Martha (1985) 'Industrial Outworking, Struggles for the Reproduction of Working-Class Families and Gender Subordination', in N. Redclift and E. Mingione (eds), *Beyond Employment: Household, Gender and Subsistence* (New York: Basil Blackwell).

Safa, Helen I. (1981) 'Runaway Shops and Female Employment: The Search for Cheap Labor', *Signs*, vol. 7, no. 2.

Safa, Helen I. (1985) 'Female Employment in the Puerto Rican Working Class', in *Women and Change in Latin America* (South Hadley, Massachusetts: Bergin and Garvey).

Stolcke, Verena (1984) 'The Exploitation of Family Morality: Labor Systems and Family Structure on Sao Paulo Coffee Plantations, 1850-1979', in R. T. Smith (ed.), *Kinship Ideology and Practice in Latin America* (University of North Carolina Press).

Tiano, Susan (1986) 'Women and Industrial Development in Latin America', *Latin American Research Review*, vol. XXI, no. 3, pp. 157–70.

Tilly, Louise and Joan W. Scott (1978) *Women, Work and Family* (New York: Holt, Rinehart and Winston).

3 Women, the Family, and the State: Hong Kong, Taiwan, Singapore – Newly Industrialised Countries in Asia[1]

Janet W. Salaff

Since the early 1970s Hong Kong, Singapore and Taiwan have entered the ranks of the 'newly industrialised countries' (NICs), based on export-led manufacturing, in which women played key roles. The successes of these countries are most impressive in an era when many Third World nations are, in contrast, suffering from a relative or even actual decline in their living standards compared with the developed nations.[2] They are grouped here because they bear many geopolitical and programmatic features in common. From them we can learn about one set of development strategies, and how these incorporate women into the new economy, polity and society.

This chapter will discuss the place of Chinese women in these three countries. The Chinese comprise 98 per cent of the populations of Hong Kong and Taiwan, and 76 per cent in Singapore, and so we are discussing the majority population. The three areas differ in size. Hong Kong and Singapore are city-states, with 5.4 and nearly 3 million people, respectively, while Taiwan, a province of China, with 19.5 million people, is 'country' size, and has a sizeable rural sector. However, all three areas suffer from limited natural resources and small populations. Half of Taiwan's 36 000 square kilometres is mountainous, and only one-quarter of the land is cultivated. To solve their developmental limitations, all three turned to export-led industrialisation programmes. Hong Kong was the earliest; Taiwan, and then Singapore followed to promote export-oriented industrialisation.

They are similar in the magnitude of their economic change: all experienced an annual rate of 10 per cent growth in their gross domestic products (GDP) during much of the 1960s and 1970s, and in the mid-1980s Taiwan continues this surging growth. Industry's share in the GDP ranged from 31 to 45 per cent in the three countries in 1977, and the share of manufacturing exceeds 25 per cent. Manufacturing is an important asset, then, and women are central in that part of the labour force that manufactures for export. After the developmental strategy of export-related manufacturing was adopted, the proportion of women in the registered labour force grew rapidly. From 21 per cent of the registered labour force in Hong Kong in 1931, 19 per cent in Taiwan in 1956, and 18 per cent in Singapore in 1957, women comprised around 34 per cent of the labour force in each of the three countries in the 1970s. Approximately 47 per cent of women in these countries now work for a wage full time.[3]

The constraints of the world capitalist economy shape the relationships among the state, economy, and society in each area. All three have strong, authoritarian states whose elites have engineered the supply of a relatively well educated and skilled, but low-paid labour force, much of it female, to far-flung world markets. Within each nation, state social policies draw the populace deeper into the commodity economy. Yet all three exclude basic social insurance provisions, thereby subjecting families, newly dependent on selling their labour to the world market and buying goods with their wages, to extreme uncertainty. The outcome is a so-called family strategy, with families turning to their own means to ensure survival. The state development strategies and the families' responses to them as they bear upon women are similar in the three countries, and form the topic of this paper.

STATE STRATEGIES IN PROMOTING EXPORT-LED INDUSTRIALISATION

Three main sets of political strategies are common to the export-led industrialisation programmes of Hong Kong, Taiwan and Singapore. They first created a climate of political stability, based on insulating the state from competing claims of class politics.[4] The interests and ideologies of state elites consequently play a determining role in shaping possible investment strategies. In all three areas technocratic developmental views prevail. Women pay little part in policy making as individuals or interest groups, which leads to their exploitation in the economic and social spheres.

The establishment of an economic infrastructure conducive to investment, and appropriate responses by elites to political-economic turning points is also important. The governments perform the key functions required for investment: provision of low-cost loans, credit, encouragement of new markets, labour force training, among others. These economic institutions are often lacking in new nations. In establishing their industrial frameworks, the three countries put into place an economy that draws on female wage labour.

Finally, the countries provide quality labour force participation through policies that make it impossible for families to continue to perform many quasi-economic activities they may once have pursued outside the money economy. Public policies further induct family members into the market to earn wages to meet old and new needs. And among the members that go out to work are women, especially young women. I turn now to the three sets of political strategies in each of the countries.

Hong Kong

Hong Kong is a colony of Britain due to revert to the People's Republic of China (PRC) in 1997 as a 'Special Administrative Region'. Hong Kong has a highly centralised administrative machinery. Fundamental policies are formulated in London, which appoints the colonial administration, headed by the governor, who in turn chooses his advisors from local men of industry and finance. Barred from holding central office, Chinese have had access solely to advisory channels to influence politics. Only in mid-1985 could Chinese become elected to the Legislative Council by the small fraction of the populace entitled to vote through an indirect electoral college and functional constituency system without political parties. Instead, Chinese mainly became elected urban councillors, popularly referred to as the 'garbage council', which oversaw urban services, half of whose 24 members are elected. Here one finds some women leaders.[5] The relatively passive indirect rule permits the Chinese to engage in economic activities, but not political activities that address political boundaries.[6] Top-down, essentially non-participatory rule remains in force.

Constrained by its colonial status, Hong Kong's geographical limitations, no natural resources, and its ambiguous, quasi-independent political relationship with China, the authorities evolved a laissez-faire approach to the economy. The public tenets of state rule are: to encourage growth, to reflect agreed-upon government policies, and to 'rule in the interest of the people'.

Undergirding laissez-faire market policies, the government provides a stable framework of laws, political controls, and fiscal and public expenditure practices. Even corruption led to dependable outcomes for investors, for example, cutting red tape. Municipal services are competently performed. Employers can count on economic policy outcomes: they know what to expect.[7]

Lacking universal franchise, the state is insulated from competing economic parties. Moreover, trade unionism is weak. Only 14 per cent of the labour force is unionised, and youths in general and the light industrial manufacturing section where women predominate are especially underrepresented. Even organised bodies have become *de facto* voluntary welfare organisations, and an insignificant force in industrial relations.[8] About a quarter of the labour force is unionised. Strikes have varied over the years but they usually are of short duration. Among the causes of trade union weakness is the political divisiveness of splits between left-, right-wing unions and independents, and the government's disinterest in supporting strong workers' groups. Hong Kong law restricts union effectiveness by not giving the workers the unequivocal right to strike. Moreover, the Labour Department has co-opted the role of trades unions in settling disputes and ensuring safety. In 1984 only 4 per cent of disputes were settled by direct negotiations between workers and their employees. Such actions lead to workers' preference for legislative protection over voluntary, negotiated arrangements.

Young adults claim to abhor politics — a claim due largely to a sense of political powerlessness. They believe the government, controlled by an elite of expatriates and wealthy Chinese, serves the elite's interest only, and would not aid them. They turn instead to individualist material goals. Women, who elsewhere in the region are quite active in the community, are uninvolved in Hong Kong.[9]

Government policies do not overtly control the economy. One finds no five-year plans, state direct investment, minimum wage, protection of local cottage industries, rent controls over commercial property, tax holidays or investment allowances. The state employs only 8 per cent of the labour force. Nevertheless, there is no institutional vacuum in the economy. Banks and experienced trading companies play the crucial institutional role in stimulating local manufacturing, purchasing and providing specifications, guaranteeing loans, and supplying credit and raw materials. Moreover, although no protection of indigenous firms is practised, established industrialists enjoyed a protected period in China prior to 1949, when they obtained knowhow, a market, connections, and capital.[10]

The state's role is nonetheless significant, starting with the reclamation of land and control of the land market. When Hong Kong experienced competition from other low-wage nations in the 1970s, the administration helped industry upgrade quality and obtain new markets. It selectively sold land to capital-intensive industry, such as the Dow petrochemical plant, although previously it was unwilling to court particular industrial sectors. It has established the statutory Vocational Training Centre to assist manpower training.

The Hong Kong state responds quickly to external shocks, which provides flexibility to its development strategies. After the 1949 Chinese revolution, the economic structure shifted from early economic ventures tied to shipping and the *'entrepôt'* economy, which had little place for women. In an *entrepôt*, goods from the place of origin are reshipped to their market. Hong Kong became instead an economy based on export-dominated manufacturing, which initially rested on low-cost labour, essentially of unmarried women. From 10 per cent of all exports in 1947, locally manufactured exports soared to 70 per cent in 1959. Transnational corporations became significant in key sectors of the economy in the 1960s, but local firms still dominate. With increased competition from other Third World countries, Hong Kong capitalists upgraded their products. From transistor radio assembly to digital watches and on to electronic circuits, from the 'rag trade' to clothes on the top end of the fashion market. Tourism and China *entrepôt* trade regained importance in the late 1970s. Manufacturing, 40 per cent of the labour force in 1966 and 50 per cent in 1971, dropped to 33 per cent in 1981. Women are so far underrepresented in such tertiary industries. But now that their part in the economy has been established, they may be able to sustain a high level of labour force participation despite the changing economic profile.

Public policies that create a quality labour force start with immigration regulation. While nearly three-fifths of the population was born in Hong Kong, half the immigrants came from cities and towns in China; and even peasants from the Pearl River delta had long contact with commercial agriculture. Shanghai migrants were especially accustomed to cut-throat economic competition. These became entrepreneurs who fueled the economy. Thus, the immigrant culture suited local industry.[11] It is further widely believed that manufacturers today convey their need for inexpensive labour to the government. Thus, at a time when Hong Kong women had had a low birthrate for years, and wages were high, the 1979 influx of boat people into the labour force dampened real manufacturing wage increases.[12]

Health care through government hospitals and outpatient dispensaries is low-cost, and basic care is adequate. The death rate is 5 per 1000 people. Women and men could expect to live 74 and 68 years respectively (at birth) in 1973. Family-planning workers are active and reach all women. The crude birthrate dropped from 20 to 17 per 1000 people in the decade before 1983. The age of marriage has risen, enabling women to receive more education and to work for a substantial period before marriage.

Full primary school in English or Cantonese Chinese education was guaranteed by the late 1960s, and three years of secondary education provided free in the late 1970s. Sixty-one per cent of youths aged 16 and 17 continued at their families' cost, reflecting the necessity to develop marketable skills in Hong Kong's competitive economy. Girls attended nearly as long as boys. Most youths (89 per cent at the turn of the 1980s) study in secondary schools where English is used, in repsonse to the international nature of the Hong Kong economy. The government funds polytechnical institutes to upgrade technical skills, but limits university places to 3.4 per cent of the age group (in 1985). Polytechnics provide a technically skilled labour force, with limited attendance for the select few, tied to the employment needs of the territory. The government regulates hours of work, and provides some recreational facilities, but gives no minimum wage or unemployment insurance. It furnishes a modicum of public assistance to the needy, but the able-bodied are ineligible, and are forced to turn to kin, or must accept any work they find. In this way, shifts in demand for labour greatly affect people's lives.

The Hong Kong government carries out one of the largest resettlement and low-rent housing programmes in the world. Public housing's capital expenditure budget in 1985 was one third of the total for the territory and is the largest single capital outlay in the budget. The government subsidises housing by providing free land as well as long term loans. It dominates the housing market. Small, high-rise public housing apartments in 'housing estates', or complexes, were home to 45 per cent of the populace in 1985. Rents are low, they range from HK$50 to HK$600 though they provide only minute spaces (averaging 36.3 square ft per person).[13] Income tests exist and family income must not exceed HK$5200; but after moving in, income has not been tied to rent. Tenants pay a median of 6 per cent of their income to public housing, as compared to the general populace which pays a median of around 20 per cent of their income for rent in the private housing sector where rents are three to four times greater than public housing. With such low rents, tenants treat their accommodations as a permanent subsidy. Some public housing units (28 per cent) are for sale at below market prices, but people are reluctant to buy, preferring rental accommodations. This changed in 1984 when, in an effort to reduce subsidies, the government stated it would peg rent to household income for those already living in public sector flats. The announcement created considerable opposition. Notably, what would be the basis of calculation of rent under the new plan? Occupants facing rent increases ask are their children's earnings to be included? The opposition, while informal, may still affect government policy.

This large-scale housing programme affects labour supply. Small factories and workshops obtain premises on the housing estates. Buses conduct the workforce to nearby factory districts. Women are likely to work near their homes, and local factories can draw on women as a labour source. The low cost of rented public housing also subsidises low wages. Further, squatters were seen as non-wage earners, outside the money economy, while people who live in public housing must earn wages. Traditionally, squatters, which are around 7 per cent of the population, paid nothing for housing (although now gangs of 'Triads' control the sale of huts which can be costly). High-rise dwellers must pay rent and utilities. Further, squatters engage in social exchange, but this declines greatly in the high-rise, where people are socially distant. Nor can they conduct subsistence economies in the high-rise as easily as they can in a squatter settlement. Resettlement thus places families in industrial time and space and propels them into the wage economy for their needs.[14]

The government does not enforce controls over wages and incomes, but the net effect of government spending is redistributive. Full employment exists, (although unemployment rose to 4 per cent of the population in the early 1980s), and the social services such as housing and health programmes improve the living standards of the poorest sectors. Thus, it has been estimated that real wages in Hong Kong increased by two-thirds in the 16 years up to 1978.[15]

Taiwan

Like Hong Kong, Taiwan is part of China, with an ambiguous political status. It is an island located off the southeastern coast of China mainland. The government has actively sought to build up the Taiwanese economy, and like the other two countries has turned to export-oriented manufacturing as the means to do so. In 1985 the Frost and Sullivan Research Group (United States) credited Taiwan with offering the best investment climate in Asia.

The 'Nationalist' Kuomintang (KMT) party of Taiwan is also insulated from local social groups. Following defeat of its party and army in the Chinese civil war in 1949, the KMT regime fled to the island of Formosa, where they took over ex-colonial Japanese properties, and the assets of the modern sector. 'Mainlanders', approximately 15 per cent of the population, monopolise high political posts, and dominate the mighty military machine, excluding 'local' Taiwan originated Chinese from leadership posts. Considerable aid from the United States through 1965 enabled the KMT to maintain its huge government bureaucracy, and one of the highest soldier/ civilian ratios in the world. Government consumed 31 per cent of Taiwan's Gross National Product (GNP) in 1954, 25 per cent in 1973, and 25 per cent in 1983. Defence spending exceeds 10 per cent of the GNP, and 8 per cent of the population is in the armed forces. Control over funds and manpower, a measure of state power, further insulates the state from local groups. Leftists and nationalists have been kept out of politics due to the perpetual war footing. Only in 1987 was martial law lifted.[16]

Taiwan does not have a strong labour movement. The Revised Labour Standards Law, passed in August 1984, has many provisions to protect workers. It was bitterly opposed by employers and economists, and is not well enforced. Unions were moribund for years; today only one-third of labour is organised, and factory management head the unions in many companies.[17] The KMT has used the perpetual conflict with the Chinese Communists to declare strikes and other labour actions illegal. Only one labour union is approved and unions are viewed as a tool of management. Nevertheless, workers without unions in their plants often desire them, but have no means to organise them. The lack of this vital bargaining weapon and labour surplus for years prevented workers from aggressively defending themselves. Unions on paper have numerous tasks, but in practice they approach the status of welfare societies. There is full employment today, but labour's impact on politics remains limited. The Constitution and Civil Laws provide equality between the sexes in the spheres of politics, education, property and some areas of family formation. But these laws are imperfectly implemented. There are three women's organisations, whose programmes stress political mobilisation against communism, not sexual equality. They direct their actions to promote family life and motherhood, extolled as women's service to the country. The Constitution grants women a 10 per cent quota of KMT posts and legislative positions. Women exceed this proportion in lower-level elected positions to the national assembly, Legislative and Control Yuans, prefectural and city councils, but there has never been a female cabinet minister. Surveys find women today to be nearly as interested in political issues as men and to vote in equal numbers with men. But only 5 per cent of women engage in community volunteer work.[18] Further, the government has recently affirmed the stress on motherhood as women's best way to make a national contribution. This emphasis may reflect the restructuring process at work in the economy, which has reduced unskilled labour, which women provided, and the concern for women to serve as an unpaid labour force to raise quality children for the new economy which goes along with the restructuring. Nevertheless, while women have gained a place even in managerial and administrative positions over the decades, and their economic momentum is likely to continue, at present only 67 of the 1900 licensed lawyers (up from 25 in 1980) and 37 of the 412 judges or prosecutors are women.[19]

The economic ideology of the KMT elite, based on the 'Three Principles of the People', of founding father Sun Yat-sen, combines private ownership of the means of production and central planning in an eclectic mix. In the 1950s, import substitution strategies strengthened the private sector. The role of public enterprises was reduced in the economy. Significant land reforms extended the control of the state into the countryside. Local Taiwanese capitalists benefited from these industrial strategies, and continue to dominate manufacturing. In 1960, American advisors and Taiwanese liberal technocrats obtained policy reforms that integrated Taiwan into the international world economy on the basis of its comparative advantage in low-wage labour. Local firms began to export: 93 per cent of the production of firms established after 1973 was exported. Investment policies are not left to the market, in contrast to Hong Kong. The Statute for the Encouragement of Investment governs investment incentives. Joint ventures and local content are promoted, in contrast to Hong Kong and Singapore, where local firms do not obtain special encouragement.[20] And the government plans soon to give tax exemptions for preferred industries.

Despite the importance of foreign capital, and the attempt to reduce the role of public enterprises in the economy, the state retains a significant share. Key industries, such as the major China Steel Corporation, are still state run, with a market oriented policy aimed at domestic functions. The combined assets of 12 national corporations was 25 billion dollars at the end of 1984, an increase of 86 times since 1956; they are worth 43 per cent of the 1984 GNP.[21]

Land reform placed a ceiling on investment in agriculture, and since political and military careers were blocked to them, propertied rural Taiwanese entered entrepreneurial careers. They reinvested profits in enterprise and commerce, not land. Industrial activities soon became widespread, and there is no economic dualism. Proto-industrial activities, such as electric looms and knitting machines in country homes and shops, are common. This decentralised pattern of economic development has shifted Taiwan's economy from agriculture to light industry, and industry is not confined to metropolitan enclaves. This strategy succeeded because colonial Japan built an infrastructure of communications and education, and which later expanded and spread more widely. The labour-intensive nature of Taiwan development made it useful to locate near rural labour sources, aided by government incentives, thereby greatly affecting rural women.[22] The structure of domestic production in 1984 was: gross agricultural product, 7 per cent, gross industrial product 51 per cent, and services 42 per cent.[23]

The three free trade export processing zones (the first of which was established in 1965), in which foreign firms bring in capital and raw materials, employ Taiwanese labour, and sell finished products overseas without having to pay the usual import duties and fees, hire mostly young rural women. In 1984 there were 80 000 workers in the zones. However, the three zones accounted for only 289 factories and 5 per cent of the workers in manufacturing in 1975. There is much labour mobility outside the zones, and women migrate to cities and towns to work, as much as the men do.[24] Thus the zones do not dominate the industrial picture.

World reccessions bear heavily on these export-oriented economies. The 'second oil crisis' of 1978 and recession of 1985 have had a severe impact on the three economies, although all three recovered. To protect itself against a recurrence, the Taiwan government, like that of Singapore, in 1978, is restructuring the economy by upgrading the capital and technology components of industry. Modern industrial parks, the Hsin Chu Science based Industrial Park, the '10 major construction projects', which had been followed by the 12 new development projects, reflect this transition. The government pledged US $40 million each year for five to six years for these projects. The government hand is crucial. In 1987 a very large scale integrated circuit manufacturer was planned, with personnel of the Taiwan Industrial Technology Institute involved. The government plans to supply nearly half the capital, the Philips Company half the remainder, and the rest will be shared by local companies. And in 1987 expansion of factory facilities and improving research and development is to account for 75 per cent of total investment by over 1000 firms surveyed. Large firms accounted for 40 per cent of those investigated.[25] The impact of the oil shock led to a drop in female employment between 1975 and 1980, but women re-entered the labour force. Nevertheless, the impact of restructuring on women's labour is not yet clear.[26]

In this closed society, rural to urban migration is the main source of new workers. Although women were legally granted inheritance under the land reform, informally they usually acquiesce to giving their brothers their proper share.[27] Thus, women were among the earliest factory applicants, leaving their brothers at home to tend the small fields.

Health standards have been improved, and the expectation of life for women and men was 73 and 68 years, respectively, in 1975, and 76 and 71 respectively, in 1985. Literacy and educational levels have risen rapidly. In 1980 nearly all children completed primary school, and most then went on to junior high school. Three-fifths of junior high graduates entered senior high school.[28] In 1987 compulsory education is being extended through 12 years. While sex differences in education were sizeable in the 1960s, by 1980 girls and boys received nearly the same years of schooling. However, by senior high and tertiary levels, they specialise in different types of training; girls in teacher's education, boys in university. And within university, education is also gender-linked.[29]

The Taiwan National Family Planning Association has been active for two decades, guided at the outset by American organisations. It disseminates birth control implements free of charge in the countryside. The crude birth rate fell from 47 per 1000 people in 1952 to 26 in 1976, and to 18 in 1985. For a long time, the Taiwan birth rate was higher than that of Hong Kong and Singapore, but it has finally dipped to the low crude rates of Hong Kong and Singapore (17 in both places in 1982). The drop is partly due to the agrarian component in the population having become urbanised in life style. Abortion was only legalised in 1985, and even then the woman's husband or guardian had to agree, but illegal abortions had been common. Finally, a rising age at marriage enables married women to work for wages for a longer period, which further depresses the birth rate. Nevertheless, as in Hong Kong and Singapore, due to women's low wages, married women are less likely to work: over 80 per cent of married Taiwan women are not economically active.

The government places the highest priority on economic growth, not income redistribution, and taxation, which has been on sales more than on firms or incomes, is regressive. Nevertheless, the rate of growth of the economy is so rapid and sustained that it has absorbed the unemployed, although underemployment is still a problem. Employers have to compete and offer slightly higher wages and fringe benefits than in the past, and even unskilled workers' wages have risen. Average per capita annual income (measured in per capita of the GNP) in 1985 was US$3144. Economic growth is considered responsible for the increased income equality over the past decades. As rural handicrafts declined, farmers sought new outlets for jobs. The proportion of net rural farm income derived from non-agricultural activities increased substantially, to 53 per cent in 1972, and to 61 per cent in 1979. The poorest families, with the least land, felt the need to earn supplementary wages first, and this has helped equalise income overall. Women's income contribution has been substantial. Women must continue to contribute because income is still unequally distributed across the populace: the lowest 40 per cent of the population obtained only 22 per cent of all personal income in 1982.[30] Rural households suffer the most from the income gap: the average non-farm household earned US$8125 in 1983, while the average farm household earned US$6300, or 78 per cent of urban wages.

Singapore

Singapore is comprised of Chinese (76 per cent), and Malays and Tamil Indians form the remainder of the population. The Chinese left southeastern China in the nineteenth and twentieth centuries in search of jobs and hoped for wealth. A colony of Britain from 1819 to 1959, Singapore is now an independent republic. It is situated off the Malay archipelago, and Malaysia and Indonesia are its geophysical neighbours.

Singapore also has a highly centralised state machinery insulated from competing local interests. Even less than Taiwan, and much less than Hong Kong, the state does not let market forces take their course. It intervenes to attract the type of investment it wants. The government is a multiparty system, opposition parties are dormant and a single party, the People's Action Party (PAP) has been constantly returned to office since independence, and holds all but one seat in Parliament. There is an active, if controlled, political life. Sovereign independence provides a sense of national purpose. These integrating and loyalty generating factors are used to enforce specific control over wages and incomes on elites and people.[31] The 'old guard' that carried Singapore from colonial to 'middle-developed' country nationhood is now grooming the second generation for political leadership, but the founder, Lee Kuan Yew, Prime Minister since 1959, remains in charge. The state is led by a highly educated, technocratic elite, which claims to represent all major interests. Labour, management, and the state participate in 'tripartite' political and economic policy-making bodies. This identification in structural terms dulls class conflict, and discourages interest group politics. The party state thus retains hegemony.

The PAP encourages union recruitment of labour, and may require companies to recognise its unions. Included here are electronics firms, in which large numbers of women are employed. Existing labour legislation is comprehensive and effectively implemented. However, only one-quarter of the labour force had ever been unionised in 1979, and since then the proportion has declined to 16 per cent (1985). Nearly all of these unionised workers are affiliated with the PAP-led National Trades Union Congress, which is headed by a government minister and run by government bureaucrats. The government has ensured labour peace, few days are lost through strikes, and other labour actions have become negligible. The fact that until now unions do not negotiate alone for improvement in workers' conditions has led to the decline in membership.

Women once played a large part in politics. Active in the anticolonial political struggle, several served in Parliament after independence in 1959. The Women's Charter in 1961, a forward-looking document, provides equal pay for equal work and outlaws polygamy.

However, fewer women now enter the political arena. For a number of years no women were fielded as PAP candidates. Indeed, PAP spokesmen proposed recently that educated women should spend more time with their families. Minister Goh Chok Tong stated in 1980, 'most women will not allow the men to do the housework' and 'women play a more beneficial role at home' than in the office. Feminists voiced concern over such public depreciation of their place, although they cannot express their concern through interest group politics. The second generation of leaders includes a number of women, and those that were elected to parliament strongly try to present their views.[32]

Of the three countries discussed here, Singapore has the largest component of foreign investment. Foreign investment fills a void, because local investors had dealt mainly in commerce and real estate prior to 1959, and were wary of taking the risks involved in manufacturing. The Singapore Chamber of Commerce failed to become part of the 'developmental elites'. The most important economic decisions are made by the young ministry technocrats and statutory boards. Foreign firms have made 76 per cent of investment commitments in manufacturing since 1976. Foreign and jointly owned firms account for 92 per cent of all exports by value. The government's macroeconomic management policy encourages foreign investment through incentives and labour controls. The state commits itself to stable, corruption-free administration, and further attracts investors, even though labour costs are high for the region.[33]

The key to Singapore's development programme is the extensive network of statutory boards, government enterprises, and state participation in private enterprise.[34] A substantial development budget devoted to social and economic infrastructure aids the economy. Local saving in state financial institutions such as the Post Office Savings Banks and Central Provident Fund help finance the development programme. The government is the main actor in the land market, and has earmarked half the land for development. The government also accounted for 20 per cent of total employment, but is cutting numbers in a move to cut red tape and privatise the economy. The tripartite National Wages Council until recently regulated wages, and the state invests in manpower training programmes to benefit private industry. These policies give Singapore a comparative advantage in export manufacturing, which this small city-state would have lacked if market forces prevailed.

The dual policy of encouraging foreign involved investors and state investment even further dampened local initiatives. Half of local capital is in 450 government-owned firms, plus 40 statutory companies, from shipbuilding to golf ranges and bird parks. But privatisation has begun the attempt to increase the role of the entrepreneur, now thought overlooked for too long with the outcome of loss of initiative and loss of top local personnel, who were creamed off by foreign companies and the government.

Government policies shifted Singapore from mainly an *entrepôt* in the 1950s, in which women played small part, to a short period of labour-intensive import substitution in the early 1960s, and then to export-oriented industrialisation after 1965. Women's role in the economy grew rapidly, especially in the manufacturing sector. Workers' wages were kept low at first, although in the early 1970s full employment was reached, and since 1979 wages climbed to their market levels. With the resulting wage increases, government shifted to promote capital-intensive activities, with manufacturing still a leading sector. Towards this end, the state in 1980 increased expenses by 20 per cent, two-fifths going towards development. Industrial and commercial development got S$1 billion. The state restructured investment incentives and set up a new national productivity council to oversee technical and skills uprgrading and increase labour productivity.[35]

In response to the 1984–85 recession, which affected the city state more strongly and for a longer period than the other two countries, Singapore again adopted radical measures: a wage freeze, reduction in employers' taxes and contributions to workers' pension funds. Quick and radical moves are possible here. The party-state now believes that the manufacturing sector cannot compete pricewise with near-NICs. Even the garment trade is upgrading from assembly line to high fashion or subcontracted brand labels (for Harrods, Macy's, Saks). It is further trying to freeze wages so as to reduce total manufacturing costs and maintain wage flexibility. And a new shift is being planned towards the financial and service sectors. Services are already 64 per cent of the GDP (1986), and the government will move to implement plans to upgrade Singapore's status as an international services, financial and computer centre. Examples include the health care industry. In order to develop exports in this field officials are beginning to look on medicine as they do electronics or financial services, integrating hardware (buildings, pill making) and software (medical skills). Here as elsewhere the line between public and private is fuzzy.[36]

Women are moving forward in the new jobs and industries, but not as quickly as men. Even so, the labour shortage and women's access to education, including technical skills, creates a demand from which women cannot be easily excluded. The need for highly skilled labour, however, appears to underlie the new 'eugenics' policy to return educated women to their homes to raise quality children for the more sophisticated industries.

Highly selective immigration policies fill labour force gaps. In the 1970s, a shortage of skilled labour led to immigrants on work permits. There were around 200 000 immigrant workers in the 1980s, most of whom were repatriated during the 1985 economic downturn, but others were again recruited in mid-1986 to meet a surge in demand in the electronics industry while keeping to the wage freeze. But state policy opposes long-term immigration. It aims to restructure the economy to do without guest workers.[37]

Medical and health care services have reduced mortality and greatly improved popular health. The expectation of life was 74 for women and 69 for men in 1980. The total fertility rate for the Chinese was 6.5 between 1947 and 1957. Then, post-1959 fertility controls brought birthrates down rapidly. At first voluntary, fertility limitation policy became stringent. In 1973, with already a crude birthrate of around 20, the government strove to attain replacement-level fertility. It introduced the Social Disincentives Against Higher Order Births, which penalised parents for bearing many children.[38] Since then the crude birthrate dropped to 17 (in 1982). The age of marriage has also risen. Women marry at an average age of 25.3, compared with 23.9 in 1975, allowing women to work longer before marriage when they might quit the labour force. There is currently a backlash, however. The state is urging educated women to resist spinsterhood (which is unusual anyway) and bear more than two children, to ensure that their so-called superior stock prevails. While dictated by eugenics, this policy is also related to the drive to raise the skill level of the populace, with middle-class women an unpaid labour force to rear their children for superior roles in society. This policy has incurred the most vocal reaction of women and men of any policy in recent years.[39] Other gender-linked family tasks are apparent. To support their family centred values, the party-state wishes to pass legislation making it compulsory for children to look after their elderly parents, meaning no doubt, wives.

In the mid-1970s, Singapore provided universal primary school, and by the late 1970s three years of secondary school. However, one quarter of the populace, mainly middle and older ages, has only primary school education. Education for girls and boys is nearly equal. Singapore's long term development plans have a human resource component built into them, with an outline of how many engineers, scientists, doctors, accountants, and labourers the economy will need. Some 20 per cent who will be unskilled labourers, will get primary school, while 20 per cent will get high school and half will be skilled technicians or fill the rank of clerks, while 5 to 10 per cent will go to university. Concern with the quality of the labour force has led to testing and streaming as early as age nine. Technical training in state-run or joint institutions follows junior high school. Higher education is not left to the market either, and is strictly regulated by national admissions policies. As in Hong Kong, a small per cent of the college-age youths are in tertiary institutions. Women have nearly an equal share of education, but courses are linked to expected gender roles.

As in Hong Kong, high-rise housing greatly affects the supply of labour. The state-provided housing by the Housing and Development Board, called HDB housing estates, housed half the populace in the mid-1970s and 76 per cent in 1985. Small factories are allotted space there, with electronics factories especially favoured, which draw on women residents as a labour force. The removal of people from squatter or *kampung* settlements (village communities) concentrates them as a labour force, and increases the expense of housing. Entry into the market economy is but the next step. Home industry has nearly disappeared, and even the shadow economy in the HDB estates serves the factory system directly. For example, instead of vending homemade food, women take in seaming for neighbourhood factories.

The housing estates aim to provide an integrating role in the political economy as well. By setting up residents' committees in them, the estates can accomplish diverse tasks, such as job information centres to sponsoring discussions on national issues.[40]

As a result of these state policies, the standard of living in Singapore has improved, full employment existed until 1985, and real wages have risen. Women's role in the economy is central to this new-found prosperity.[41]

FAMILY STRATEGIES IN ENCOURAGING WOMEN TO WORK

Families in the three countries have developed similar strategies in response to opportunities for employment. Implied in the concept of family strategies is a corrective to individualistic views of women wage-earners, motivated by personal interest and gaining power as a result of access to wages. Instead, in these societies family roles propel women to work and reap the benefits of their employment. Families are not just attracted by wage work opportunities for their offspring, but also have been forced by necessity to send members to work. They are decreasingly able to live off the land, to grow or make goods themselves. The penetration of the money economy forces them to depend on earnings to survive. They must buy food, clothing, furnishings, education, and housing. Families thus exploit the environment to get cash, but do so without the bounds of social structure. The following discussion sets out the structures that influence families' strategies of encouraging daughters to work.

I first turn to the work experiences of women in Hong Kong, Taiwan and Singapore in the mid-1970s, the height of the export-oriented industrial strategies in the three areas. I compare material from the following sources: my in-depth study of 28 unmarried working- and middle-class women in Hong Kong, research by Linda Gail Arrigo and Lydia Kung on Taiwan factory women the same ages, case histories by myself and Aline Wong of 100 young Singapore Chinese married women, from working- and middle-class backgrounds, half of whom were employed, and finally my research on older Taiwanese women.[42] This comparison shows how state strategies and the survival and family upgrading strategies of Chinese families have led to similar patterns of women's work in the three areas. Unmarried women dominate the female labour force, and married women are less likely to work, and if they do, less likely to stay in the formal sector. This single-peaked work pattern resembles that found in North America at the turn of the century.[43] North America today, in contrast has a double-peaked work pattern, with women working during the periods after they leave school and after their children are school age. This is not the case for the Chinese women under study here.

Structural reasons for the single-peaked labour force pattern include demographic pressures, especially a high dependency ratio, the

Chinese family type and the family life cycle stage. These will be discussed in turn.

Demographic Pressures

The demographic pressures, notably the high dependency ratio, created a special situation, which probably was not experienced in this form during earlier historical periods when higher mortality limited the surviving births. The high post-World War II birthrates in the three areas, with improved health conditions, meant that women born between 1948 and 1960 had many brothers and sisters. In Hong Kong, for example, women the age of the mothers of the young employed women I studied in the 1970s, aged 40 to 44 in 1971, averaged 4.3 live births. Comparable large families are found among Singapore and Taiwanese mothers of the same age cohort. This demographic phenomenon created a high dependency ratio, as measured by the ratio of the wage-earners to dependents. In the families of my sample of 28 Hong Kong women, dependency ratios of over 1:4 to 1:9 were common when respondents were youngsters, that is, about 1960 (Table 3.1). There was usually only the father as the single earner, and only when his contribution diminished — having become ill or having died, taken two wives or deserted the family — did the mother go to work. For another example, two-fifths of the fathers of men in the 100 Singapore couples studied were early teenagers, compelling their mothers, brothers and sisters and themselves to work. Most mothers were burdened with many small children, labour-intensive household chores and insufficient help at home, and they lacked education or industrial labour force experience. In Taiwan they had farm tasks to perform. Such mothers rarely worked for a wage outside the home.

But after these states propelled the populace out of the subsistence economy, the high dependency ratio made the need to earn money overwhelming. The demographic situation also suggested the means to do so — by sending children out to work. Thus, young women who went to work after primary school entered the new low-waged manufacturing work just then opening up in the 1960s, and the dependency ratio markedly improved. In my study of Hong Kong working daughters, I found that the dependency ratios improved to 2:4, and even 3:7 in 1965, because of the daughters' entry into the labour force (Table 3.1). Several years later, when unmarried work-

TABLE 3.1 *Ratio of wage earners to family dependents, 1960 to 1974*

Respondents	1960	1965	1970	1973	1974
Working Class					
A-li	1:8	3:7	3:7	4:6	4:6
I-ling	1:4	2:4	3:3	3:3	3:3
Mae-fun	1:7	3:5	4:3	4:3	3:3
Wai-gun	1:7	3:6	3:6	4:5	5:4
Upper Working Class					
Ming	1:6	1:7	3:5	3:5	3:5
Middle Class					
Ju-chen	1:9	2:7	3:7	4:6	3:6

ing daughters were aged 25 or so, the dependency ratio even reversed itself, with more workers than non-workers in many cases.

Although their wages were low, young women were able to support themselves, and as they gained work experience they could contribute more to the family coffers for survival, or even modest family prosperity (Table 3.2). The same was true for the unmarried Taiwanese women that Kung and Arrigo studied.

When young women married, they typically entered the household of their husband's parents, which created an extremely favourable dependency ratio, especially where the newlyweds lived patrilocally (with the husband's parents). In the family structure of married Singapore women, several adults were old enough to work. It was therefore usually unnecessary for the new bride with only a modest education to remain in the labour force, since she could not earn much in the kinds of women's jobs that were available. She would be requested to quit her job and do the housework, and might thereby free other younger unmarried daughters to continue their employment. Married women might, however, continue to work if they had above-average education and could work in the slightly better paying women's jobs, so long as other women were willing to undertake the housework in their stead. Nevertheless, when young women had children, they found it difficult to remain at work in the prevailing low-paid women's jobs. They simply did not earn enough to justify giving their homemaking burdens and obligations to others.

Moving on to a later life-course stage, we find that women have a greater chance to come into their own when they become mothers-in-law and grandmothers. It is this point when the dependency ratio

TABLE 3.2   *Occupational profiles, family members and income*

Occupation of several respondent's family members	*Household income per month*		*Percentage contribution of all daughters to household income, 1973*
Mae-fun	*1963*	*1973*	
Father[e]	$ 85	$120	
Mother[a]			
Sister[c]	25	80	
Mae-fun[c]	25	80	42%
Brother[e]		100	
(seven members in family)	$135	$380	
Wai-gun			
Father[d]	$ 50	$ 80*	
Mother[b]	30	60	
Wai-gun[c]	20	80	52%
Sister[c]		70	
(nine members in family)	$100	$290	
Suyin			
Father[e]	$ 15*	$ 20*	
Mother[b]	30	60	
Suyin[c]	30	120	73%
Sister[c]	30	100	
(eight members in family)	$105	$300	
Chin-yiu			
Father[f]	$---*	$200	
Mother[a]			
Chin-yiu[e]	30	160	66%
Sister[f]	30	170	
Sister[c]		70	
(seven members in family)	$ 60	$600	
I-ling			
Father[d]	$---*	$200	
Mother[b]	30	60	
I-ling[d]	30	100	28%
(six members in family)	$ 60	$360	

* Father contributing little due to unemployment, layoffs, illness or residence elsewhere.
[a] Never worked.
[b] Unskilled.
[c] Semiskilled.
[d] Skilled.
[e] Low-paid clerk.
[f] Well-paid clerk.
All dollars are given in US dollars, at the rate of $HK 5 = $US 1.

improves once again and, from the older woman's perspective, she is the one to benefit.

Type of Family

Families long looked forward to the transition to an improved dependency ratio. Parents thus tried to stretch out the period, within limits. Their goals were structured by the type of family that prevailed. Students of the Chinese family distinguish three conceptual units. The patriliny is the family core, composed of men linked by descent, and with equal rights to inherited property.[44] This family type is dominant in the three areas discussed here. It is true that few families in the two city-states inherited land, and Taiwanese land-holdings are small. Immigrant families in Hong Kong, and to some extent, Singapore, grew up without a full set of paternal kin, and in Taiwan, rural to urban migrants might also leave their kin behind. High wartime levels of mortality also meant a low probability of survival of grandparents and parents in the three areas.

Even though an ideal form of patrilocal household cannot come into existence everywhere, the patriliny still remains a guiding goal for behaviour, and so it is crucial for families to bear sons for economic reasons. In these industrial settings daughters earn less than sons, and only in Singapore do parents have some enforced contributory retirement savings. Parents also aim to continue the family line, and this further endears sons to them. In such a patrilineal family, ties of women to their kin cause potential loyalty conflicts, which the patriliny attempts to dilute. Daughters are expected to sever their ties with their parents on marriage, and so more fully turn their loyalty and energy to their husband's line.

The patrilineal concept affects strategies toward daughters' training and employment. When the young women born after the Second World War were growing up there was rarely enough money to train both sons and daughters in these three societies. Looking towards the future, parents saw daughters as 'goods upon which one loses', while boys were the future of the family. Thus, in the 1950s and 1960s, girls received less schooling than boys. Certain that they would work for only a few years until their marriage, with enough education to give them literacy, but not enough for them to enter skilled jobs with a future, young women were a prime labour force for low-waged export-oriented industries.

Turning to post-marital patterns, in Singapore patrilocal residence was common for young couples in 1975, and three-fifths of the couples I studied had once lived with kin, most with the husband's family. By the time one or two children were born, just under half of the families studied still lived with kin, and two-fifths of the couples studied lived with the husband's parents. In Taiwan, recent retrospective survey data finds that the same proportion had lived with their parents after marriage, and most with the husband's side. They were not expected to remain there. The eldest son married first by custom, and brought his wife into the household of his parents. He usually had children soon after marriage. From a low dependency ratio, the family then had a higher dependency ratio. When the next son planned to marry, it was hard to put all couples under one roof in a high-rise flat. The first son and his wife and children typically moved out, and the newlyweds took their place, improving the dependency ratio once again.

The second conceptual family unit, the domestic or economic family (*chia*) focuses on present-day economic survival, rather than the line of inheritance. The domestic unit contributes to the common budget. Since it draws on all available labour power, it includes women in these efforts. Ties to women's kin are tolerated and even may be encouraged if they contribute to the well-being of the household. The family's drawing upon the labour of the children stems from the domestic family.

The third family unit is formed by the bonds of sentiment between women and their children. Since the mother lacks the same rights as her husband in the line, she compensates by building bonds of support with her children. Emotional exchanges underlie these bonds of support. Where the father is emotionally distant from his offspring, as is common in Chinese families, the mother can more easily build up these alliances. Based on her Taiwan research, and applicable to Hong Kong and Singapore, Margery Wolf calls the female-centred family the 'uterine family'.[45] The willingness of daughters to contribute to the economic family, despite their exclusion from the patriliny, family inheritance and family future, is ensured by the sentimental bonds of support built in this family unit.

We can easily note that these several concepts of family can come into conflict. While people will attempt to minimise the conflict of expected behaviours,[46] at times conflict cannot be avoided, and the result may be particularly painful. An example is the case of a young Hong Kong working daughter, Wai-gun, depicted in Tables 3.1 and

3.2 above, who contributed her wage, first as an electronics assemb-
ler, then as a higher-paid garment seamstress, to the family budget
since she was 12 years old. In 1971, when I first met her, she was only
one of three contributors, and the only child to earn a living, in a
family of nine members. By 1974, however, two younger siblings
entered the labour force, and there were five wage-earners and four
dependents. Wai-gun's place in the domestic economy was now
becoming less essential. She was allowed to use more of her money
for recreation and leisure time, and hobbies. She was also preparing
to marry. Her intended was an eldest son whose father lived in the
Philippines, and who lived with his mother in Hong Kong. The
couple planned to marry in the near future, and saved money for the
event. Unfortunately, Wai-gun's father became critically ill, while
her mother, whose health was never strong, also began to deterio-
rate. Soon neither parent earned money, the father died, and the
family dependency ratio unexpectedly in 1976 took a turn for the
worse. Three older children supported three younger children, and
the ill mother. Now Wai-gun could not withdraw her earnings from
the household and thus she could not marry. At this time, her fiancé
was under pressure from his father to further the family line. He was
expected to marry and bear a son in the patrilineal tradition. Thus,
the two potential partners were enmeshed in different family concepts — Wai-gun in the domestic circle, her fiancé in the patrilineal
system. Their relationship predictably broke up under the conflicting
definitions of family demands.

In sum, the young girl who matures into adolescence and then
early adulthood finds her worklife determined by the demographic
pressures of the period. The three types of family units form the
bounds within which demography is defined. These are the long-term
stress on males due to the line concept, the short-term stress on
women's earnings due to the domestic economy concept and the
bonds of affection between mother and daughter that propel her to
add to the household economy, an outcome of the concept of the
uterine family of affection.

The Family Life Cycle

The Division of Labour in the Household

The numbers of family members and their contribution to the

household division of labour vary by cycle of the family. Expected household tasks for the younger unmarried women living at home in Hong Kong, Taiwan and Singapore during the period under study are shaped by the large family size. William Goode notes that sheer size in an organisation entails rules of interaction, authority, obedience and emotional intimacy.[47] Robert Winch focuses on the number of functions the family fills: the more functions filled, the more need there is for a strict definition of roles by age, sex, generation and lineage.[48] The family at the stage we are studying here is sizeable enough to require a number of rules which are generally accepted.

First was early training of children to participate in family tasks. By age five most learned many necessary tasks, and by age 12 on the eve of their entry to wage work, all hauled water, cooked, washed clothes. As they neared adolescence the older girls took in putting-out work (plastic flowers, transistor assembly, pressing metal eyelets, beading). They did this as part of a family-wide project, carried out in the home and they received no individual wage or recognition. This was most common in Hong Kong, the earliest entrant to the international world economic order. In Taiwan, young girls often had tasks that were associated with their agricultural roots or housekeeping: they fed the pigs or nipped the ends off bean sprouts. Singapore girls similarly performed subsistence work, helped in family hawker enterprises or did domestic work in other households.

With this bridge of hard work to perform household tasks and work in family putting-out projects, working-class Hong Kong and Taiwan daughters entered the paid labour force between ages 12 and 14; the Singapore girls studied started to work a few years later when factories began to reach out for them. Middle-class families in all countries were more likely to delay the entry of their daughters to the workforce until they completed some portion or all of high school and they went to work at around age 16.

Not only were tasks divided by age but sex roles marked different expectations. The daughters went to work after having completed primary school, so that the period during which they would contribute to the domestic economy would be a long one. They entered before reaching age 14, and were child labour in the accepted definition of the International Labour Organisation. They would leave the domestic family upon marriage. Their brothers, however, were to be contributors to the domestic economy throughout their lives, albeit unevenly due to their own domestic economic burdens. If there were a sum of money available for only some of the children to study, the boys were therefore chosen. They could repay the family back at a higher rate of return.

The lengthening of the daughters' years of contribution to the domestic economy was accomplished not only by their early entry to the labour force but parents might also postpone their daughters' exit through marriage. Hong Kong parents sought a full decade of daughters' income contribution, the number of years moulded perhaps by the need to ensure younger siblings' completion of schooling at an ever higher rate. If the daughter was herself a younger sibling, the length of time she needed to contribute her wages to the household economy was reduced. Even so, younger daughters sought to repay their parents for the costs of their upbringing. Social class differences came into play. The lower-middle and middle-class daughters with the longest period of education also entered the labour force at an older age. They then were expected to contribute to the family budget and as a result delayed marriage past the period of working-class women.

Kung's study of Taiwanese factory women similarly stresses the daughters' desire to repay their parents for the cost of their upbringing. Although Kung did not study middle-class women, the 1980 census of Taiwan reveals that marriage age is directly associated with educational level in Taiwan.[49] Among the reasons for this delay is undoubtedly the period of post-educational employment, much of which aids the families.

A newly married woman's right to work is also decided upon as part of a household-wide strategy. Here, too, the division of labour takes its mark from the household size, where many people may be accommodated and many functions performed. The older generation sets the division of labour. In situations of patrilocal residence, where there are several adults in the household, the elders can choose the women with the strongest wage-earning power to work.

Actually, few Singapore women in our study were in this happy situation. Few could earn a wage that justified leaving their homemaking burdens to others. After all, women are designated to take over men's homemaking burdens, and work for a wage lower than would be charged if men paid full market value for the services needed to support them.[50] Thus women's wages are set by the presumption that they are dependents on others, and do not themselves support others. Women's wages are further depressed by the large number of women who compete for a narrow range of jobs. Consequently, only 18 per cent of Singapore women with two

TABLE 3.3   *Comparison of the residences of full-time wage-earning wives and homemakers, Singapore ca. 1975*

	Wives' employment status					
Form of residence	*Wage-earners*		*Homemakers*			*Total*
	%	*(number)*	%	*(number)*	%	*(number)*
Stem or extended	65		31		49	
Neolocal	35		69		51	
	100	(52)	100	(48)	100	(100)

children were still in the labour force in 1973, and similarly under 20 per cent of ever-married Taiwan women were economically active in 1980.

In order to go out to work, women must find others to do the household chores, child care, and other internal ministering of the household for them. In a large household, there was considerable work to do. However, a large household with a strong dependency ratio also has the potential for a division of labour in which young women can find back-up services of others in their homes. Our Singapore research of the mid-1970s showed that the factories' demand for women was crucial in determining who would go to work and who would remain as backup workers in the home. Women with above-average education, some technical skills, and longer industrial employment experience were most often chosen for better paying factory work. Thus, although most women in our sample had worked prior to marriage, many had helped in traditional types of work on farms, in workshops or small factories packing peanuts, making gold paper used to burn for the dead, or in soy sauce factories. Their labour force experience could not command a good post-marital job. Those married women who worked were among the better educated, the women with superior class backgrounds in our sample.

In addition, women whose families were in great need, whose husbands were quite poor, might also work for a wage, but typically they could only get low-paid work. They were then highly subsidised by other women in the household, who responded to their great need. Alternatively, some of them might do non-industrial work in the neighbourhood, take in washing, wash floors part-time for neighbourhood women. This underground economy work was not registered in labour force statistics.

That household support is the key in aiding married women to

TABLE 3.4   *Interaction patterns of working wives and housewives, Phase 1,*
Singapore ca. 1975

	Wives' employment status			
	Wage-earners		Homemakers	
	%	*(number)*	%	*(number)*
Isolates	10		35	
Interactors	90		65	
	100	(52)	100	(48)

work is seen in a comparison of full-time wage-earning women and
homemakers in our study (Table 3.3). Women who lived in the same
home with other kin (stem or extended households) were more likely
to work than women who lived neolocally. In addition, however, a
number of women carved out support systems that crossed household
walls and drew upon several kin in a community area. These women
are 'interactors'[51] (Table 3.4). Thus, wage-earners invariably had
kin-based support systems to help them out.

For example, one Singapore woman, Tan Giok Bee, a domestic
servant in the mid-1970s had received only four years of primary
school, quit to care for her five younger siblings, until at age 17 she
entered domestic service like her mother and her older sister. She
worked six days a week for only S$180 a month for foreign families
living in Singapore.[52] She left temporarily to care for each of her
three newborn daughters. After the first birth she tried another line
of work and spent a year making incense sticks but found that she
could not fit the fixed factory hours with her demanding regime of
household tasks. One of her daughters was subject to epileptic
seizures, and caring for this child imposed an added burden on her. 'I
prefer to work as an *amah* (domestic servant) because I don't have to
keep strict hours on this job. Sometimes I can go home early or
choose my own day off, when I have to take my daughter to the
hospital on a working day.' Her husband, Poh Wah, a tinsmith, also
earned a poverty-line wage of S$250. The couple lived with their
three daughters in a rented two-room HDB flat with elder Mother
Tan. Tan Giok Bee's mother-in-law helped care for the children, but
because the elderly woman was not well, Tan Giok Bee still had to do
much of the housework, the errands and services entailed in mother-
ing. Tan Giok Bee gave mother-in-law a small sum of cash in

exchange for the child care help. A typical day's chronology of household care arrangements for Giok Bee is given in Table 3.5. (Poh Wah was, we note, not part of these arrangements.)

Many working women who lived in small households found it necessary to engineer child care arrangements of this type. With the wider help, however limited, Tan Giok Bee was thus enabled to put in a full working day, but she could not manage to work at the higher paying factory jobs just then opening up. Her earnings were not enough to live on and she 'borrowed right and left' from her mother, who lived with two working sons and one daughter. Without the help of kin, Tan Giok Bee could not afford to work for the low wage she earned. In turn, she could support her mother-in-law, at a modest level. Interviewed six years later, Tan Giok Bee told us that her mother-in-law had passed away. Giok Bee's household burden had even increased somewhat. Although her eldest children could care for themselves, the girls did not do the housework. Giok Bee was pressed into a heavier double day than before and she had to reduce her working hours to do so. Other women also enter and create complex interpersonal relationships, and may, if their husband's mother cannot help them, draw from relatives on both sides, which helps them to remain in the labour force after marriage. In turn their work often gives employment and needed support to their kin.

The Consequences of Women's Work

Families reward women for their employment and their input to the household. Women get something out of their input, which keeps them in the exchange. Part of what they get is material, sometimes they also obtain an enlarged role in the family. Finally, they see that their family truly need their material input, they feel some satisfaction in meeting this role. They feel they meet their filial obligations, as daughters. Thus the exchange can be interpreted as part of the three types of family forms. The patriline requires women to support the family of the male line (their parents or their husbands after marriage); the economic family demands an input for families in the material economy. And the uterine family ties give emotional satisfaction to women that help out at home. Thus, the exchange is neither entirely material nor is it of short term, reciprocal, duration.

Working Hong Kong daughters widened their sphere of decision making as it affected their social lives. So long as they could put in a

TABLE 3.5　*Chronology of help for domestic servant Tan Giok Bee in 1975*

6.30	Tan Giok Bee rises to prepare breakfast for her three daughters (ages 8, 10 and 11).
7.00	Giok Bee takes middle daughter to primary school, then continues to the neighbourhood market to shop for the day's vegetables.
8.00	Giok Bee does the day's laundry by hand.
9.00	Giok Bee leaves home for her job.
9.00–12.30	Mother Tan cares for the two children at home, cooks and serves them lunch.
13.00	The younger and elder girls walk to primary school for the afternoon session.
14.30	Giok Bee returns from work, takes a nap and on alternative days prepares dinner for the family.
19.00	Giok Bee's husband returns from work to eat dinner.
20.00	Poh Wah goes out for an evening of drinking with his coworkers.

Chronology of help for Tan Giok Bee in 1981

6.30	Giok Bee rises.
7.00	Giok Bee markets for the day's vegetables.
7.30	Giok Bee cooks breakfast and lunch for her three daughters (ages 14, 16 and 17).
7.30	The younger two girls leave for secondary school and the eldest goes to work as a dental receptionist.
9.00	Giok Bee leaves home for her job as a household servant.
14.00	Giok Bee returns home and does the day's laundry by hand.
15.30	Giok Bee takes a nap and on alternative days prepares dinner for the family.
19.00	Poh Wah returns from work to eat dinner.
20.00	Poh Wah sits in front of the colour television for a quiet evening at home.

good-sized proportion of their wages to their family budget, they kept a portion for their own spending money. They could thereby join peer activities, dress better and use their free time in ways decided upon by themselves. By entering the spreading consumer economy, they became enmeshed in the new capitalist system.

Similarly, Taiwan daughters enjoyed a period of friends, participating in the newly expanding consumer culture and group dates. These opportunities were more accessible when the working daughters lived in factory dormitories and less accessible when the girls lived at home.[53] Working daughters could not greatly expand their input into decision-making processes in their families in either setting and their wages did not confer upon them power to realign their dependence on the family itself.

In Hong Kong, opting out (becoming a 'swinging single') was limited by the expectation that women remain at home until marriage, despite their earning money. This expectation is reinforced by aspersions cast on the sexuality of women who leave home as loose women. But in addition, since the housing market is dominated by the state's public housing, given only to families by need criterion, plus a very expensive private market, it would be hard for most women earners to live alone or with other women. They cannot leave. Taiwan factory women lived in the main in tightly supervised dormitories and the women who moved into private flats found it was too expensive to meet the obligations to their families. Those who could live at home and commute to work did so, to save money. Work did not confer a period of accepted physical independence from the family. However, women who lived apart from their families, in factory dormitories, had the greatest chance to choose recreational activities and friends of their own.

Although working daughters obtained a meaningful outcome from their employment, their employment cannot entirely be seen as a transaction between two equal parties, in which they have power to work or not to work. Unmarried Hong Kong, Taiwan and Singapore women have less power in their households than their parents. Also, married women are so closely dependent on others in their homes in order to work that they are not free agents either.[54]

Married Singapore women were unlikely to perceive their employment as a form of independence, since their money went to their families. Even middle-class women saw their work as only possible if they could successfully field their family obligations to others. Women with their own money enjoyed an enlarged sphere of action. With their funds they bought clothes for their children, rounded out the family budget, provided small sums to their mothers or other kin, which could not legitimately be drawn from their husband's or the wider household budget. They could join peer outings with workmates on special occasions and purchase presents with their earnings. However, in virtually all cases studied, married women placed the major part of their earnings at the disposal of their family, usually their nuclear family. The freedom gained was not an individual form of liberty. Rather, they obtained a widened sphere for their small nuclear unit in the extended, usually patrilineal, construct.[55]

The material consequences of women's work were crucial, much more so than a widening of their proper sphere. Household purchases varied by the dependency ratio, a product of the life cycle. When, as young unmarried daughters, women first entered the labour force within the context of a high dependency ratio, their wages helped their families buy necessities — rent and food for the entire family. Medical care was an optional but costly item and families improved their care when extra money became available. Married Singapore women in the poorest households, typically those with a difficult dependency ratio, also placed their wages at the disposal of the family. Working women's income enabled extended education for younger siblings past the years provided by their governments. Married women could help pay for tutors for their own children, to improve their performance on competitive state examinations.

An example of the daughters' importance in this regard is the case of the elder sister in a Hong Kong family of five girls. Still unmarried at age 29, she earmarked one-third of her factory earnings for the education of her two youngest sisters. All of her sisters had the opportunity to continue school past primary 6, the eldest only reached primary 4. The youngest went further in her studies than the oldest girls. The eldest's economic assistance was to continue until the next two working sisters could assume the entire burden themselves.

As the dependency ratio improves, daughters in working-class families can contribute toward an improvement in the family living standard through raising the education of their younger brothers. But since everyone in the society is in pursuit of more education, there is a spiralling of credentials and youngsters must remain in school longer just to keep in the same place. Nevertheless, the ability to raise younger brothers' education was most feasible when daughters had been working for a decade. Telephones, televisions, small semi-automatic washing machines and other goods add to household comforts and are made possible by the combined earnings of the employed children, notably the working daughters.

Middle-class girls also contribute their earnings; for example, many help their parents launch a small business, such as hawking, knitting or garment shops. The high savings propensity of the Chinese in Hong Kong, Singapore and Taiwan, has been documented and their willingness to risk investment in the local economy.[56] Earnings of the children, added to the family budget, thus in turn boost the export-oriented manufacture economy. The extent to which children aid their parents in building small funds of capital for investment in these countries is worthy of future study.

As they age, however, women may have a chance to take direct control over their expenditures. A 1984 survey of married couples in Taiwan found that on average they spent US $113 on their parents a month if both spouses worked (this sum was 8 per cent of their income). Twenty-six per cent of the parents depended entirely on the children, 36 per cent depended partly on their children to live. Sixty per cent of the couples surveyed did not live with the parents, 30 per cent did and in 17 per cent of the cases the parents lived with each of their sons in turn, a common Taiwan solution for spreading the burden of support among offspring.[57] The Taiwan labour force survey looked into the expenditure patterns of employees by age and reports that spending patterns of women in their late fifties differed greatly from their younger female counterparts. In the cohort of these Taiwan women, these typically are married with grown and even married children. They have the greatest freedom to spend money on themselves. A study that I have conducted on firms that include older women as blue collar employees confirmed that women that have a solid family structure and are not in broken families, are finally able to use their earnings as 'pocket money'. This factory or service sector wage is often the first real sum of money they have ever fully controlled. They spend their earnings variously on renting video tapes, gambling, group outings and excursions, dinners and drinking. One factory section is known plant wide for the leisure activities organised by one such, a fifty-five year old line worker who is in charge of the informal group. Apart from investing in household furnishings for a new apartment, in the main she felt free to spend her earnings on her enjoyment, depending on her husband, son and daughter-in-law to maintain the household economy.

Her co-workers stressed to me that that this dowager was able to enjoy herself because she did not have a 'double day'. In my view, also crucial was the strength of the filial tie, which meant that her son and daughter-in-law were willing to support their mother and permit her this modicum of freedom with her earnings. It is quite possible that the current period is an unusual one, in which the youths are willing still to meet their obligations in line with the three types of family forms. Later cohorts, brought up in school systems and society that do not so much extol the elderly, and with fewer siblings with whom to share this care may find the burden of the aged too heavy.[58]

Then the need for society to come forth with a universal social insurance system will be unprecedented.[59]

Thus, we have come full circle. The states of each of the three areas discussed here, Hong Kong, Taiwan and Singapore, have boosted their economies, making crucial steps to develop export-oriented economies. They drew upon the inexpensive labour of unmarried women and to a lesser extent that of married women. They propelled the families into the money economy which required families to increase their access to cash. Parents held control over their daughters' labour and their daughters dutifully went to work in support of the families they would soon leave upon marriage. With the earnings, parents made ends meet but eventually some, especially those in Hong Kong and Taiwan, hoped to accumulate capital themselves to invest in small-scale enterprises, some of which served local populations and others of which formed part of the export businesses.

The working women of these three countries were conscious of their place as earners in the family economy. They knew their need to earn was due to family necessity, linked both with demographic demands — a large number of siblings — and with the loss of a 'natural economy' and new needs and aspirations in the consumer economy. At the same time, they witnessed an explosion of wage-earning opportunities over their working lifespan. The ideology of market capitalism conveys the wish to be free. Since their households control their labour, these women do not enter the work force as independent individuals. Hence, they do not internalise this wish to be free. They feel the surge of 'freedom' in terms of consumer goods and a widening sphere of choice but at the same time they retain their sense of obligation to the family unit. Interest in political activities is not fuelled by the state apparatus, and their sense of individual rights is not developed. Consequently, the overriding concern of many of these women is to promote their own interests within the family context. In such a setting, feminist concerns that ride on a sense of justice regarding formal rights and rights compared with men is often not developed. But, as I have tried to show, the lives of these women are undergoing great change along with the economy and their position in the changing family unit. The outcome of these forces is a dynamic vitality which, while not the same as that felt by middle-class western women, is nonetheless profound.

Notes

1. This is a revised and updated version of an article which first appeared in Lynne B. Iglitzen and Ruth Ross (eds) *Women in the World: 1975–1985 The Women's Decade*. Second, revised edition (Santa Barbara, California: ABC-CLIO Press, 1986) pp. 325–57. Permission to reprint is acknowledged with thanks. The three areas discussed (in association with the Republic of Korea) are commonly referred to as the 'newly industrialised countries' of Asia. Strictly speaking, the areas discussed here include only one country, the Republic of Singapore. Indeed, Hong Kong is a colony which will become a Special Administrative Region of the People's Republic of China (PRC) in 1997. Taiwan's political status is in dispute and is referred to both as Taiwan province of the PRC or the Republic of China. As shorthand, I will refer to these areas as 'countries'.

2. *World Bank Report* (Washington DC: World Bank, various years).

3. Hong Kong Housing and Population Census, 1931 (Hong Kong unpublished statistics); *Hong Kong Housing and Population Census* (Hong Kong Government, Census and Statistics Department, 1971); S.C. Chua, *State of Singapore: Report on the Census of Population, 1957*; *Report on the Labour Force Survey of Singapore 1979* (Singapore: Research and Statistics Division Ministry of Labour, 1980); *An Extract Report on the 1980 Census of Population and Housing, Taiwan-Fukien Area, Republic of China* (Taipei: Census Office of the Executive Yuan, ROC, 1982); Director-General of Budget, Accounting, and Statistics, *Year Book of Labor Statistics* (Taipei: Executive Yuan, ROC various years).

4. Bruce Cumings, 'The Origins and Development of the Northeast Asian Political Economy: Industrial Sectors, Product Cycles, and Political Consequences', *International Organization* vol. 38, no. 1 (Winter 1984), pp. 1–40; Stephan Haggard and Chen Tun-jen, 'State Strategies, Local and Foreign Capital in the Gang of Four', paper prepared for the 1983 Annual Meeting of the American Political Science Association, Chicago, 1983.

5. An example is the reformist leader, Elsie Elliot, OBE, who is the urban councillor representative of a sizeable housing estate and a school principal. She has been reelected for years. See her publication *A,B,C's of Hong Kong* (or, 'Avarice, Bureaucracy, and Corruption of Hong Kong').

6. Siu–Kai Lau, *Society and Politics in Hong Kong* (Hong Kong University Press, 1982).

7. Frances M. Geiger and Theodore Geiger, *The Development Progress of Hong Kong and Singapore* (New York: Macmillan, 1975); Mary Lee, 'Work Suspended,' *Far Eastern Economic Review* (henceforth, *Review*) (21 August 1981) pp. 32–3.

8. David Chaney and David Podmore, *Young Adults in Hong Kong: Attitudes in a Modernizing Society* (University of Hong Kong, 1973); Joe England and John Rear, *Chinese Labour under British Rule: A Critical*

Study of Labour Relations and Law in Hong Kong (Hong Kong: Oxford University Press, 1975); H.A. Turner, et al., *The Last Colony, but Whose?* (Cambridge University Press, 1981).

9. Lau, op.cit., chapter 4; Chaney and Podmore, op.cit., pp. 46, 60; Sherry Rosen, *Mei Foo Sun Chuen: Middle Class Families in Transition* (Taipei: Orient Cultural Service, 1976).

10. Haggard and Chen. See note 4.

11. Lau, see note 6.

12. Christopher Howe, 'Growth, Public Policy and Hong Kong's Economic Relationship with China', *China Quarterly* 95 (September 1983), pp. 512–33.

13. The exchange rate is approximately HK$5=US$1.

14. Tamara Hareven, *Family Time and Industrial Time* (Cambridge University Press, 1982); Lau, op.cit.; Larissa Adler Lomnitz, *Networks and Marginality: Life in a Mexican Shantytown* (New York: Academic Press, 1977); Keith Hopkins (ed.) *Hong Kong: The Industrial Colony* (Hong Kong: Oxford University Press, 1971).

15. Turner et al., see note 8. Chapter 6.

16. Richard E. Barrett and Martin King Whyte, 'Dependency Theory and Taiwan: Analysis of a Deviant Case', *American Journal of Sociology*, vol. 87, no. 5, pp. 1064–89; Cumings, see note 4; Council for Economic Planning and Development, Republic of China, *Taiwan Statistical Data Book 1984* (Taipei, 1984), pp. 23, 156; Thomas Gold, *State and Society in the Taiwan Miracle* (New York: M.E. Sharpe, 1986); A.H. Amsden, 'Taiwan's Economic History: A Case of Etatism and a Challenge to Dependency Theory', *Modern China 5 (1979)*, pp. 341–80.

17. Lydia Kung, *Factory Women in Taiwan* (Ann Arbor: UMI Research Press, 1983).

18. Esther S. Lee Yao, *Chinese Women: Past and Present* (Mesquite TX: Ide House, 1983).

19. *Free China Journal*, 23 February 1987, p. 2.

20. Barrett and Whyte, see note 16; Cumings, see note 4; Walter Galenson (ed.) *Economic Growth and Structural Change in Taiwan* (Ithaca, New York: Cornell University Press, 1979); Haggard and Chen, see note 4; Samual P.S. Ho, *Economic Development of Taiwan 1960–70* (New Haven: Yale University Press, 1978).

21. *Free China Journal*, 2 March 1987. The exchange rate at this time was approximately NT40= US$1.

22. Kung, see note 17.

23. See Director General of Budget, Accounting and Statistics, Executive Yuan, various years, in *Free China Weekly*, 8 February 1987, p. 4.

24. Kung, see note 17.

25. *Free China Journal*, 2 March 1987.

26. There is some discrepancy in the labour force statistics. The *Yearbook of Labor Statistics* indicates that women's share in the labour force peaked in 1973, at 34.56 per cent of the labour force; between 1973 and 1980 the trough was in 1976 at 31.91 per cent of the labour force. However, the 1980 census report claims that women's employment was only 29 per cent of the labour force in 1975 and 27 per cent in 1980 (*An Extract Report,*

p. 113). The oil shock had less of an impact on women's work in the former than in the latter statistics.

27. Myron Cohen, *House United, House Divided* (New York: Columbia University Press, 1976).
28. Yao, op.cit., p. 209.
29. *An Extract Report*, Table 13; Council for Economic Planning and Development, p. 302.
30. Barrett and Whyte, see note 16; Council for Economic Planning and Deveploment, p. 54; Department of Agriculture and Forestry, Taiwan Provincial Government, *Report of Farm Record-Keeping Families in Taiwan, 1979* (Taipei, 1980), p. 20; *Free China Review*, 17 July 1983, p. 3.
31. Geiger and Geiger, see note 1.
32. V.G. Kulkarni, 'Designer Genes', *Review*, 8 September 1983, pp. 23–4; Linda Lim, 'A New Order with Some Old Prejudices', *Review*, 5 January 1984, pp. 37–8.
33. Linda Lim, 'Multinational Export Factories and Women Workers in the Third World, A Review of Theory and Evidence', in Nagat M. El-Sanabary (compiler), *Women and Work in the Third World* (Berkeley: University of California, Centre for the Study, Education, and Advancement of Women, 1983). In 1985 average wage costs for production workers were US$2.44 an hour in Singapore, 70 per cent above that of South Korea and Taiwan, and 37 per cent above Hong Kong. *Review*, 21 August 1986, p. 79, and 12 June 1986, p. 116. Total labour costs rose 40 per cent since 1980, compared with 10 per cent in Taiwan and marginal rates in Hong Kong. The government hopes that workers in loss-making companies will take pay cuts to link firms with profits.
34. Geiger and Geiger, see note 7.
35. Linda Lim, 'Singapore's Success: The Myth of the Free Market Economy', *Asian Survey*, vol. 23, no. 6, June 1983, pp. 752–64.
36. Report of the Economic Committee, *The Singapore Economy: New Directions* (Singapore: Ministry of Trade and Industry: February 1986); *Review*, 26 June 1986, p. 70.
37. *Review*, 12 June 1986, p. 114.
38. Janet W. Salaff and Aline Wong, 'Country Study of Incentives and Disincentives in the Family Planning Program of Singapore', New York, paper prepared for the United Nations Fund for Population Activities, 1984.
39. Kulkarni, see note 32.
40. *Review*, 15 October 1982, pp. 30–2.
41. Siow Yue Chia, *Export Processing and Industrialization: The Case of Singapore* (Bangkok: International Labour Organisation and Asian Regional Team for Employment Promotion, 1982).
42. The Hong Kong, Singapore and Taiwan studies employed purposive sampling to meet quotas. The ages of the Hong Kong women studied were 20 to 24 in 1973 and they were studied over a several-year period. The Singapore women were married, with at least one child and aged 20 to 30 when interviewed in the mid-1970s. They were also studied over time, the mid-1970s and early 1980s; the Taiwan data covers women of

all ages with particular types of work experience. The latter is still in process.

Lydia Kung engaged in a two-pronged study of an ethnography of a market town and neighbouring agrarian communities and participant observation in an electronics factory west of Taipei (the capital city). Most of her respondents were unmarried. Arrigo similarly studied an American electronics firm in depth, through participant observation, survey and case study methods. Although Kung and Arrigo did not explicity select their sample of women workers within a particular age bracket, the labour force participation pattern of Taiwan women limits most workers to essentially the same ages of the Hong Kong and Singapore women studies, that is, their early twenties. For further discussion of sampling and other findings, see the following studies: Linda Gail Arrigo, 'Taiwan Electronics Workers', in Mary Sheridan and Janet W. Salaff (eds), *Lives: Chinese Working Women* (Bloomington: Indiana University Press, 1984), pp. 123–45; Kung; Lydia Kung, 'Taiwan Garment Workers', in Sheridan and Salaff, pp. 109–22; Janet W. Salaff, *Working Daughters of Hong Kong* (Cambridge University Press, 1981); Janet W. Salaff, *State and Family in Singapore* (Ithaca, New York: Cornell University Press, in preparation).

43. Valerie Kincaide Oppenheimer, *The Female Labor Force in the United States: Demographic and Economic Factors Determining its Growth and Changing Composition* (Berkeley: University of California, Institute of International Studies, 1980) Population Monograph Series, no. 5.
44. Arthur Wolf and Chich-shan Huang, *Marriage and Adoption in China, 1845–1945* (Stanford University Press, 1972).
45. Margery Wolf, *Women and the Family in Rural Taiwan* (Stanford University Press, 1972).
46. William H. Goode 'A Theory of Role Strain', *American Sociological Review*, no. 25 (August 1960), pp. 483–96.
47. William J. Goode, *The Family* (New York: Prentice-Hall, 1982).
48. Robert F. Winch, *The Modern Family* (New York: Holt, Rinehart and Winston, 1963).
49. *An Extract Report*, 62.
50. Michele E. Barrett and Mary McIntosh, *The Anti-Social Family* (London: Verso, 1982).
51. 'Interactors' are couples whose wives or husbands visited the same kin two or more times a week. Typically kin cared for their children during the week which helped wives work. Some women or their husbands worked with kin. Many of the exchanges that occurred aimed to reduce the homemaking burdens of these young mothers. Thus, women could often draw upon this support system and go out to work.
52. In Singapore dollars, at the approximate rate of S$2.25 = US$1.
53. Kung, *Factory Women*.
54. Kung, *Factory Women*, pp. 200ff.
55. Cohen, see note 27.
56. Marjorie Topley, 'The Role of Savings and Wealth Among Hong Kong Chinese', in I.C. Jarvie and Joseph Agassi (eds), *Hong Kong Society: A Society in Transition* (London: Routledge and Kegan Paul, 1969) pp. 167–227.

57. A Survey by China Youth Corps, reported in *Free China Journal*, 17 June 1984.
58. Charlotte Ikel.
59. A recent 'Conference on Economic Development and Social Welfare in Taiwan', sponsored by the Academia Sinica, Economics Research Centre, held in January 1987 in Taipei, stressed this issue.

4 Female Employment and Export-led Development in Ireland: Labour Market Impact of State-reinforced Gender Inequality in the Household[1]

Jean L. Pyle

This paper examines the relation between women's participation in the wage economy and household relations in the context of an export-led development strategy and international investment in the Republic of Ireland (hereafter referred to as Ireland).

The economic development process in Ireland 1961–81 exhibited characteristics which have been shown in other countries to result in substantial growth in measures of women's participation in the labour force — a shift in economic structure from agriculture to service and industry and export-led growth involving the influx of multinational corporations.

However, observation of two measures of women's changing roles in the labour force — the female labour force participation rate and the female share of total employment — indicate that Irish women were not able to substantially enhance their aggregate position in the labour force during the growth associated with the outward-looking development strategy. Both of these measures of the position of Irish women in the labour force became among the lowest in the Western European Organisation for Economic Co-operation and Development (OECD) during this period and showed a startling lack of response to the dramatic social and economic change experienced in Ireland during this period.

Detailed examination of female labour force participation data reveals that Ireland differed from other countries by the exceptionally low participation of married women. In seeking an explanation for why this might have occurred I explore the feminist argument that male domination in the household can negatively impact on the labour supply decision of married women. This line of reasoning has much relevance in the Irish case but cannot explain how such unequal gender relations could be perpetuated in light of forces (such as the preferences of multinationals in incoming industries for female workers elsewhere) which would tend to erode it.

However, a survey of state policies suggests that these unequal gender relations in the household were maintained by a range of family and reproductive rights legislation which constrained the labour market supply decisions of women. I argue that unequal gender relations in the household as reinforced by state policy were the cause of the perpetuation of the low female labour force participation rate of married women and the low overall labour force participation rate of women in the face of forces generated by export-led development which would tend to increase them. I close by outlining the implications this case study offers as a contribution to the development of a theoretical framework for understanding women's roles in the economy.

WOMEN'S LABOUR FORCE PARTICIPATION DURING IRELAND'S ECONOMIC DEVELOPMENT, 1961–81

A number of aspects of the Irish economic development process would have been considered likely to result in the increased participation of women in the paid labour force: the export-led development process with an inflow of multinationals which elsewhere hired substantially female workforces; the shift of economic activity from the agricultural sector to the industrial and service sectors; and the necessity that Ireland conform to European Economic Community (EEC) social policy directives regarding equality between the sexes.

The rationale for why the first two of these characteristics of the development process would be expected to increase female labour force participation is as follows. The utilisation of an export-led development strategy, accompanied by an influx of multinational corporations into a country, has been widely characterised at both general and case study levels of analysis as involving extensive use of female labour, leading to increases in the female labour force participation rate. It has been argued that in contrast to import substitution development which has a dampening effect on women's share of industrial employment, export-led development is largely based on female labour (Sen, 1981; Ward, 1985). This phenomenon has been documented by a variety of country studies, for example Singapore, the Philippines, Malaysia and industry analyses such as electronics and clothing (Chapkis and Enloe, 1983; Grossman, 1980; Gruńwald and Flamm, 1985; Lim, 1983; Wong, 1981).

In addition, empirical work in industrialised countries during the post-war period shows that women's participation rates have risen as proportionately more of the labour force were employed in the industrial and service sectors (Ciancanelli, 1983; OECD, 1979; Tilly and Scott, 1978; Weiner, 1985).

These processes occurred together in Ireland. First, the Irish government implemented the export-led development programme in the early 1960s by gradually widening free trade agreements and by immediately establishing a programme of financial incentives to attract foreign direct investment in industrial sectors. The Industrial Development Authority, a semi-autonomous state body, established promotional facilities abroad and aggressively courted selected firms in other countries which it deemed to meet its social and economic criteria for potential investors.

The Irish industrial promotion effort in the 1970s was considered 'one of the most highly intensive and organized of its type among competing countries' (NESC, 1980, pp. 12–13). Ireland was perceived as an attractive site for foreign direct investment and has been widely characterised as having created an 'environment in which capital can thrive' (Minard, 1 February 1982). The financial and trade incentives (export profits tax relief and complete freedom to repatriate profits, liberal depreciation allowances and a package of non-repayable cash grants of 35 per cent to 50 per cent of assets based on regional location) combined with a wide range of other subsidies (100 per cent employee training grants, loan guarantees and interest subsidies, advance factory space and duty free importation of capital equipment), relatively lower labour costs, political stability and a well-educated workforce, made Ireland an attractive competitor for foreign direct investment. The main source was the United States and Ireland experienced the third fastest rate of growth of United States foreign direct investment during the period 1966–77, behind only Singapore and South Korea (Flamm and Grunwald, 1979). United States Department of Commerce data support the contention that investors could prosper in Ireland. United States firms in Ireland 1977–80 earned an average 33.7 per cent yearly rate of return on manufacturing investment, more than twice the average rate of return on United States investment in the EEC (16.8 per cent) or in all countries (14 per cent).

Further, many of the firms locating in Ireland were in manufacturing industries which elsewhere had hired greater proportions of female employees than the average share of women in manufacturing in Ireland (30 per cent in 1970). Although sector data which is comparable internationally is limited, some comparisons can be made with respect to the electronics industry. This sector experienced an influx of firms in Ireland during the 1970s. Survey data collected by James Wickham and Peter Murray (1983) indicate that 51 per cent of the workforce or 72 per cent of non-craft production workers in the Irish electronics industry were women in 1981. This is substantially lower than proportions in Malaysia and Mexico at the same time. Rachael Grossman (1980) reports that 90 per cent of assembly workers in electronics plants in Penang were women. Joseph Grunwald and Kenneth Flamm (1985) have shown that 82 per cent of electronics production workers in Mexico in 1980 were female.

Secondly, as export-led development progressed, Ireland changed from a relatively undeveloped agricultural economy into an industrial and service economy. The proportion of the labour force employed in the agricultural sector fell from 36 per cent in 1961 to 17 per cent in 1981 while the percentage in the industrial and service sectors rose from 64 per cent to 83 per cent.

Thirdly, an integral part of the Irish export-led development strategy was attainment of membership in the EEC. This was necessary to attract foreign direct investment because it offered foreign firms an export-production platform in Ireland with tariff-free access to markets in the EEC. However, membership in the European Economic Community required that Ireland reform social policy to conform with EEC directives on equal pay (1975) and equal treatment with regard to access to employment, vocational training, promotion and working conditions (1976). This would also be expected to enhance women's participation in the Irish labour force.

However, in spite of these three structural changes and their upward impact on women's labour force participation elsewhere, Table 4.1 shows that the labour force participation rate for Irish women was virtually unchanged from 1961–81, remaining at just

TABLE 4.1 *Measures of women's participation in the labour force, Ireland, 1961–81+*

	1961	1966	1971	1975	1979	1981
Labour force participation rate‡, women aged 15+	29.4*	29.1*	28.0*	28.5	28.7	29.7
Female share of the labour force§	26.4	26.3	26.4	27.8	28.9	29.1

* Rates for these years were calculated from ratios in which the datum in the numerator was for ages 14+.
‡ 'Gainfully occupied' women aged 15 and over as a percentage of all women aged 15 and over, where 'gainfully occupied' includes those 'at work' and 'unemployed, having lost or given up previous job'.
§ The per cent of total employment which is female.
+ Abstracting from some of the details of these two measures, the female share can rise when the female labour force participation rate remains constant if male labour force participation rates fall (as they did in Ireland and many other countries during this period).
SOURCES Calculated from tables in *Census of Population in Ireland*, various years; *Labour Force Survey 1979*.

under 30 per cent. The female share of the labour force rose slightly from 26.4 per cent in 1961 to 29.1 per cent in 1981. (The footnotes to Table 4.1 explain the measures and how one can rise when the other is constant.)

These surprising results become even more striking when viewed in the context of average levels of female labour force participation and/or female share of the labour force for both Western European OECD countries and another small export-led economy for which data is available for a comparable period, Singapore.

The unchanging Irish female participation rate contrasts markedly with the dramatic increases experienced in Italy, Portugal, Netherlands, Luxembourg, Denmark, Norway and Sweden. By 1981 the labour force participation rate of women in Ireland had become one of the lowest in the seventeen Western European OECD countries, slipping from a ranking of tenth in 1961 to fourteenth and falling well below the average (unweighted) of 39.7 per cent. The female share in Ireland became the lowest in the Western European OECD by 1981, falling well below the average (unweighted) of 37.3 per cent (Pyle, 1985).

The contrast is even sharper when a comparison is made to export-led growth in Singapore. Both women's labour force participation and the female share of the labour force in Singapore nearly doubled 1957–79: the former rising to 41.9 per cent, a level 45 per cent higher than that in Ireland and the latter rising to 33 per cent.

The levels of female labour force activity in Ireland were less than Western European averages in 1961; these differences not only persisted during this period but widened. The virtual lack of change in female participation during Irish export-led growth was a dramatically different experience from the near 100 per cent increase in Singapore. Why was there little increase in female participation rates in Ireland at a time when structural changes were occurring (export-led growth, shift of economic activity from agriculture to industry and services, enactment of EEC directives) that were considered likely to increase female labour force activity?

We can begin to develop an answer for why this lack of response occurred by disaggregating the labour force participation rates by age and marital status. This reveals the components of the relatively unresponsive aggregate labour force participation of women and establishes a basis for assessing how they differed from similar measures of women's labour force participation in these other areas.

The age-specific labour force participation profile presented in Figure 4.2 suggests that the female labour force in Ireland throughout this period was young. Rates were highest for the 20–24 year-old age group, and dropped off sharply thereafter. This profile changed in only minor ways during these two decades. In 1961, 41 per cent of the female labour force was under 25 years of age; in 1981, 42 per cent.

This pattern differed sharply from that of Irish men, women in other EEC countries and women in Singapore. Figure 4.2 also shows that Irish males had higher labour force participation rates for all ages, with strikingly different participation rates after age 25. Comparison with age-participation profiles of women in other EEC countries for 1974 in Figure 4.3 shows that activity rates for Irish women aged 25–64 were substantially below the Community average. By 1979, activity rates for all women under 50 in Singapore exceeded those for Irish women (Pyle, 1985).

Labour force participation rates of Irish women by marital status are presented in Table 4.4 for three categories: married, single and widowed. The female labour force was primarily single throughout this period. The participation rate of married women was very low, although it experienced a spurt from 1971–75. This profile also contrasts dramatically with that of Irish men, as shown in Table 4.4. Men's rates exceeded women's in every category during this period,

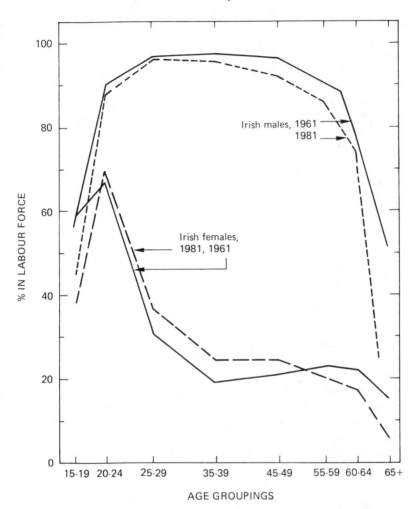

SOURCE   *Census of Population*, 1961 and 1981.

FIGURE 4.2   *Male and Female Age-Participation Profiles, Ireland, 1961 and 1981*

with the largest differentials occurring in the category 'married'.

Comparisons which can be made during this period to labour force participation rates by marital status in other Western European countries indicate that different participation rates for married women were the source of the major difference between Irish female labour

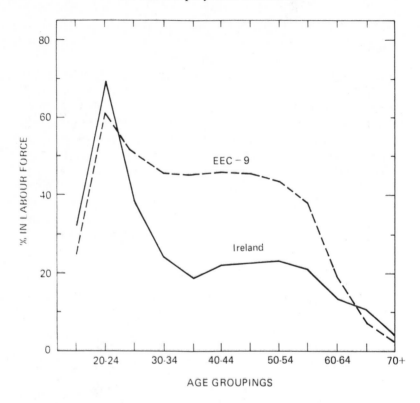

SOURCE   Brendan Walsh, *The Unemployment Problem in Ireland* (Dublin: Kincora Press, 1978) p. 18.
FIGURE 4.3   *Female Age-Participation Profiles, Ireland and EEC Average, 1975*

force participation and that in the other countries.

Table 4.5, based on data from around 1970, shows that although the participation rates for single and widowed Irish women were comparable to those of other Western European OECD countries, that of married Irish women was strikingly low. This disparity continued through the two decades under examination. In 1980 the labour force participation rate of married Irish women was about 15 per cent, less than half the EEC average of 37 per cent (*Working Party on Child Care Facilities*, 1983, p. 19).

Comparison with changes in Singapore during this period reveals that rates of Singaporese single, married and widowed women rose to levels which exceeded those in Ireland. In 1979, 26.8 per cent of married women in Singapore were employed, whereas only 15.2 per cent were in Ireland (Wong, 1981).

This look at more detailed female labour force participation data suggests that Ireland's low aggregate labour force participation of women can be largely attributed to the comparatively low participation of married women and raises several questions. Why were the labour force participation rates of married women in Ireland so low? Why weren't they rising to levels comparable with the other Western European OECD countries and Singapore? Are there factors in household relations and the way in which power relations within the home impact on labour supply decisions which could have resulted in such relatively low participation even in the light of incoming multinationals in industries which elsewhere hired large proportions of female workers?

IMPACT OF MALE DOMINATION IN THE HOUSEHOLD ON FEMALE LABOUR SUPPLY

Feminist analysis offers the argument that women's labour force participation can be constrained in a patriarchal society. The body of feminist theory which locates the subordination of women in the household would assert that male domination can be maintained systematically via social relations in the household, where males effectively control material resources, decision making, and female labour time as well as by fertility levels and the delegation of child care responsibilities to women.

The relevance of this explanation for the relatively unresponsive female labour force participation rates in Ireland during the export-led development programme can be explored by examining first whether the Irish household was patriarchal and secondly how male domination in the household could affect female labour supply.

That the Irish family was patriarchal for most of this century has been well documented. Irish economist-historian Mary Daly reviews the literature regarding rural life in Ireland in the 1930s and urban life in the 1940s which depicted the marked subordination of women to men — including marriages arranged for women by men, women eating after the men, and separate socialising (Daly, 1981). David Schmitt's study of authoritarianism in Irish democracy in the late 1960s and early 1970s mentions the continuation of male dominance:

TABLE 4.4   *Labour force participation rates of men and women aged 15 and over in Ireland by marital status, 1961–1981*

Marital status	1961*	1966*	1971*	1975	1979	1981
		Women				
Single	60.5	62.0	59.8	57.1	55.0	54.9
Married	5.2	5.3	7.5	14.5	15.2	17.4
Widowed	26.2	22.2	19.3	14.7	12.8	11.4
		Men				
Single	77.5	75.8	70.8	70.4	68.3	67.4
Married	90.8	90.2	89.9	85.6	85.0	84.8
Widowed	51.7	47.6	45.0	35.8	28.9	30.2

* Ages 14 and over.
Note that in contrast to census data collection procedures in many other countries, data has not been collected in Ireland for the category 'separated and/or divorced'. This is because divorce is illegal in Ireland and therefore neither 'divorced' nor 'separated and/or divorced' is an officially recognised census category. The growing number of women who return themselves on census forms as 'other' (that is not married, single or widowed) have been lumped with the 'married'. Because of this, the labour force participation rate of married women is a somewhat inflated figure.
SOURCES   Calculated from tables in *Census of Population in Ireland*, various years; *Labour Force Survey 1979*.

'within the home the major decisions are traditionally made by the male head-of-family, whose word — especially in economic matters — is absolute' (Schmitt, 1973, p. 46). His review of the literature in the 1960s regarding male dominance reveals its multiple dimensions; in addition to the position accorded the husband-father, sons were deferred to by both mothers and sisters.

The extensive analysis of Damian Hannan and Louise Katsiaouni in the 1970s traces the changes in the economic, cultural and social environments of interspousal relationships in rural farm families since the 1930s and 1950s. They found that, although changes had occurred which allowed some wives more input into particular aspects of family decision-making, one-half of the families still conformed to the model of the traditional patriarchal family which was *strictly* defined (Hannan and Katsiaouni, 1977, pp. 5, 113, 116). Although the extremely patriarchal organisation of household relations of the 1930s and 1940s had been somewhat loosened (for example, marriages were no longer arranged), social relations in the Irish family throughout the two decades 1961–81 could only be described as fundamentally patriarchal.

TABLE 4.5 *Female activity rates by age and marital status, selected OECD countries, 1970 (percentages)*

	Total 15+	15–19	20–24	25–34	35–44	45–54	55–64	65+
Single								
Austria	63	60	84	89	88	83	40	7
Belgium	46	34	71	78	72	67	38	5
Finland	50	32	64	84	83	80	53	5
France	56	35	69	84	81	78	61	14
Germany	66	65	85	89	88	85	55	11
IRELAND	56	39	87	85	72	64	51	22
Italy	44	38	57	63	57	51	25	7
Spain	43	38	53	55	51	47	38	12
Sweden	44	29	58	72	73	71	53	5
Switzerland	70	59	90	93	91	85	69	21
Married								
Austria	38	58	53	45	46	45	23	4
Belgium	27	44	54	40	30	25	11	2
Finland	53	47	60	63	64	56	35	5
France	40	50	62	53	45	43	28	4
Germany	35	58	55	41	41	39	22	6
IRELAND	7	11	15	9	7	7	7	3
Italy	21	20	29	27	25	24	12	3
Spain	7	11	10	7	7	8	7	2
Sweden	37	35	45	40	48	48	28	3
Switzerland	31	54	48	35	35	34	23	6
Widowed								
Austria	10	*	*	42	46	42	17	2
Finland	24	*	*	75	80	72	39	3
France	15	*	*	70	71	67	40	3
IRELAND	19	*	*	44	47	42	31	11
Spain	10	*	*	37	39	28	16	3
Sweden	13	*	*	42	56	57	32	2
Switzerland	21	*	*	61	66	63	42	8

* Signifies less than one thousand in each category.
SOURCE   United Nations. *The Economic Role of Women in the EEC Region* (New York: United Nations, 1980) p. 15, Table II.4.

Secondly, male domination of social relations in the household impacts on female labour supply decisions in two interrelated ways as indicated in Figure 4.6 — by the general importance of the male in household decision making (which includes the woman's labour supply decision) and via the indirect impact of fertility levels.

The first link between male domination in the household and

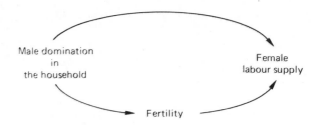

FIGURE 4.6   *The Effect of Male Domination in the Household on Female Labour Supply*

female labour supply can be documented by regression analyses revealing the importance of the husband's 'preferences' in the labour supply decisions of married women, the second by using demographic data regarding the level of and the change in Irish fertility rates.

With respect to the direct effect of the importance of the male in household decision making on female labour supply, analysis of survey data has shown that husbands' opinions regarding their wives' participation in the labour force have been of major importance in the labour supply decision of Irish women. The regression analysis of factors affecting the labour supply behaviour of non-farm married women run by Brendan M. Walsh and B.J. Whelan revealed that the husband's approval of married women working had a significant influence on participation of married non-farm women in the labour force. 'The increase in labour force participation associated with the "husband approves" response is the largest coefficient obtained for any variable (in the transformed equation), and its contribution to R^2 is also the greatest' (Walsh and Whelan, 1973–74, p. 23). Correspondingly, the disapproval of the husband would have a negative impact on labour force participation.

The results of this neoclassical analysis of Walsh and Whelan suggest that the female labour supply decision is not simply based on the 'preferences' of that individual alone, as assumed by the neoclassicals, but rather, in the case of a married woman, is fundamentally influenced by the 'preferences' of another, the husband. The wife's decision and therefore her labour market options may be constrained by her subordinate position in the household, by the existence of unequal power relations between the sexes.

Fine-Davis' analysis of 1978 survey data indicates that the importance of the husband's viewpoint persisted throughout the period. Perceived approval of the husband was the second most important correlate between characteristics of housewives and potential labour force participation (Fine-Davis, 1983).

Male domination in the household can also affect female labour supply indirectly via its impact on fertility levels. It can be argued that male domination increases fertility and, in turn, fertility and labour force participation are negatively correlated. The theoretical relationship between patriarchy and fertility levels has been explored by Nancy Folbre who argues that unequal gender relations in the household govern reproductive decisions by affecting the internal distribution of the costs of children. She suggests that to the extent men have patriarchal control over women they can shift the costs of raising children on to women and disproportionately reap benefits of children. This applies to more narrowly described cases where males have patriarchal control over adult children (Folbre, 1983) and to the broader situations where children are eventually the supporters of social security which men disproportionately benefit from whether they have children or not (Folbre, 1984).

The correlation between the power of the fathers/husbands and fertility has been shown empirically to exist in Ireland by the Hannan-Katsiaouni study. It revealed that larger numbers of children were linked with greater male power in the home and that, the younger the children, the greater the dependence of women (Hannan and Katsiaouni, 1977, p. 116).

Examination of total fertility data shows that fertility in Ireland has been the highest of the Western European OECD countries by a very wide margin. Table 4.7 shows that fertility rates for most countries fell below 2.0 in the 1970s whereas Ireland's remained well above 3.0. Irish fertility changes also contrast dramatically to trends in Singapore during these same years where the average number of births per woman fell from more than six to just under two (Fawcett and Khoo, 1980).

Total fertility rates have been found to have an inverse relation with labour force participation rates of women in industrialising countries. In his review of the literature on the relationship between fertility and labour force participation rates, Guy Standing (Standing, 1981) concludes that statistically significant results consistently arise when fertility variables such as the presence of a child under six and the number of children under eighteen in the household are used as independent variables in cross-section or time-series multiple regression analyses for industrialised countries.

TABLE 4.7   *Total fertility rates Western European OECD countries,*
1960–1980

	1960	1980	Change
(unweighted) averages	2.64	1.89	−0.75
IRELAND	3.8	3.3	−0.5
Austria	2.7	1.6	−1.1
Belgium	2.5	1.7	−0.8
Denmark	2.5	1.7	−0.8
Finland	2.7	1.6	−1.1
France	2.7	1.9	−0.8
Germany	2.3	1.4	−0.9
Greece	2.2	2.3	0.1
IRELAND	3.8	3.3	−0.5
Italy	2.3	1.8	−0.5
Luxembourg	2.3	1.5	−0.8
Netherlands	3.1	1.6	−1.5
Norway	2.8	1.8	−1.0
Portugal	3.0	2.4	−0.6
Spain	2.8	2.5	−0.3
Sweden	2.2	1.7	−0.5
Switzerland	2.3	1.5	−0.8
United Kingdom	2.7	1.8	−0.9

SOURCE   *World Tables*, Third Edition, vol. II, Social Data, 1983.

According to his analysis, it is most likely that fertility will depress labour force participation rates of women under the following conditions: where the structure of the labour market does not offer work alternatives such as flexible hours or homework; in societies where the time-intensity and quality of child care is high; where alternative forms of child care are not available; or where the motivation of mothers to work, as shaped by past experience and the nature of work available, is low.

During the period of time under study, Irish society exhibited at least three of these characteristics (that is, a labour market structure not offering flexible hours, high expectations for quality of child rearing, and lack of alternative forms of child care). Therefore, it could be assumed that the high fertility rate in Ireland had a major constraining effect on the labour force participation of married women. This is supported by the Walsh-Whelan regression analyses. Their results revealed that the presence of children under 14 years of age had a significant negative impact on the labour force participation of married women (Walsh and Whelan, 1973–74, p. 22).

To conclude, examination of the feminist argument has found that Irish society was patriarchal during this period and that both the direct and the indirect ways in which male domination can affect female labour supply decisions were present in Ireland during this period. The feminist explanation appears relevant — that is that measures of female participation in the labour force remained low and unchanging from 1961–81 because Ireland was a patriarchal society in which the appropriate role for women was in the home. The evidence suggests that this was enforced by the importance of the husband's opinion in the wife's labour supply decision and by high levels of fertility, which are associated in countries such as Ireland with low participation rates.

But, I would argue that, in light of evidence from other patriarchal societies undergoing similar types of economic change, this line of reasoning is not sufficient. Although it offers an explanation of why labour force participation rates of married women might be low in a closed society it does not explain how patriarchal domination in the household is reproduced in an open economy. In pursuing export-led growth Ireland opened itself to influences which in other cases have reduced the dependence and subordination of women *vis-à-vis* men and resulted in substantial increases in married women's labour force participation (for example Singapore). The arrival of foreign firms in Ireland, many in industries seeking female labour, the enactment of EEC compatible social legislation which extended female rights in the workplace, and the exposure to cultural changes elsewhere (different lifestyles for women, dramatically lower fertility rates elsewhere in Western Europe) — all would tend to undermine patriarchal domination. Furthermore, this approach does not offer an explanation of why fertility rates remained so high in Ireland or why the labour force participation of married women rose suddenly from 1971–75 only to resume its very slow rate of increase from a strikingly low base.

Patriarchal domination in the Irish household appears to offer an explanation *if* the reasons for its persistence can be determined. Were there social structures which reinforced household gender inequalities during the period of economic change which had tendencies to erode it? A survey of Irish social legislation reveals the answer — an extensive range of policies which supported and reproduced male domination in the household. It also provides an explanation for the persistence of high fertility and the puzzling jump in married women's participation rates.

THE IMPACT OF STATE POLICIES ON GENDER EQUALITY IN THE HOUSEHOLD

From their foundation in the Irish Constitution which defined the appropriate role for women as in the home, state policies established and perpetuated unequal gender relations internal to the household in two ways. First, a range of family law and reproductive rights legislation placed women once married in a subordinate position for life. These unequal family relations in turn limited women's freedom to freely choose to enter the labour force. Second, employment policies in effect through most of this period precluded the option of paid employment external to the household for most married women. In particular, the marriage bar prohibited the employment of women after marriage in many sectors of the economy. This eliminated the possibility for most wives of establishing some degree of economic independence and thereby reinforced dependence on and subordination to the husband.

This range of policies ensured that Irish married women remained in an unequal position in the household — legally subordinate and economically dependent. Irish society was patriarchal and state employment and family policies were not only designed to preserve it but also sustained it against the erosive forces generated by the export-led development process.

The Constitution of 1937, in its specification of Fundamental Rights, addressed the importance of the family and the role of women in society in Article 41, 'The Family':

41. 1. 1. The State recognises the Family as the natural, primary and fundamental unit group of Society, and as a moral institution possessing inalienable and imprescriptible rights antecedent and superior to all positive law.

2. The State, therefore, guarantees to protect the Family in its constitution and authority, as the necessary basis of social order and as indispensible to the welfare of the Nation and the State.

41. 2. 1. In particular, the State recognises that by her life within the home, woman gives to the State a support without which the common good cannot be achieved.

2. The State shall, therefore, endeavour to ensure that mothers shall not be obliged by economic necessity to engage in labour to the neglect of their duties in the home.

The traditional family was the core institution of the society; women belonged at home and mothers should not work. There were a myriad of policies implemented with this Constitutional viewpoint in mind. The structure of the Irish legal system curtailed the rights of married women and their range of choice, placing them in positions of subordination to their husbands. It was considered appropriate that a husband had primacy in household decision making, deciding where and how his family might live. Exit from marriage was almost impossible. Divorce was illegal throughout this period under study (1961–81); state financial support in the cases of desertion was difficult to obtain; laws regarding abuse in marriage, particularly sexual abuse, gave women little to no protection. Further, women faced few options in exercising control over biological reproduction. Abortion was illegal and access to contraceptives was limited throughout this period.

To elaborate with respect to family law, the ultimately powerful position of the husband in household decision making has been described as follows by the Commission on the Status of Women:

> There is a presumption in law that where a husband and wife are living together, the wife has authority to contract on his behalf in all matters concerning the supply of necessaries for the husband, herself and the household. The goods and services so contracted for must be suitable in kind, sufficient in quantity and necessary in fact according to the conditions in which *the husband chooses his wife and family shall live*. In deciding what are necessaries of life, the criterion is not primarily the husband's means but the standard at which *he decides* his family shall live. Where the husband supplies the wife with necessaries or with the money to buy them he has the power to cancel the authority of his wife to contract on his behalf or to pledge his credit.

The Commission describes the economic roles of the husband and wife and the distribution of benefits among family members from them under common law during this period:

> The day's work of a housewife looking after children at home is fully committed to the purposes of the family and the Constitution recognises this. The day's work of the husband in earning an income is on the other hand, in the eyes of the law, committed to the purposes of the family only to the limited extent outlined above. He has the right to profit fully from his wife's work at home.

She, in the eyes of the law, can claim from the profits of his work only necessaries plus such further addition to the family's standard of living as *he — not she — may decide* (*Report to Minister for Finance*, Commission on the Status of Women, 1972, p. 174). [emphasis mine]

In addition, although the Constitution specified the desirability of a woman working in the home, the legal system has not guaranteed her equal input into decisions regarding the disposition of the home nor any claim to a portion of its value. The Married Women's Status Act of 1957 established the right of women to own property and enter contractual agreements but the family residence continued to be owned typically by the male, who could dispose of it and its contents without the consent of his wife. The issue was not addressed until, under pressure from the Commission on the Status of Women, the Family Home Protection Act was enacted in 1976. It prevented the sale of the family home without the consent of the wife, but still guaranteed her no portion of its value unless it can be shown that she actually contributed toward home payments.

Compounding this lack of power in household decision making, Irish wives had few options legally or economically in the event of marital breakdown. For example, if the husband became abusive, it wasn't until the late 1970s that the wife had even limited legal recourse. (He could be barred from the home for up to three months if she or the children were in danger, but the police did not have the power to arrest a husband violating this order.) There was no relief for marital sexual abuse. Marriage presumes the right of the husband to sexual relations; therefore he could not be prosecuted for raping his wife.

If the husband deserted the wife and children, she had to prove desertion to obtain social benefits. This was difficult. The problem was often compounded by the issue of domicile. 'Wives, minors and lunatics are given the domicile of dependency' (Martin, 1977, p. 91). The domicile of a married woman is considered to be that of her husband, even if he has deserted and moved abroad. This has adverse implications for married women in terms of nullity, divorce, illegitimacy, succession and inheritance.

Divorce is illegal in Ireland according to the Constitution. The only legal recourse available is to obtain an annulment, a divorce granted by the High Court based on adultery or cruelty, or a separation deed. The first two are expensive and time-consuming and, under the terms of the latter, neither party can remarry during the lifetime of the other. English divorces may be recognised under certain conditions but acceptance of them in Ireland can be arbitrary and discriminatory. For example, Irish courts have upheld an English divorce awarded to an Irishman residing in England while his wife was in Ireland. The second wife was considered the legal wife, eliminating any claim of the first to his property. However, a similar case involving an Irish woman obtaining a divorce in England was not upheld by Irish courts. Her children from the second marriage were considered illegitimate (*Progress Report on the Implementation of the Recommendations in the Report of the Commission on the Status of Women*, 1976, p. 70).

Women and their dependants were particularly vulnerable economically in cases of marital breakdown, much more so than men. The problems women experienced through most of this period in obtaining financial support (public assistance or maintenance from the husband) were intensified by discriminatory employment policies — the marriage bar, protective legislation and training and apprenticeship programmes.

The marriage bar was the most damaging of these employment policies to the labour market prospects of married women. Barring the employment of married women has been an issue throughout the existence of the Irish Republic. Motivations for such a ban have been based both on the ideology that the appropriate role for the married woman was tending the home, husband and children, and on the fear that they would compete with men and single women for available jobs. In the 1930s the government banned married women as national teachers and in 1956 they were barred from positions in civil service.

By the 1960s the marriage bar meant that 'in general, females employed in clerical jobs in service industries, banks, local authorities and semi-state bodies are required to resign from their employment on marriage' (*The Commission on the Status of Women*, 1972, para. 252). This practice was mimicked by some private sector employers.

Since the service sector was the major source of employment for women in Ireland (62 per cent of females employed in 1961 and 75 per cent in 1981 were in the service sector, with one-third and two-fifths of these in the public sector in these respective years), the marriage bar limited a broad arena of opportunities to a certain type of worker: single women or males. A married woman could only be reinstated in cases of hardship, meaning where she could prove desertion.

Under pressure from the Commission on the Status of Women in Ireland and various women's groups, the marriage bar was phased out during a four year period, 1973–77, with the major thrust of its removal occurring early in the period. The Employment of Married Women Act, 1973 removed it from the Civil Service; it was removed from local and health authorities shortly thereafter; and the Anti-Discrimination Bill, 1975 made it illegal in the private sector.

Augmenting this network of legal inequalities which maintained male domination in the household was the fact that all women, even married women, encountered government legislation which limited their control over biological reproduction and/or curtailed their sexual freedom. Access to contraceptives was limited. Even in the late 1970s it was illegal to advertise or import contraceptives for sale; they could be imported for personal use only. There were only six Family Planning Clinics in the Republic, three of which were in Dublin (Martin, 1977, p. 125). Although the Family Planning Act of 1979 allowed contraceptives to be sold, it was only by a physician's prescription and only to married couples for bona fide family planning purposes. Abortions are illegal in Ireland (now by a 1983 Constitutional amendment approved by the electorate after a year of bitter debate).

To summarise, this survey of state family law and employment policies suggests that the persistence of male domination in the patriarchal household and its two-fold impact on the labour force participation of married women — via the powerful overall position of the male in household decision-making and via high fertility rates — during this period of economic and social change can be attributed to state policy. The importance of the husband's preferences in the labour force participation decision of the wife demonstrated in the previous section is clearly underwritten by legal and economic inequality in the household, which has placed the female in a materially disadvantaged position.

In addition, in light of the legal structure regarding reproductive rights and male prerogatives in the household in Ireland, I would suggest that the Irish fertility rate was the highest among Western European OECD countries largely because of state policy. Fertility was high because of the limited options for controlling reproduction (based on state policies which constrain access to reproductive options) *and* the overall dominance of the male in the household (which was reinforced by state policy). Given the right of the husband to sexual relations and the limited birth control options, male domination translates into high fertility rates. In turn, these high rates augment inequality in the household by increasing the wife's workload in home duties and child care.

This survey has also suggested an explanation for the sudden spurt in the labour force participation of married women 1971–75. The increase coincided with the elimination of the marriage bar from most sectors which had been subject to it. Since it has been shown elsewhere that this jump was not due to demographic changes, it is likely that it reflected the termination of this constraint on wives' labour force participation (Pyle, 1985).

CONCLUSIONS

This examination of state policy provides us with answers to the major questions raised regarding the low labour force participation rate of married women (a major component of the surprisingly low and unchanging aggregate female participation rate of Irish women) and the manner in which male domination in the household could be maintained during export-led growth and curtail the labour supply of married women.

This analysis has suggested that male domination in the Irish household was maintained and fertility rates remained at such high levels during this period because they were reinforced by state policy — family law and reproductive rights legislation. This combination suppressed the labour force participation rate of married women and, in turn, kept the aggregate participation rate low.

There are at least three implications of this case study for the construction of a theoretical framework for understanding the economic roles of women as growth and development occur. First, it underscores the importance of examining household relations in determining female labour supply — in particular, the ways in which gender inequality can impact on a woman's decision to enter the labour market. The Irish case indicates that this can occur via male domination which directly inputs on the labour supply decision and indirectly via fertility levels.

Secondly, it shows that male domination in the household can be perpetuated by a variety of state policies — both employment policies and family law and reproductive rights legislation. It alerts researchers to the importance of firstly adding this dimension, the state and its role in maintaining gender inequality in the household, to the analysis; and secondly analysing a wide range of policies.

Lastly, it suggests that to incorporate women into the labour force attention must be directed to altering all policies which sustain gender inequality in the household — employment policies *and* family law and reproductive rights legislation. It shows that altering only employment policy has a very limited impact on female labour force participation if male domination in the household persists. In the Irish case, eradicating the marriage bar over the period 1973–77 resulted in a spurt in the participation rate of married women but their participation rates remained stable at very low levels due to the lack of change in family law and reproductive rights legislation which perpetuated female subordination in the Irish household.

Note

1. The author would like to acknowledge the support of Jean A. Larson in the pursuit of this research.

References

Central Statistics Office (1961, 1966, 1971, 1979, 1981) *Census of Population* (Dublin: CSO).
Central Statistics Office (1975, 1977, 1979) *Labour Force Survey* (Dublin: Stationery Office).
Chapkis, Wendy, and Cynthia Enloe (1983) *Of Common Cloth, Women in the Global Textile Industry* (Amsterdam: Transnational Institute).
Ciancanelli, Penelope (1983) 'Women's Transition to Wage Labor: A Critique of Labor Force Statistics and Reestimation of Labor Force Participation of Married Women in the United States 1900–1930', unpublished doctoral dissertation, New School, New York.
Commission on the Status of Women (1972) *Report to Minister for Finance* (Dublin: Stationery Office).
Daly, Mary E. (1981) 'Women in the Irish Workforce from Pre-industrial to Modern Times', *Journal of the Irish Labour History Society*, 7 pp. 74–82.
Fawcett, James T. and Siew-Ean Khoo (1980) 'Singapore: Rapid Fertility Transition in a Compact Society', *Population and Development Review*, 6, 4 (December), pp. 549–79.
Fine-Davis, Margret (1983) 'Mothers' Attitudes Toward Child Care and Employment: A Nationwide Survey', in *Working Party on Child Care Facilities for Working Parents* (Dublin: Stationery Office).
Flamm, Kenneth and Joseph Grunwald (1979) *Observations on a North-South Complementary Intra-Industry Trade* (Washington, DC: Brookings Institution).

Folbre, Nancy (1983) 'Of Patriarchy Born: The Political Economy of Fertility Decisions', *Feminist Studies*, 9, 2 (Summer), pp. 261–84.

Folbre, Nancy (1984) 'The Pauperization of Motherhood: Patriarchy and Public Policy in the United States', *Review of Radical Political Economy*, 16, 4 (Winter), pp. 72–88.

Grossman, Rachel (1980) 'Bitter Wages: Women in East Asia's Semiconductor Plants', *Multinational Monitor*, 1, 2 (March), pp. 8–11.

Grunwald, Joseph and Kenneth Flamm (1985) *Global Factory: Foreign Assembly in International Trade* (Washington, DC: Brookings Institution).

Hannan, Damian and Louise Katsiaouni (1977) *Traditional Families?* (Dublin: The Economic and Social Research Institute).

Lim, Linda (1983) 'Multinational Export Factories and Women Workers in the Third World: A Review of Theory and Evidence', in Nagat M. El-Sanabary, compiler, *Women and Work in the Third World: The Impact of Industrialization and Global Economic Interdependence* (Berkeley: Centre for the Study, Education and Advancement of Women, University of California) pp. 75–90.

Martin, Janet (1977) *The Essential Guide for Women in Ireland* (Galway, Ireland: Arlen House).

Minard, Lawrence (1982) 'Xenophobia is very Uncommon Here', *Forbes* (1 February 1982).

National Economic and Social Council (NESC) (1980) *Industrial Policy and Development: A Survey of Literature from the Early 1960s*, prepared by Eoin J. O'Malley (Dublin: NESC).

Organisation for Economic Co-operation and Development (1979) *Demographic Trends 1950–1990* (Paris: OECD).

Progress Report on the Implementation of the Recommendations in the Report of the Commission on the Status of Women (1976) a Report by the Women's Representative Committee (Dublin: Stationery Office).

Pyle, Jean L. (1985) 'Sex Discrimination and Public Policy in an Open Economy', unpublished doctoral dissertation, University of Massachusetts at Amherst.

Schmitt, David E. (1973) *The Irony of Irish Democracy* (Lexington, Massachusetts: Lexington Books).

Sen, Gita (1981) 'Capitalist Transition and Women Workers — a Comparative Analysis', paper presented at the Fifth Berkshire Conference on Women's History, Vassar College, Poughkeepsie, New York, 11 June 1981.

Standing, Guy (1981) *Labour Force Participation and Development*, second edition (Geneva: ILO).

Tilly, Louise A. and Joan W. Scott (1978) *Women, Work and Family* (New York: Holt, Rinehart and Winston).

United Nations (1980) *The Economic Roles of Women in the ECE Region* (New York: UN).

Walsh, Brendan (1978) *The Unemployment Problem in Ireland* (Dublin: Kincora Press).

Walsh, B.M. and B.J. Whelan (1973–74) 'The Determinants of Female Labour Force Participation — An Econometric Analysis of Survey Data', *The Statistical and Social Inquiry Society of Ireland* XXIII, 1, pp. 1–33.

Ward, Kathryn (1985) 'Women and Transnational Corporation Employment:

A World-System and Feminist Analysis', paper presented at the meetings of the American Sociological Association, Washington, DC.

Weiner, Lynn (1985) *From Working Girl to Working Mother*. (Chapel Hill: University of North Carolina).

Wickham, James and Peter Murray (1983) 'Women Workers and Bureaucratic Control in Irish Electronics Factories', paper presented to the British Sociological Association.

Wong, Aline K. (1981) 'Planned Development, Social Stratification, and the Sexual Division of Labor in Singapore', *Signs*, 7, 2 (Winter), pp. 434–52.

Working Party on Child Care Facilities for Working Parents (1983) report to the Minister for Labour (Dublin: Stationery Office).

World Bank (1983) *World Tables*, vol. II *Social Data*, 3rd edn. (Baltimore: Johns Hopkins University Press).

5 Wage Earning Women and the Double Day: the Nigerian Case
Jane L. Parpart

INTRODUCTION

The relevance of western feminist scholarship to the study of Third World women has been a matter of considerable debate for some time. At the 1976 Wellesley conference on women and development, Third World women argued forcefully against the assumption that all women are oppressed by men. They rejected western feminists' preoccupation with patriarchy and insisted that global inequities, not men, were the main enemy facing Third World women. Indeed, Third World men were seen as potential allies in the fight against imperialism and class oppression — both considered more problematic than gender inequality. This theme surfaced at the UN Decade for Women meetings in 1975 and 1980 and, though perhaps less stridently, in 1985.

The force of these arguments alarmed western feminists, many of whom drew back from the apparently dangerous business of cross-cultural feminist analysis. The study of Third World women became the preserve of development specialists who preferred practical action to 'impractical' academic discourse (Papanek, 1986). The concerns of western feminists were declared irrelevant for Third World women, who needed basic services, such as clean water and better health care not lectures on patriarchy. This has been particularly true in Africa, where the recent economic crisis has preoccupied development planners and academics alike.

However, in recent years some scholars and development specialists have begun to recognise the relevance of some feminist concerns to the condition of African women. The fact of reproductive labour on a generational and daily basis has been incorporated into the analysis of the working rural women and petty-traders. Increasingly scholars and development agents acknowledge that African women's reproductive burdens and domestic duties reduce their access to the

161

education and experience necessary for securing waged employment or obtaining the capital needed to establish a successful business. It is no accident that African women work predominantly in agriculture and petty-commodity production — both occupations that mix well with domestic obligations (Bay, 1982; Oppong, 1983; Rogers, 1980; The WIN document, 1985).

Surprisingly, the study of wage-earning women in Africa continues to be largely ignored as an area for comparative analysis despite apparent similarities with the West. The separation between domestic (private) work and waged (public) work holds in both cases. Wage-earning women in Africa have to balance their domestic and waged work responsibilities just as wage earning women in the West do. But the problem of the double day, which has become a major preoccupation of feminists concerned with women and work in the West, has been declared inappropriate in the African case. In a recent publication, *Women and Class in Africa*, Janet Bujra claims that 'African petty-bourgeois women rarely are immersed in domestic concerns' (1986, p. 135). Educated African women with paying jobs, according to Bujra and others (Robertson, 1984; Lloyd, 1974), have an army of servants to release them from the perils of reproductive labour. According to these authors, wage-earning women have become, in some ways, a kind of sexual labour aristocracy — pampered, self-indulgent and certainly not victims of the double day.

This paper challenges that assumption, arguing that both reproductive and productive labour must be examined in specific historical contexts and on a daily material basis, before one can determine the amount and nature of work performed. Neither servants nor advanced technologies necessarily free a woman from some aspects of the daily work of reproducing the labour force, and surely nothing frees women from the work of reproducing people. This chapter examines the Nigerian case and suggests that while wage earning women in southern Nigerian cities have always been a minority, and often an educated and privileged minority, most of these women have to perform both productive and reproductive work, albeit in a uniquely Nigerian manner. Furthermore, as in the West, this double burden has affected career patterns, limiting many women's access to positions of power in the political and economic arenas and consequently their ability to influence the state and to effect change.

WOMEN, WORK AND THE FAMILY: THE LATE NINETEENTH CENTURY

The cities of southern Nigeria are particularly instructive on this matter as Nigeria has a long history of western educated women. In the early 1880s missionaries began providing education for girls and these educated women became the wives of the emerging elite, mostly educated Christian men. But the missionaries' initial enthusiasm for progressive female education waned when they discovered they were inadvertently producing headstrong young women. Victorian wives were supposed to be 'proper' Victorian ladies, providing healthy Christian family-oriented environments for husbands and children, not questioning Victorian values. In order to fulfill this role, women's education was toned down and began to emphasise the niceties of caring for a husband and children and providing an elegant home. Victorian standards of dress, hygiene and manners dominated the curriculum (Mann 1985, pp. 78–9; Echeruo, 1977, chapter 3). As an article in an 1883 Lagos newspaper claimed, the Female Institution in Lagos only provided its students with 'that sort of smattering of education, that is comprised solely in playing the piano, and a fondness for dress' (Echeruo 1977, p. 53).

Elite women were trained to fill their proper place at home, not to enter male dominated occupations. The few women who did work outside the home were relegated to teaching and sewing — the two occupations deemed suitable (if undesirable) for Victorian women (Mann, 1985, pp. 30–2). The ideal woman remained at home, devoting herself to her family and the community.

Thus elite women's educational and occupational prospects were shaped by Victorian middle-class ideology. These women were expected to reproduce the people, the culture and the standard of living of the elite. In the nineteenth century, many elite women achieved this goal. They married elite males in Christian marriage ceremonies and devoted their lives to their husbands and children. Supported by retinues of servants, they organised their households to reflect and sustain the high status of their husbands. Their lives were taken up with the details of middle-class life, reflected in 'the family portraits with father in starched collar, mother in bustle and children in sailor suits' (Lloyd 1974, p. 58). Levees, soirées and private parties filled the evenings of the elite, demanding prodigious organisational skill from its women (Echeruo, 1977, p. 31). The daily and generational labour needed to sustain this life required considerable effort and management skills, and no doubt many hours of unpaid work, even with servants. At this point we can only conjecture about the time involved, but comparative data from the busy lives of Victorian middle-class English and American women (Lewis, 1986; Oakley, 1974) suggest the need to re-examine the amount of effort required to supervise a large household in Victorian Lagos.

Because most elite women in the nineteenth century did not work outside the home, for the most part they did not bear the double burden of reproductive and productive labour, although they certainly worked hard managing their households. However, in the late nineteenth century, colonialism reduced the economic opportunities open to African men in southern Nigeria and the ability (and will) to sustain 'proper' monogamous Victorian marriages waned. An earlier pattern of polygamy reappeared in a new form — the 'outside' wife. Christian wives were increasingly deserted or neglected by husbands preoccupied with their extra family obligations. The social stigma of divorce left few wives choosing that option. But even respectable Christian widows often had to struggle with outside wives and children over their husband's estate. By 1890, Christian marriage was receiving a bad press, and concerned parents sought ways to protect their daughters from the vagaries of married life among the Christian elite.

WOMEN, EDUCATION AND WAGED LABOUR

Concerned middle-class parents decided to set up schools designed to educate women for employment in the hope that their daughters could cope with fiscally irresponsible husbands if they had waged jobs. The Lagos elite, led by Felicia Ayodele (Benjamin) Wright, opened the Lagos School for Girls in 1907. The school proposed to offer girls 'a sound moral, literary and industrial education' and 'to render [them] fit to cope with any and every emergency [in] . . . life' (Mann, 1985, p. 89, citing *Lagos Weekly Record*, 1906). In 1927, a secondary school for girls, Queens's College, was established in Lagos much more as the result of pressure from Lagos women's organisations than of government initiative. This school provided vocational skills as well as training for domestic life (Mba, 1982, pp. 62–3). The elite also sponsored schemes to train women for employment in hospital and office work (Mann, 1985, pp. 89–90).

By 1915, educated middle-class women began to work outside the home in larger numbers both to ensure their own security and that of their children. Some entered business or farming as that combined more easily with family commitments, but these women were also the first to seek careers in politics, the professions and the colonial service (ibid., 1985, pp. 90, 117). Initially elite families preferred their daughters to enter the teaching profession, which Victorian sensibilities considered one of the few acceptable ways for women to earn a living. Gradually, however, they began to recognise the need to broaden women's employment options, and in the 1920s the elite-dominated Lagos Women's League (LWL) began lobbying the government to upgrade working conditions for African nurses. As this happened, nursing began to attract increasing numbers of African women and between 1923 and 1934 the number of nurses in training rose from 50 to 140. By 1944, the Medical Department employed 289 women as nurses, midwives and asylum attendants (Denzer, 1987, pp. 3–4). The LWL pressured the government to open other positions in the civil service to women as well, particularly in the Posts and Telegraphs and the Printing Departments. Colonial officials viewed these suggestions with scepticism and often outright hostility, as most accepted the dictum that women's (both African and British) place was in the home. This philosophy coincided with and reinforced Nigerian patriarchal culture, which supported colonial preference for Nigerian males in waged employment. In the face of these pressures, only a few well qualified and persistent women managed to obtain government jobs. By 1939, only 260 females worked in the Nigerian civil service (ibid., pp. 8, 10–14).

However, as in the rest of the world, the Second World War provided new opportunities for women's employment in Nigeria. The number of female Medical Department employees rose from 167 in 1939 to 289 in 1944. During the war the number of women employed in the Printing Office more than doubled and female telephone operators increased from 12 to 19. Traditionally male-dominated clerical positions opened up to women as well. In 1939 the government employed only one woman clerk; in 1944 there were 58. Many of these jobs were temporary, but they provided crucial work experience for future employment and proof that women could perform supposedly 'male' work, often for lower pay (ibid., 1987, pp. 4–12).

Encouraged by gains in women's employment opportunities and a resurgence of nationalist fervour, Nigerian Women's organisations, particularly the Lagos Women's League, intensified demands for better educational and occupational opportunities for Nigerian women. In 1944, the Women's Party, organised by Mrs (now Lady) Oyinkan, revived the LWL's campaign and lobbied government for more female employment, equal pay for equal work, more training institutions for women, and better conditions for domestic servants and girl hawkers. The government responded by setting up a committee which, while recognising the need to provide more civil service employment for women, openly stated its preference for hiring women in minor administrative posts and for the establishment of a separate grade for women clerks (ibid., pp. 12–16). As a result, while women employees were for the most part stuck in dead-end jobs, at least more of them were able to secure waged employment. Moreover, opportunities for waged labour expanded further in the 1950s, especially after the establishment of regional self-government in 1956 and the resulting expansion of the civil service (Mba, 1982, pp. 64–5).

In response to these opportunities, the number of girls' schools grew rapidly during this period and female enrolments increased. The nature of the curriculum changed also, with more technical and vocational training available. The number of women receiving tertiary education increased as well. In 1948, when the university College of Ibadan was founded, only four out of 104 students were female. By 1957, deliberate encouragement of female students resulted in 31 female students that year and 92 by 1961 (ibid., pp. 65–6).

Educational and occupational opportunities for women gradually increased as independence neared, although never equalling those available to men. Independence in 1960 brought some improvements in education. In 1960 females constituted 37 per cent of the primary students, 18 per cent of the secondary school students and 7 per cent of the students in post-secondary institutions. By 1974, these figures had risen to 40 per cent, 33 per cent and 15 per cent respectively (Ware, 1983, p. 14). The small percentage in tertiary education reflected the continuing dominance of males in the educational sectors. Furthermore, women were clustered in the arts and social sciences rather than engineering and technical courses (Alo and Adjebeng-Asem, 1985, pp. 6–7). Between 1980 and 1983, female enrolment was negligible in the faculties of technology, agriculture, forestry and veterinary medicine at the University of Ibadan. Women made up only 5 per cent of the faculty of technology. At the Polytechnic at Ibadan in 1983/84, less than one per cent of engineering students were female (Longe, 1985, p. 9). In the next year, the University of Lagos reported 21 female students against 282 men in engineering (Olurode, 1985, p. 10).

This male bias in education, among other factors, limited female access to waged jobs, particularly in the professions. Most Nigerian women remained locked into agriculture and the informal sector. However, some women were able to compete successfully in the waged labour market. In 1963 Nigerian women held 14.9 per cent of professional, technical and related positions; 9.6 per cent of clerical positions; 60.3 per cent of sales positions; 26.3 per cent of the jobs in service, sport and recreation; 23.5 per cent of the jobs in craft work; and 2.1 per cent of the jobs in transport and communication. They were listed as 9.6 per cent of the farmers or fisherwomen in Nigeria at that time as well. While Nigerian women were 24.1 per cent of the recorded labour force, they were predominantly either family workers or, to a lesser extent, self-employed. Only about 5 per cent of the salaried employees were women (Fapohunda, 1983, pp. 50–1).

Women's employment possibilities have improved somewhat since 1963. In 1977, women constituted 3.9 per cent of general managers and directors; 8.7 per cent of economists; 5.2 per cent of the architects; 6.9 per cent of estate surveyors and valuers; 3.3 per cent of the agricultural engineers; 15.1 per cent of the general practitioners; 12.4 per cent of the paediatricians; and 7 per cent of the university lecturers. As in most of the world, women predominate in the less skilled, more poorly paid professions. In 1977 Nigerian women were 84.3 per cent of the dieticians and nutritionists and 80.2 per cent of the nurses, but while they dominated primary school teaching only 7 per cent of university teachers were women (Agheyisi, 1985, pp. 148–9). As in the past, most women worked in the informal sector (especially cottage and craft industries or trade) or on family farms, and women overall constituted only about 8 per cent of the waged labour force (WIN document, 1985, p. 49). The 1981 Manpower Survey reported female participation of 13.3 per cent in private and public sectors of the formal economy. However, women continue to be clustered in nursing, secretarial and teaching professions. Only a small proportion engage in paid employment in professional, technical and senior administrative activities (Sambbo and Jemerigbe, 1985, p. 3). Women's participation in waged labour continues to hover between 10 and 15 per cent. It will probably remain at that level as long as the economic crisis continues to require labour rationalisation and thus pit women workers against the more entrenched male labour force (Zdunnek, 1987, pp. 11–12; Fapohunda, 1986, pp. 143–4; Osoba, 1985, p. 5).

THE DOUBLE DAY AND WOMEN'S EMPLOYMENT
BEFORE THE OIL BOOM

How do we explain these educational and employment patterns? There can be no doubt that reproductive responsibilities and expectations have kept many Nigerian women out of school, and thus out of waged jobs, particularly jobs with high status and salaries. Large families have always been the norm, and prevailing fertility levels in the rural areas remain at six or seven children per woman (Adeokun, 1985, p. 7). The domestic burdens associated with such large families have shunted most Nigerian women into petty commodity production, trade or farming, which mixes more readily with domestic duties and requires less schooling. But even though this type of work provides greater flexibility for balancing material, domestic and occupational demands, the double day is still a problem. A recent study discovered that Nigerian women traders work about 670 to 735 minutes a day, while their farmer or unemployed husbands average from 0 to 420 minutes per day (Aluko and Alfa, 1985, pp. 169, 172; Ogunlesi, 1985, Table 2).

But have wage-earning wives endured similar burdens? In the past, as we have seen, educated Nigerian women in the southern urban centres ran large complicated households. When these women began entering the job market in larger numbers after 1915, most of them tried to maintain high standards for their households and their waged responsibilities. We need more detailed research before we can determine the degree to which the double day afflicted these women, but we can be sure that social pressures to maintain middle-class standards in the household did not abate when middle-class women entered employment.

Before the oil boom in 1973, household help was readily available for the more affluent urban households, and many less affluent households had poor relations live with them to help with domestic chores. The question at issue is the degree to which this labour relieved wage-earning women of domestic concerns. While servants undoubtedly performed the more onerous household work, often in very difficult circumstances, the evidence suggests that household help, even well-trained help, never entirely removed domestic responsibilities from women in charge of large middle-class and even working-class households. According to several informants, life as a working mother was always busy. They recalled endless days and general complaints of fatigue and overwork among working mothers, even those with plenty of servants. Problems with house help often arose, and those problems were the wife's responsibility. When house help fell ill or disappeared, it was the wife's responsibility to assist or replace servants. When poor relatives doubled as household help, resentment over work loads often flared into family quarrels, which invariably fell on the wife to solve. The well-to-do preferred contractual servants but many less affluent families had to rely on help from poor relatives — always an unreliable and difficult labour pool (interviews, Lagos and Ife, 1986; Olurode, 1987, pp. 16–18).

Many duties had to be performed by the wife, with or without servants. Sick children had to be tended to, homework had to be checked and husbands often refused to eat food unless it was prepared by the wife. Purchases of clothing, household items and even some foods had to be monitored by the wife. Entertaining in a 'proper' middle-class style demanded close supervision of servants often only marginally trained in the niceties of middle-class living standards. Thus even women with servants still had much to do. Even if much of that labour was managerial, it took time and effort. More marginal middle- and working-class women had less help, and consequently exploited it more. As a result, they often had to bear with servants' resistance to their demands. Thus, while house help assisted with reproductive labour it clearly did not remove it (interviews, Lagos and Ife, 1986).[1]

The double burden of the well-staffed working mother's household is highlighted in a newspaper article about a teacher, Mrs Aribola Ademola, who has a loyal retinue of staff, including a cook, house-girl, gardener and drivers. Even with all this help, she says that 'coping with her kind of life and house chores is not an easy task because you are a mother, wife, head-mistress and you have to be everywhere at the same time.' Even with a high level of organisation, she still has to 'see it [each day] through [by] sheer determination and guts'. (*Punch*, 2 September 1986). Clearly, having a large retinue of servants has not reduced the managerial obligations and many of the duties of this working mother. I suspect most middle-class working women lived at the same hectic pace.

NIGERIA SINCE THE OIL BOOM

The problems of juggling employment and domestic labour have increased dramatically since the oil boom began in 1973. With the oil boom, sky rocketing prices and rising expectations reduced the availability of affordable household help. The minimum wage shot up and opportunities for employment expanded. Professional servants with western cooking skills were able to demand higher wages. Competition for highly trained house help intensified and only the very rich were able to hire well-trained Nigerian house help, especially in the cities.

This competition has intensified because domestic service has acquired a bad name in Nigeria. As tales of easy wealth spread, Nigerian men and women began to expect more of their lives than domestic service, which had an often deserved reputation as an unattractive, servile way to make a living — something no self-respecting Nigerian wanted to do. This attitude was reinforced by a media that pictured house servants as virtual slaves (which indeed sometimes they were). For example, Samuel Mbah tells of the arduous unhappy existence of one such house help, whom he describes as in 'total submission' to the 'madam's pre-dawn military style orders' (*Guardian*, 17 September 1986). Such descriptions fuelled the growing distaste for domestic work.

The steep rise in rental prices encouraged many people to rent out their servants' quarters, leaving servants to find housing in the expanding urban slums (interview, Ibadan, 1986). Furthermore, the new housing blocks for junior civil servants barely accommodated most Nigerian families, let alone a live-in servant. As a result, one of the major attractions of domestic service, namely the provision of minimal family housing, declined, further reducing the desire to enter domestic service.

The introduction of free universal education for children in 1976 changed matters as well. Parents who had previously been happy to send unschooled children to work in affluent relatives' homes, now felt they should send their children to school. Parents who kept children out of school were regarded as irresponsible, and employees (even relatives) who kept children from school were regarded in the same light. As a result, poor relations from the rural areas who had been available as scullery maids and unskilled domestic workers suddenly expected to go to school, and it became increasingly difficult to keep them at home (Olurode, 1987, pp. 16–17). Relatives had never been seen as a very happy solution to domestic help as they often resented being given orders. Their poor English and 'uncivilised' behaviour worried parents intent on bringing up 'proper' middle-class children. Besides, most rural relations knew little about middle-class life and had to be taught the fundamentals of hygiene and cleaning before they could be of any help. Once these children were no longer available during the daytime, their utility for the wage-earning mother declined. Increasingly, working mothers in Lagos and other cities consider relatives as household help more trouble than benefit. (Fapohunda 1982, p. 280; Olurode 1987, pp. 14–15). However, many middle-class wives cannot afford purely contractual house help. Out of 120 women employed at the University of Lagos (UNILAG) in 1986, 75 per cent had housemaids and of those 64 per cent of their housemaids were relatives. The majority of these housemaids attend school, despite bitter complaints that the housewives 'serve housemaids more than the housemaids have time to serve them' (ibid., pp. 15–16). Of course, such tensions and resentments only worsen working conditions for both employer and employee.

Increasingly working women have come to prefer contractual arrangements to help them with child care and domestic labour. Since Nigerians generally dislike domestic service, many wage-earning women, especially in Lagos, have turned to foreigners for house help. People from the poorer neighbouring French-speaking countries are more available as house helpers. But this source has often turned out to be both expensive and unreliable. Agents represent these workers, and women have to hire helpers through them. The agents frequently collect deposits from more than two clients. The agents demand a finder's fee for each house help hired and travel costs from the territory of origin to the employer's home. Often these domestic workers have actually been in the city, so the transport fee is simply pocketed by the agent. This scam, of course, encourages agents to keep these servants circulating among Lagosian households as each new hiring provides another transport fee. Foreign workers quit frequently, often moving to a neighbour's house, who has unwittingly paid the transport fee for their new 'imported' helper. Robberies have increased as well; departing house servants often take the VCR and other goods when they leave. Several informants reported robberies by house help (interviews, Lagos and Ife, 1986; Olurode, 1987, pp. 14–18) and newspapers regularly carry accounts of the latest scam being pulled on unsuspecting households.

Even if an employer manages to keep a foreign house helper for some time, these helpers often fail to provide the standard of care middle-class mothers require. One informant recalled that her helper from Benin just moped around the house waiting for her boyfriend to pick her up (interview, Lagos, 1986). A newspaper article in *The Sunday Times* described a Benin housemaid who fed the baby with rotten milk and a houseboy who sexually assaulted the employer's child (15 June 1986). Working wives also worry that ambitious housemaids may seduce their husbands. The wives employed at UNILAG reported instances 'where some smart and pretty housemaids snatched their "oga" husbands'. Such stories explain the preference for housemaids under 15 years. Some women refused to travel out of town for fear of leaving their husbands with impressionable and seductive young housemaids (Olurode, 1987, pp. 16–18). Such horror stories abound in the press, and fuel growing concerns about household help.

As a result, many working mothers have started turning to day care centres for the solution to their child care problems. But these centres are scarce, expensive and not always reliable. Activists have been pressuring the government to ensure that privately operated day care centres are licensed and regularly inspected in order to ensure safety, but progress is slow (*Sunday Times*, 15 June 1986). Nurseries are developing and this is becoming a booming business, but not everyone can afford to send their children to them (*Punch*, 2 September 1986). This is particularly true for women with smaller incomes because day care expenses are usually paid for out of the mothers' monthly income (Adeyoyin and Akinware, 1985, p. 17). The limited facilities, expense and time required to prepare, deliver and pick up babies at the centres is a continual drain on the energies and resources of young working mothers (Fapohunda, 1982, pp. 283–85). One informant, for example, reported getting up at 5 a.m. to prepare breakfast, get children ready for school and get herself ready for work. After delivering the children to school and daycare, and working all day she picked up the baby, cooked supper and did some cleaning. By 8 p.m., she fell asleep totally exhausted, only to repeat the whole schedule the next day (interview, Lagos, June, 1986).

As domestic help becomes scarcer, more expensive and less reliable, more working women in Nigerian cities are struggling to perform both waged and reproductive labour without regular household help. Twenty-five per cent of Olurode's sample (120 women) had no housemaids (1987, p. 15). A number of informants reported that they and many of their friends are resorting to weekend help; they muddle through without servants during the week. These weekend employees certainly help with the hard domestic work, but leave the working mother with many hours of household labour during the week. And as household budgets reel under the drop in oil prices, the economic slump and rising inflation, even this help becomes more dispensable than food, clothing or housing.

This change is bringing many Nigerian working mothers face to face with the dilemma facing most working mothers in the West — namely, who will help with the household work. As in the West, the degree to which husbands will take on such tasks is limited. Husbands increasingly deliver and pick up children at school, help with the shopping and do some household repairs. Some help with various chores around the house though rarely with more menial and thus less 'masculine' activities such as cooking and clothes washing (di Domenico, de Cola and Leishman 1987, pp. 128–9).[3] But the major burden of child care and household labour still falls on the woman. Indeed, Grace Aluko and Mary Alfa interviewed two elite families and discovered that the husbands did no cooking and cleaning while the wives spent between 220 and 150 minutes per day doing so. In contrast the husbands spent 240 minutes on social obligations while their wives spent none (1985, pp. 168, 170). Even men who used to do kitchen and household chores while living abroad, often revert to type under pressure from relatives and friends, who ridicule 'henpecked husbands' who help around the house (interviews, Lagos and Ife, June 1986). Wives are reluctant to push husbands too much as there are all too many single women willing to offer potential sugar daddies a more supportive environment. This competition over men, aggravated by the increasing divorce rate, the threat of losing custody of children in a divorce, and the difficulties of changing a long established sexual division of labour, inhibit many women from pressing too hard for change (Pittin, 1985, pp. 176–81).

Instead, working mothers are beginning to ask their children for more help. Informants reported making chore rosters for both male and female children, though admitting that female children did more work around the house. However, while children are being asked to do more household chores, the potential labour from this source is limited by middle-class families' desire to maintain quality child care and to ensure their children's education. Middle-class working mothers value their children's education more than their household labour (interviews, Lagos and Ife, 1986; di Domenico, de Cola and Leishman, 1987, p. 129).

The most apparent result of these changes has been an increase in wage-earning women's workload. Working women in southern Nigerian cities increasingly suffer from the double day that afflicts most working women in the West. They rise as early as 5 a.m. to get the children ready for school. The children must be properly dressed as 'a badly dressed child always reflects badly on the mother'. Mothers must arrange for day care until they get home or monitor the household help. Once at home, they have to supervise or prepare supper while the average husband relaxes. After supper, dishes are done and clothes readied for the next day. Di Domenico et al.'s study discovered that many of the women in their sample 'spend their leisure time doing housework, caring for their children, or simply sleeping after their chores are finished'. Around all this, the middle-class wife is expected to supervise her children's homework and to inculcate middle-class values that will ensure her children's success in Nigeria's competitive job market. Weekends are taken up with shopping, family events and supervision of weekend help (interviews, Lagos and Ife, 1986; di Domenico, de Cola, Leishman, 1987, pp. 128–9; Ogunlesi, 1985, p. 3).

Husband-care takes up a good deal of time as well. Durojaiye Ilori discovered that Nigerian working mothers living without husbands spent about an hour and a half a day *less* total worktime than those with husbands at home (1982). Educated husbands in elite marriages often have higher expectations both of companionship in marriage and of standards in the home, thus increasing required family-time for harried working wives. Many husbands insist that the family be put before career demands, and refuse to let their wives go to evening meetings or to travel on the job. Several informants complained that their husbands would only eat their cooking, so they had to cook meals even with a servant in the house. Others worried that their husbands would look for a girlfriend if they (the wife) became too successful (interviews, Ife, 1986). As one writer put it, 'many of our men cannot cope with successful women' (*Guardian*, 8 October 1986). This theme surfaces repeatedly in the popular press, along with stories about gold-digging girlfriends (*Guardian*, 24 December, 1986) and keeps women attentive to their husbands' needs.

CAREER PATTERNS AND THE DOUBLE DAY

How does this increased domestic labour affect working mothers' careers? The general consensus is that these reproductive burdens harm the careers of working mothers, whether they are professionals or unskilled industrial workers. Eleanor Fapohunda reported that 'more than half of the working mothers interviewed in Lagos, both self-employed and salaried, claimed that being a mother affected their progress at work' (1982, p. 285). Di Domenico, de Cola and Leishman discovered that the middle level urban worker had the greatest difficulty with both job satisfaction and child care arrangements (1987, p. 126). But even more highly skilled women professionals had problems. Fapohunda discovered that academic women's domestic burdens hinder productivity and the ability to travel for conferences or research purposes. The current crisis in daycare and household help have only made matters worse, leaving all of Fapohunda's informants fatigued and less competitive within their professions (1983a). Carolyne Dennis discovered that managers at the Odu'Atex factory in southwestern Nigeria rarely promoted women, and inadequate daycare for small children provided a welcome excuse for maintaining a steady turnover of female employees (1984, p. 117).

A recent symposium organised by the Lagos State Women's wing of the Nigerian Labour Congress cited both domestic duties and husband care as primary problems facing Nigerian career women. The 300 delegates agreed that 'most women turn down promotion to higher responsibilities which entails working late nights or extensive travelling'. They also recognised husbands could be a problem, admitting that 'the dedicated career wives with mistrusting husbands may have a harder job getting higher than their husbands' noses' (*National Concord*, 16 March 1987).

Legal efforts to remove discrimination against working mothers have backfired in many instances. Many managers accuse women employees of excessive absenteeism and emotionalism and use the cost of improved maternity benefits as an excuse to employ more men. This has been particularly true in non-professional occupations where women have been hired for their lower wage rather than skill (see chapters in Fashoyin, Oyekanmi and Fapohunda, 1895). Carolyne Dennis discovered that improved maternity benefits were a disincentive for hiring women and a case study of the Odu'Atex factory revealed a marked predilection for hiring single women for short periods (1984, p. 115). Ibadan's industrial labour force was 15.5 per cent female in 1976 but had fallen to 12.6 per cent by 1980. The number of men employed in private factories increased by 37.5 per cent over this period, while the number of women employees decreased by 9.3 per cent. This decrease, according to Catherine di Domenico, is largely due to government regulations which are ostensibly drawn up to protect women, but also serve to discourage employers from hiring them (1983, pp. 259–61).

Are there any solutions in sight? Most women are left to find their own solutions. They rearrange their schedule so they can work before the children get up or after they go to bed. They figure out ways to slip back to the office at quiet periods when they can do some work. They bully children, relatives and husbands into helping with household chores, and above all, they work longer days and enjoy less leisure (interviews, Ife, 1986). Urban working mothers are deliberately limiting family size as another obvious strategy to reduce domestic labour. This is particularly true of educated wage-earning women (Farooq, Ekanem and Ojelade, 1987, pp. 80–2).

Some women have reduced their work by eliminating the burden of husband care. Successful career women are often single. A woman doctor admitted that few female doctors have intact homes (*Guardian*, 1 October 1986). As the Nigerian Labour Congress meeting put it, 'evidences abound that women who make it to the top by dint of hard work, dedication to work and firmness are usually single women who are divorced, separated, widowed or have never married'. The meeting defended the single career woman, claiming that 'contrary to the general belief that spinsters are loose and frustrated, a lot of single women are happy and it is yet to be proved that they commit more sexual atrocities than their counterparts who are married . . . there is absolutely nothing wrong in choosing to remain single' (*National Concord*, 16 March 1987). As the number of single mothers increase, they are gradually becoming a more accepted part of Nigerian society. This appears to be a growing population and at least a partial solution to the problem of balancing career and domestic responsibilities (Pittin 1985, p. 176).

However, marriage is still desired by most women, as it provides both social status (that is, legitimacy as an adult) and sometimes access to male prestige and resources. As a result most working mothers prefer to remain married and bear the full brunt of the double day, while trying to maintain as much economic autonomy as possible. Some women with very wealthy husbands solve the problem by opting out and returning to the home. But the current divorce rate, unfavourable inheritance laws, as well as the general expectations that wives will provide financial support for the family keep most women economically active (Mack, 1978). One out of every five marriages in Nigeria ends in divorce, and many legally married women receive no monetary support for themselves and their children. Newspaper articles (and reality) advise women to prepare for divorce, even if happily married. One such article warns women to find 'legitimate and moral ways of making yourself financially secure . . . a woman should take full or part-time employment'. She should have friends of her own, save separately, never leave insurance and bank statements solely with her husband, and 'should no longer expect too much out of marriage . . . Prepare yourself so that when your loving husband leaves you, you will still have two things to cling to — your life and your sanity' (*National Concord*, 22 December 1986). The totally dependent wife is a rarity in southern Nigeria. Thus the economic realities of marriage and the ever present threat of divorce leave most women with little choice. They must earn money one way or another. For those women in waged employment with long hours and demanding requirements, this has become an increasingly onerous task.

Despite these difficulties, Nigerian women show no sign of giving up their quest to successfully combine domestic and career responsibilities. Leading professional women publicly exhort women to commit themselves to the determination and hard work necessary for success (Dr Bolanle Awe, *Guardian* 10 December 1986). But while professional women generally acknowledge the importance of marriage and family life, they do not see this as a reason to abandon career goals. As one writer put it, 'A woman's primary role is in the home. . . . But nothing should keep her from doing whatever she wants in life' (*National Concord*, 1 December 1986).

CONCLUSION

The double day, so central in the western feminist literature on women and work, clearly applies to the Nigerian case as well. It often takes a different form — the Nigerian extended family, polygamy and more ready access to servants has affected the conditions of reproductive labour for wage earning women in Nigeria. But the ultimate responsibility for the family's daily and generational reproduction has always fallen primarily on the shoulders of Nigerian women and when they enter waged employment, like wage-earning women in the West, they take on the double day as well. Their domestic labour may be more managerial than manual, but it still requires time and effort.

However, this double burden must be analysed in specific historical contexts because it varies with the material and cultural circumstances of a woman's life. In the Nigerian case, we have seen that middle class women in the cities of southern Nigeria were caught up in a drive to replicate Victorian living standards in the late nineteenth century. These women had plenty of servants, who performed much of the more onerous household labour. But the ideology of the day required the 'lady of the house' to maintain middle-class living standards, which required considerable supervision of servants as well as the personal attention needed to guarantee that these standards of behaviour would be adopted by the next generation.

The double burden, however, did not affect petty-bourgeois Nigerian women until the early twentieth century, when economic constriction and changing marriage patterns drove them increasingly into the waged labour market. These wage-earning women were still responsible for running large middle-class households, and several informants testified to the difficulty of that task. Servants altered the nature of reproductive work, but did not eliminate it.

Conditions of reproductive and productive labour change over time, and Nigeria is no exception to that rule. Since the oil boom in 1973, the lives of wage-earning mothers of all classes in the cities of southern Nigeria have grown more like those of their Western counterparts. Servants are expensive and often unreliable. The very wealthiest women can afford good household help, but today most working women cope by hiring weekend help, using day care, limiting family size and cajoling children and occasionally husbands into helping with domestic chores. Some white collar and industrial workers cannot afford any household help and struggle to cope by themselves. But professional women report widespread fatigue and overwork as well. Many survive by stretching themselves to the limit of their endurance and by compromising their career goals.

Do these conclusions have wider implications? I think they do. First, this chapter suggests that feminist categories of analysis can and should be applied cross-culturally, but always in specific historical and cultural contexts. By doing this we will be less apt to assume away similarities between women in different parts of the world. We will find it more difficult to dismiss the reproductive labour of a certain class or ethnic group, and will instead try to understand the concrete manifestations of women's reproductive and productive labour in different cultures and time periods.

Second, this paper highlights some of the problems facing wage earning women in southern Nigeria. Reports of similar problems are surfacing in many other African countries. Inadequate day care and unreliable servants may appear trivial in comparison to the problems facing women among the urban and rural poor, but it is important to remember that Africa's wage-earning women are a small but potentially influential sector of the female population. These women have the opportunity to influence policies which could benefit women as a whole. Anything that inhibits their progress and their ability to perform at an optimal level, reduces women's visibility in the state and the economy and consequently their ability to affect change.

Finally, while differences exist between Nigerian and Western wage earning women, it is important to recognise some of the similarities facing women as they struggle with the double day. For it is only as we begin to see global patterns that women can begin to lobby to change the sexual inequities facing women all over the world, whether they labour in the fields or struggle to balance career and home in the relatively privileged world of waged employment.

Notes

1. This chapter is based on written sources and supplemented by a number of in depth interviews in Lagos, Ife and Ibadan. To protect confidentiality, exact names have been omitted. I want to thank Drs Simi Afonja and Lilian Trager for their support and help with this project.
2. In a study of 676 urban working mothers, Catherine di Domenico, Lee de Cola and Jennifer Leishman discovered that 85 per cent of their sample would prefer to have their children cared for by day-care centres if the charges were reasonable (1987: p. 130).
3. Traditionally Yoruba men were only responsible for certain household jobs: fitting wooden handles to knives and axes, preparing a broom out of the midrib of the palm-leaf and mending broken calabash bowls and platters. Consequently, Yoruba men can use 'custom' to reject increased workloads in the house (Fadipe, 1970, p. 88). Similar traditions existed among most Nigerian ethnic groups.

References

Adeokun, Lawrence A. (1985) 'Reconciliation of Reproductive and Productive Roles of Women', presented at Seminar on Nigerian Women and National Development, Institute of African Studies, University of Ibadan, 20–21 June.

Adeyoyin, F.A. and M.A. Akinware, (1985) 'Child Custodianship among Selected Working Mothers: A Case Study of Work and Family Roles in

Lagos', presented at Seminar on Nigerian Women and National Development.

Agheyisi, Rachel Uwa (1985) 'The Labour Market Implications of the Access of Women to Higher Education in Nigeria', in WIN, *Women in Nigeria Today*, pp. 143–57.

Alo, Oladimeji and Selina Adjebeng-Asem (1985), 'Collective Bargaining in Women's Occupations: the Case of Nigerian Clerical Workers', presented at the Seminar on Nigerian Women and National Development, 20–21 June 1985, Ibadan.

Aluko, Grace B. and Mary O. Alfa, (1985) 'Marriage and the Family', in WIN, *Women in Nigeria Today*, pp. 163–74.

Bay, Edna (ed.) (1982) *Women and Work in Africa* (Boulder: Westview Press).

Bujra, Janet (1986) 'Urging Women to Redouble their Efforts . . .: Class, Gender and Capitalist Transformation in Africa', in Claire Robertson and Iris Berger (eds), *Women and Class in Africa* (New York: Holmes and Meier).

Dennis, Carolyne (1984) 'Capitalist Development and Women's Work: a Nigerian Case Study', *Review of African Political Economy*, 27/28, pp. 109–19.

Denzer, La Ray (1987) 'Family Employment in the Government Service of Nigeria 1885–1945', presented at Seminar on Women's Studies: The State of the Art Now in Nigeria, Institute of African Studies, University of Ibadan, 4–6 November.

di Domenico, Catherine, Lee de Cola and Jennifer Leishman (1987) 'Urban Yoruba Mothers: At Home and at Work', in Oppong, 1987.

di Domenico, Catherine (1983) 'Male and Female Factory Workers in Ibadan', in Oppong, 1983, pp. 256–66.

Echeruo, Michael J. (1977) *Victorian Lagos: Aspects of Nineteenth Century Lagos Life* (London: Macmillan).

Fadipe, N.A. (1970) *The Sociology of the Yoruba* (Ibadan University Press).

Fapohunda, Eleanor (1986) 'Nigeria: Women and Industrialization in Anglophone West Africa', in E. Fapohunda, E.M. Allam, S. Solomon and L.T. Mukuras (eds), *Women and the Industrial Development Decade in Africa* (Addis Ababa: Economic Commission for Africa, ATRCW/86/05, Research Series).

Fapohunda, Eleanor (1982) 'The Child-Care Dilemma of Working Mothers in African Cities: the Case of Lagos, Nigeria', in Bay, 1982, pp. 277–88.

Fapohunda, Eleanor (1983) 'Female and Male Work Profiles', in Oppong, 1983, pp. 32–54.

Fapohunda, Eleanor (1983a) 'Male and Female Career Ladders in Nigerian Academia', Michigan State University, Women in International Development, Working Paper no. 17.

Farooq, Ghazi, Ita Ekanem and Sina Ojelade, 'Family Size preferences and Fertility in South-western Nigeria', in Oppong, 1987.

Fashoyin, Tayo, Felicia Oyekanmi and Eleanor Fapohunda (eds) (1985) *Women in the Modern Sector Labour Force in Nigeria: Issues and Prospects* (Lagos: Leamson Printers).

Ilori, F. Durojaiye (1982) 'Time Allocation of Working Mothers and its Implications for Fertility in Nigeria', presented at International Conference on Research and Teaching Related to Women, Concordia University, Montreal, 26 July–4 August.

Imam, Ayesha, Renee Pittin and H. Omole (1985) *Women and the Family*, edited Proceedings of the Second Annual Women in Nigeria Conference (Dakar, Senegal: CODESRIA Book Series).

Lewis, Jane (ed.) (1986) *Labour of Love: Women's Experience of Home and Family 1850–1940* (London: Basil Blackwell).

Lloyd, Peter C. (1974) *Power and Independence: Urban African's Perception of Social Inequality* (London: Routledge and Kegan Paul).

Longe, Remi (1985) 'Educational Disparity as a Barrier to Women's Participation in Technological Development in Nigeria', presented at Seminar on Nigerian Women and National Development.

Mack, Delores E. (1978) 'Husbands and Wives in Lagos: The Effects of Socioeconomic Status on the Pattern of Family Living', *Journal of Marriage and the Family*, 40, 4, pp. 807–16.

Mann, Kirsten (1985) *Marrying Well: Marriage, Status and Social Change among the Educated Elite in Colonial Lagos* (Cambridge University Press).

Mba, Nina (1982) *Nigerian Women Mobilized: Women's Political Activity in Southern Nigeria, 1900–1965* (Berkeley: University of California, Institute of International Studies, Research Series, no. 48).

Nwabara, Comfort (1987) 'Women and Work in Nigeria', presented at Seminar on Women's Studies.

Oakley, A. (1974) *The Sociology of Housework* (New York: Pantheon Books).

Obi, Regina (1987) 'Women in the Urban Economy in Nigeria', presented at Seminar on Women's Studies.

Ogbuagu, Stella (1987) 'The Place of Women in the Nigerian Economy: A Look at the Federal Civil Service', presented at Seminar on Women's Studies.

Ogunlesi, Modupe O. (1985) 'Women in Paid Employment: Work and Family Roles', presented at Seminar on Nigerian Women and National Development.

Olurode, 'Lai (1987) 'Women and Work: The Housemaid Question', presented at the seminar on Women's Studies.

Olurode, 'Lai (1985) 'Inequality and Infringement of Rights of Nigerian Women', presented at Seminar on Nigerian Women and National Development.

Oppong, Christine (ed.) (1987) *Sex Roles, Population and Development in West Africa* (London: James Currey).

Oppong, Christine (ed.) (1983) *Female and Male in West Africa* (London: George Allen and Unwin).

Osoba, Adenike (1985) 'Women's Participation in the Nigerian Labour Force: Constraints and Prospects', presented at Seminar on Nigerian Women and National Development.

Papanek, Hannah (1986) 'Coming out of the Niche: Intellectual Consequences of Segregating Advocacy Research on Women and Development', presented at Women and Development Conference, Pembroke Centre for Teaching and Research on Women, Brown University, Providence, Rhode Island.

Pittin, Renee (1985) 'The Control of Reproduction: Principle and Practice in Nigeria', in Imam, Pittin and Omole (eds), *Women and the Family*.

Robertson, Claire (1984) *Sharing the Same Bowl: A Socio-economic History of Women and Class in Accra, Ghana* (Indiana University Press).

Rogers, Barbara (1980) *The Domestication of Women: Discrimination in Developing Societies* (London: Tavistock).

Sambo, Adesina and H.I. Jemerigbe (1985) 'The Participation of Women in the Labour Force: Constraints and Prospects', presented at Seminar on Nigerian Women and National Development.

Ware, Helen (1983) 'Female and Male Life-Cycles' in Oppong, 1983, pp. 6–32.

Wellesley Editorial Committee (1977) *Women and National Development: the Complexities of Change* (The University of Chicago Press).

Women in Nigeria (WIN) (1985) *The WIN Document: Conditions of Women in Nigeria and Policy Recommendations to 2000 AD* (Zaria, Nigeria: WIN).

Women in Nigeria (WIN) (1985) *Women in Nigeria Today* (London: Zed Press).

Zdunnek, Gabriele (1987) 'Development Towards Poverty: The Work of Women in the Urban Labour Market', presented at Seminar on Women's Studies.

6 Women, Work and Social Change in Algeria
Marnia Lazreg

This paper explores the conditions under which women participate in the labour force in Algeria. The significance of the analysis presented in the following pages lies in its avoidance of the religious paradigm which has typically privileged Islam as an explanation of gender inequality in societies such as Algeria where this religion is predominant.[1]

I will, instead, pursue the line of thinking developed by Alice Clark (1968) in her reconstruction of working women's lives in the eighteenth century, and echoed in one form or another in the more recent literature on women and development (Sen and Grown, 1987). Clark (preface) alerts her readers to the 'difference between reality and the commonly received generalizations as to women's productive capacity' which, if obscured, results in the invisibility of women's work. Within the context of North Africa and the Middle East, the invisibility of women's work as expressed in low statistics is often seen as causally related to the inhibiting influence of religion on women's ability to work.

WOMEN IN GOVERNMENT STATISTICS

The 1977 census indicates that women account for 6 per cent of the labour force or a 2.5 per cent activity rate. A 1985 statistical report published as an update of the census reveals an increase of 6 per cent in the proportion of working women (Office National des Statistiques, 1965, p. 43). Considering that this report does not give any indication as to the method used to calculate the increase, I propose to base my analysis on the 1977 national census data. This, however, does not mean that there has not been any change in the size of the women's labour force. It simply means that given the nature of the demographic and economic changes that have taken place since 1977 (namely increased migrations to urban centres, further devaluation of agricultural work among men, growth of the construction works industry which attracts primarily men, liberalisation of currency transfers to promote private business, and changes in the land tenure system affecting previously state-owned estates) it is unclear whether the increase among women workers reflects greater job opportunities for women or a simple replacement of men who left unattractive positions for better prospects.

Algerian feminist F. Hakiki (1980, pp. 37–108) pointed out that the 1977 census does not adequately reflect the reality of women's participation in the labour force. Often, women who had declared themselves 'occupied' were listed as being partially 'occupied'. In addition, analysts have drawn attention to the fact that the census was taken in February, a time of low agricultural activity. This resulted in an undercounting of the proportion of women engaged in agricultural work. In fact, the number of women workers in rural areas was found to have inexplicably diminished by 15 100 since 1966.

Women working for a salary tend to be concentrated in urban centres where 83.8 per cent of all women work. It is estimated that two women out of one hundred are 'active'. The category 'active' refers to three situations: women who were already employed when the census was taken; those who had worked before but were unemployed when the census was taken, and those who were looking for work for the first time. This definition obscures the fact that many women who did not declare their intention to look for a job may indeed have wished to have one. Similarly, the category 'housewives' (which according to the census included 3 613 407 considered 'neither active nor unemployed!') does not distinguish between those who are housewives by choice and those who are compelled into housework. For example, there are young women who do housework while waiting to be married or to reach the required age before being admitted to a vocational school.

Among those who work in urban centres, 73 per cent are engaged in the professions (with 30 per cent in scientific and liberal professions, and 27.63 per cent in the services). Unlike other women in the Middle East as studied by Nadia Youssef (1974, pp. 34–41), Algerian women account for 19.11 per cent of workers in administrative services as compared with 21.5 per cent men (Ministere de la Planification, 1977, p. 49 and 69).

Among rural women, 59 per cent are employed in services, while 25 per cent are engaged in agricultural work. Table 6.1 presents a summary of women's salaried work.

TABLE 6.1   *Percentage distribution of the employed female population
according to the sector of the economy*

	Total	Urban	Rural	Metropolitan
Agriculture	5.59	1.58	25.59	0.35
Heavy industry	14.62	15.61	9.66	16.62
Hydrocarbon	1.09	1.21	0.53	1.57
Other	1.65	1.94	0.21	2.48
Construction and public transport	2.05	2.14	1.61	2.50
Transportation and communications	3.26	3.68	1.17	4.89
Commerce	3.32	3.61	1.85	4.42
Administration	53.75	54.69	49.09	48.80
Other service	10.25	11.02	6.40	13.15
Undocumented	4.42	4.52	3.89	5.22
Total	100.	100.	100.	100.

SOURCE   1977 General Census (Algerian Ministry of Planning).

The low participation of women in industry is similar to men's (17.2 per cent) and reflects the labour saving, capital intensive nature of Algerian industry (Ministere de la Planification, 1977, p. 37).

The age distribution of women in the labour force displays characteristics similar to those of women in industrialised societies. Except for rural women who enter the labour market before the age of 14, women work for a salary between the ages of 20 and 24 (26.75 per cent of all urban working women). Employment rates diminish among women aged 24 to 39, then increase until they reach age 49.

The educational characteristics of women in the labour force merit mentioning. While only 15 per cent of gainfully employed men have a diploma, 46 per cent of women do, and 49 per cent of them received highly specialised training (as compared with 19 per cent men). The 9th grade diploma (or Brevet) is the most common among women while the 6th grade level diploma is most frequent among men (ibid., pp. 69–73). In other words, salaried work for women is a function of education while it is not so for men. In addition, working women may be relatively more educated than working men, but their education does not beget positions of responsibility. Indeed, 25.45 per cent of women were employed as middle managers and only 3.71 per cent of them hold executive positions.

Educational opportunities for women are real. Nevertheless they cannot be overemphasised. Indeed the enrolment of girls in schools lags behind that of boys. For example, 93.36 per cent of boys aged six are enrolled in schools against 79 per cent of girls. By age 15, the number of girls attending school drops to about one-quarter of the number of boys (Office National des Statistiques, 1985, pp. 67–8).

The statistics concerning women in the labour force leave out a sizeable portion of women who work in the informal sector of the economy. These women, often illiterate, provide services that are unavailable in the official market place. In small towns and urban centres women often work as *dellalat* or saleswomen going from door to door to sell their merchandise on credit. *Dellalat* sell gold jewellery, received from jewellers or from other women who made trips to Saudi Arabia within the context of a pilgrimage to Mecca or to neighbouring Morocco where gold tends to be cheaper. The occupation of a *dellala* is an old one dating back to the times when women of good breeding did not go shopping for themselves but were brought all the goods they needed to their homes. The typical *dellala* was an older widowed woman who made a living on the commissions she received from shopkeepers. While today's *dellala*, in a small town, may still be an older widowed woman, she can also be a middle-aged woman who has travelled to Saudi Arabia, Morocco and more frequently to France. An increasing number of female relatives of immigrants to France smuggle luxury items (such as lingerie, soaps, perfumes and cosmetics), fashionable clothing and even shoes. In larger towns, these women do not see themselves as *dellalat* but as businesswomen. Nor do they go from door to door. Customers go to their houses to buy items from them (Jansen, 1987, pp. 211–22). Women also cater to other women's needs by setting up beauty salons in their homes. They thus make a good living that is not taxed by the state since they operate without a license. Finally, the old tradition among women to sew clothes for shopkeepers continues. This form of cottage industry makes it easier for women with large families to earn some money at their leisure.

The apparently low participation of women in the labour force as defined by the state is a function of a number of structural factors three of which merit close scrutiny, namely, the nature of the Algerian economy between 1962 and 1978, demographic growth and family relations.

THE ALGERIAN ECONOMIC STRUCTURE

I have analysed elsewhere (Lazreg, forthcoming) the ways in which the organisation of the economy along Islamic socialist lines between 1962–78 resulted in the exclusion of illiterate women and unskilled male workers from the salaried labour force. In agriculture, Islamic socialism has been until recently characterised by the state's appropriation of the large estates abandoned by the former French colonists. These estates were placed under the nominal management of rural workers and administered by state employees. A series of land reforms aimed at redistributing the land among landless and impoverished peasants did not succeed in increasing food production to make Algeria self-sufficient. Women have generally benefited little from the agrarian reforms. In 1976, the year that the late President Houari Boumediene launched a major land redistribution drive, 13 women for every 100 men were allotted some land (Baghriche and Chaulet, 1980, p. 115). Yet, women have demonstrated their ability to do agricultural work. During the war, rural women whose husbands and/or older sons left their land to join the Army of National Liberation filled in for them. In addition, in recent years, as men left their jobs on socialist estates, they were replaced by women when no teenage boys were found to do the work (pp. 105–6).

On privately owned farms, women usually raise chickens, tend and gather lentil crops, fetch water and garden. These activities have been gradually diminishing in importance. Indeed, the commercialisation (and rationalisation) of chicken raising, and the increased mechanisation of agriculture have not only resulted in the deskilling of women but also made them more dependent on the fluctuations of the agricultural labour market.

In addition, since 1978, the new Algerian government of Chadli Bendjedid has embarked upon a slow but determined policy of privatisation of agricultural production. Large socialist estates are in the process of being broken up and measures have been taken to facilitate the acquisition of landed property by those who ostensibly promise to make it profitable. Thus, a special appeal has been made in the past year to young people (essentially males) to become farmers. After a period of time, the farm leased to them becomes their property. It is not unrealistic to see these new farmers using a cheap and available female labour force to produce for the market.

Thus, while the organisation of agriculture along socialist lines (between 1962–78) was carried out theoretically in a gender-blind fashion, its reorganisation in capitalist terms does not appear to be more open to women.[2] Admittedly, gender has only recently emerged as an issue to be addressed by development planners. Nevertheless, the United Nations sponsored Decade for Women failed to sensitise Algerian leaders to the problem of salaried work for women, be they rural or urban.

In industry, Algeria proceeded on the assumption that if it invested intensively in the development of a manufacturing and transformative capability, it would soon be able to make the machinery necessary to mechanise agriculture. Therefore, a highly modern and capital intensive industry would have a pulling effect on agriculture and expand the industrial sector by supplying small entrepreneurs with the required equipment. This has meant that only skilled workers could be hired in the new, large scale factories. Where skills were needed (as in steel works and petrochemicals) it was men who were trained for the jobs. Hence, the low participation of women in these industries. In this sense, Algeria's economic development programme as it was devised in the 1960s, as well as its revision in 1978, systematically ignored the large reserve army of unemployed women.

DEMOGRAPHIC GROWTH

The demographic factor plays as significant a role in impeding women's access to salaried jobs as the structure of the economy. It has also been used as a ploy for confining women to the informal sector of the economy.

The Algerian population has almost tripled since 1962 rising from 8 449 000 to about 20 841 000 in 1984 (Office National des Statistiques, 1985, p. 15). The annual growth rate stands at 3.4 per cent making Algeria one of the fastest growing Third World nations. This demographic growth can be explained in historical as well as political terms.

At the beginning of the colonial period, the Algerian population decreased by 20 per cent as a result of new diseases introduced by the colonists (such as tuberculosis), epidemics of cholera, typhus (in 1869–72), a major famine (in 1868), and military campaigns following the rebellions that took place in the late 1860s and early 1870s. Population growth picked up between 1920 and 1954. However, it was checked by the war of national liberation (1954–62). The high fertility registered throughout the colonial era was counterbalanced by equally high infant mortality (Benissad, 1982).

After independence (1962) a baby boom ensued which the government welcomed. Indeed, Algerian leaders saw population growth as a secondary issue to economic development (Oubouzar, 1976, pp. 193–4). There was also a sense in which Algerian leaders conceived of population growth as an asset. Wasn't neighbouring and hostile Morocco growing equally fast? Wasn't Egypt making claims to the leadership of the Arab world based on its size rather than its achievements? Finally, a large population would permit economies of scale when the newly designed model of industrial development entered its productive phase.

For the average Algerian woman, the invisible producer of this surplus population, high population growth has meant bearing and rearing seven children (the exact statistic is 6.9). It would be misleading to argue that women bear children to please the state since no official appeal was made to that effect. Nor do they maintain high levels of fertility to consciously make up for the loss of life during the war. An answer to a woman's propensity to bear seven children is to be found not only in the political economy of Algeria, but also in the nature of gender relations, women's self-perceptions as well as a diffuse social orientation towards children.

Analysts have generally attributed high fertility rates in North African and Middle Eastern societies to the role played by religion, Islam, in men's and women's lives (Fekkar, 1979, pp. 135–46). Yet, the Koran does not contain specific injunctions about the ideal family size. Nor does it oppose contraception (Mussallam, 1986). However, in the popular culture having children is as desirable as having wealth. Indeed, it is not uncommon to wish somebody prosperity as well as *posterity*. 'Let your house be filled [with children]' is frequently part of a prayer performed by older people on behalf of younger relatives or friends.

To assuage people's anxiety about reducing their fertility for no apparent reason to them except that it is difficult for the state to keep up with population growth, the government appealed to religious leaders to issue two *fetwa* or promulgations (one in 1968, the other in 1982) explaining that the use of contraceptives is not anti-Islamic. Other Middle Eastern countries such as Tunisia and Egypt had used *fetwas* making it easier for Algeria to do the same. That the 1968 *fetwa* had little effect on women's and men's fertility demonstrates that, short of using coercion (as was the case in Singapore and China) reproductive behaviour is not easily amenable to adjustment by religious or political decree.

The literature on the failure or success of methods of fertility control in the Third World is too vast to summarise here. I will, however, focus on two major factors that are relevant to the Algerian situation, namely, motivation and gender roles within the family (Freedman, 1979).

To reduce their fertility couples must be motivated to do so. In a child-oriented society such as Algeria having children is a norm that both women and men accept. For women in particular, it is a source of empowerment. Algerian women share with other women across cultures a concern for their ability to procreate which is undoubtedly related to their female identity. However, unlike some women in industrialised societies, Algerian women rarely wish or decide not to have children.[3] In general, when they choose to limit their fertility, they use modern contraceptives after they have borne their fifth child (Adjali, 1985, p. 101). While the ideal family size that couples wish to have varies with their education and social class, it is always higher than the replacement level of two children per woman.

This situation does not reflect only the value placed on children as social and economic assets. It also reflects the premium attached to the reproductive and home-making functions performed by women as well as a relative lack of opportunities for employment outside their homes. Therefore, while motivation to reduce fertility exists among women, it is counteracted by their social definition as mothers and housewives. As a result, the individual desire for children (perhaps in smaller numbers) becomes indistinguishable from the socially induced necessity to have them. The reproduction of women's child-bearing role is embedded in the prevailing economic system which as seen above is built around the exclusion of women from the salaried labour force. The near absence of state sponsored day care centres, except for central government employees and some state-owned corporations, makes it difficult for women who work or seek work to also take care of their children. Working women must therefore rely on relatives or older daughters to babysit for them. Hence, the family emerges as a crucial institution in both hampering and facilitating paid work for women.

THE FAMILY

The Algerian family has historically exhibited paradoxical features. On the one hand it offered resistance to policies aimed at annihilating it. On the other hand, it was open to changes that left some of its members bereft of their authority. Often subjected to contradictory political forces, it has managed to reassert its power over the minds of its members, women and men.

During the colonial era, French legislators deliberately and systematically attempted to destroy the Algerian family's economic and social foundations. This was done through land expropriations, massive uprooting of tribes (both in the first half of the nineteenth century and during the 1954–62 war), reforms of family and property laws, and naturalisation laws requiring Algerians to renounce their 'personal status' which essentially meant their religious/family status (Julien, 1964; Ageron, 1974).

While the old extended family underwent a process of contraction often resulting in the formation of more or less nuclear families, ties between kinship groups survived spatial dislocations. At the same time, parental authority (especially the father's) was undermined by the rise of a new, post Second World War generation of young men, educated in French schools and eager to obtain legal, political and economic rights with the French colonists. The war for independence enabled this generation to sacrifice the values of marriage and the family for the sake of the struggle for freedom. This affected the women who joined the war more than the men. By stepping out of their socially ordained roles as dutiful daughters, wives and mothers, women compromised their future. For, there was no way for them to know the extent to which they would be reintegrated in their society at the end of the war without incurring a stigma stemming from their involvement in a traditionally male activity (Amrane, 1980, pp. 201–23).

Few, if any, women were ostracised because of their participation in the war. Nevertheless, the war had a destabilising effect on the family which was compounded by the fact of independence. One of the major achievements of the post-colonial era has been a dramatic increase in the proportion of females attending schools (Office National des Statistiques, 1985, pp. 67–8). Woman's access to education has broadened their horizons and raised their expectations. It is not uncommon to read in the major weekly, *Algerie Actualite*, letters written by young women complaining about their male relatives. In addition, the general structural changes that have accompanied independence (namely, a quickened pace of urbanisation, frequent travels to France where 900 000 Algerian immigrants live and work, the spread of television throughout the nation and changing life styles) have also undermined the old consensus over the 'naturalness' of the homemaking vocation of women. These changes have also had the effect of raising anxiety among men in relation to their attitudes towards women.

While giving women greater access to education has not been actively opposed by men in their roles as fathers or opinion leaders, the sexual division of labour within the family has not been challenged either. Working mothers must shoulder the double burden of paid work and housework. Socially privileged women who can afford house helpers often refrain from working outside their homes in state or corporate businesses for fear of incurring a loss of status. This has led some of them to start their own businesses using their husbands' contacts to secure licences, capital, office space, raw materials (especially wool and cotton).

The existing sexual division of labour in the family is reproduced among the post-independence generation through education. Elementary schools typically use textbooks portraying girls and boys in conventional terms. This is a remarkable phenomenon considering that it takes place within the context of a state-sponsored co-educational policy.

In urban centres, a severe housing shortage has further impeded any change that might affect the sexual division of labour within the family. One of its unintended consequences, however, has been to delay marriage. Those who nevertheless do get married and must cohabit with their parents and siblings find it difficult to save their marriage from an early divorce. Although statistics on the effects of the housing shortage on divorce are not readily available, it is a well-known fact among residents of major urban centres such as Algiers, Oran and Annaba, for example, that a lack of private housing causes frictions and conflicts between couples. Housing is also a cause of stress on women who must work harder at keeping their cramped apartments tidy and clean.

Housing shortages also have the effect of hindering women's ability to seek alternative lifestyles. Indeed, women who do not get along with parents or male siblings must endure their situation for longer periods of time. Finally, living in cramped quarters makes young women's activities more easily scrutinised by their older male relatives.[4]

The housing crisis is compounded by a water shortage which has led to state mandated cut-offs in most neighbourhoods except for selected residential areas. The water shortage affects Algiers more severely than other urban centres because of its size. Water cut-offs follow an erratic pattern often leaving housewives without water all day. Service is frequently restored in the middle of the night or at dawn. This has meant that women stay up late or wake up early to fill up any available water storage utensil for use during the day. Discussions I had with a female medical doctor from the city of Algiers in the summer of 1986 revealed that a number of women have developed psychological problems directly linked to the stress they experienced as a result of the water shortage. The construction of a dam in Algiers vicinity has not brought about the expected relief as rainfalls in the past two years have been insufficient.

It is unclear why the water and housing shortages have not been alleviated since the mid 1960s. At any rate, women have borne the brunt of the state's failure in satisfying these basic needs. There is a sense in which the cohesion of the family has been formally reinforced by the sheer spatial constraint. Hence, the housing crisis has caused the family to prevent transformations in gender roles. Indeed, women's access to education, their openness to the world outside the family as conveyed to them through the media, and their rising expectations are circumscribed by a lack of spatial mobility as well as alternatives to the family (such as women's hostels, boarding houses and/or women's centres).

Yet, women's conditions are seen by policy makers as requiring greater control. In July 1984, a family Code was issued codifying family and property laws. The Code put an end to a legal system that had until then combined the haphazard application of the *shari'a* with a number of pre-independence reforms (Lazreg, forthcoming). It generally reinforces the authority of the father and the husband while making some concessions to women. For example, women are required to obey their husbands. Polygamy is restricted but not abolished. A woman can become the legal guardian of her children should her husband die or become incapacitated. A noteworthy aspect of the Code is its recognition of women's limited access to salaried work by making it incumbent upon men to support their families.

CONCLUSION

Given the nature of Algeria's economic development policy, demographic growth and family formation, it is hardly surprising that women's participation in the salaried labour force is statistically low compared to men's. Nevertheless, labour statistics in Algeria as elsewhere in the Third World hide a whole range of economic activities, some paid, others free but socially necessary. Women do work against a number of institutional odds (such as large and overcrowded families, lack of day care centres, water shortage etc.).

The state's unwillingness to confront the significance of women's work makes it easier to ignore it while at the same time benefiting from it. Women ensure both the maintenance of the existing male labour force by taking care of their husbands, and/or unmarried sons' needs and its reproduction. In rural areas, women often replace, at a low cost, a male population of workers continuously in flux. Finally, women (primarily illiterate) constitute an important part of the informal sector or parallel economy.

The non-transformation of women who work in the informal sector into salaried labourers is a result of the state's reluctance to accept women's right to earn a wage regardless of their marital status. In so doing, the state enables businessmen (primarily in the garment industry, crafts and jewellery) to realise capital accumulation at a minimal cost. The liberalisation of the socialist economy which has been under way for the past few years will undoubtedly accelerate the use of illiterate women's labour power while keeping them unorganised and dependent on their employers' needs.[5]

The invisibility of women's work clearly transcends the Algerian case. It is a phenomenon that also characterises other developing societies. One of its consequences has been to provide economic planners and heads of governments with useful alibis. Indeed, since women are statistically nearly absent from the paid labour force, there seems to be no compelling need to create jobs for them. The family is assumed to take care of them. The urgent task for planners is then to create jobs for men, as heads of households. It is assumed that as development programmes become implemented, women's access to the labour market will be made easier. Yet, recognising that women are already engaged in the economic process but in unpaid or insufficiently paid occupations would lead to strategies aimed at expanding and up-grading the quality of their work.

There remains a question to be raised about the liberating potential of work given the Algerian context. Paid work is liberating only if housework (short of being remunerated) is minimised and if child rearing is not left to women only. That socialist states usually make efforts to provide institutional supports to working women need not be reiterated here. That the Algerian state, claiming as it did at least until 1978, that it was socialist, but woefully neglected to inscribe the woman question on its political and economic agenda requires further analysis. To argue as is often done that the Islamic nature of Algerian socialism is responsible for women's problems is insufficient. There is no injunction in the Koran against women working outside their homes, assuming that people conduct their lives according to the Book. In addition, as has been shown, women have always worked when necessity or circumstances required them to do so.[6]

This paper analysed some of the structural roots (other than religion) which might shed light on the complex and historically evolving relationship between gender roles, women's work and development policy. A great deal of research remains to be done on the ways in which the Algerian economy based as it is on fluctuating oil and natural gas revenues, dwindling immigrants' remittances and capital intensive industry, necessitates the invisibility of the bulk of women workers and their maintenance as a non-salaried labour force.

Notes

1. I have addressed in some detail the pitfalls of using Islam as the ultimate cause of gender inequality in Algeria and the Middle East. See my 'Feminism and Difference: The Perils of Writing as a Woman on Women in Algeria'. *Feminist Studies*, 14, 1, 1988. See also 'Unravelling the Religious Paradigm: Gender and Politics in Algeria'. *Signs* (forthcoming).
2. It is interesting to note in this respect that, in August 1987, a TV documentary featured a woman who owned and managed a large olive grove. Few details were provided about the circumstances that led her to own the property.
3. We must keep in mind the fact that in western societies where presumably women have greater access to the job market and need not worry about their ability to bear children to keep their husbands, women still worry about their fertility. That fertility is tied to one's identity is attested to by women who take fertility drugs or use surrogate mothers to bear their children for them. The average Algerian woman who uses the service of the Health and Family Planning centre (or Centre de Protection Maternelle et Infantile, PMI) is usually 26 years old, illiterate and has already had five children (M. Adjali, 1985, p. 101).
4. I have been privy to a case where a young female PhD in political science could not stay at home with her parents and three brothers with whom she did not get along. Unable to find any housing in Algiers, she was compelled to leave the country.

5. A similar process has taken place among the lace makers of Narsapur, India. Although they are crucial to the export-oriented lace industry, these women who work at home, are defined as housewives doing housework (See Maria Mies, 1982, especially chapter 7). I am not suggesting that the absolute equivalent of the putting out system established in Narsapur is already in place in Algeria. However, the women who peddle jewelry, clothes and a variety of luxury items are the functional equivalents of the lace makers.

6. It should be noted that a survey carried out in Algiers, in 1970, showed that attitudes towards women working outside their homes varied with social class rather than religious beliefs. See, 'Direction du Plan et des Etudes Economiques', (1970) *Enquete Socio-Economique*. IV, Roles Assignes aux Hommes et aux Femmes, (Alger: AARDES, pp. 11–16).

References

Adjali, Malika (1985) *L'Espacement des naissances dans le Tiers Monde. L'Experience Algerienne* (Alger: OPU).

Ageron, Charles-Robert (1974) *Histoire de l'Algerie Contemporaine* (Paris: Presses Universitaires de France).

Amrane, Djamila (1980) 'La Guerre de Liberation Nationale 1954–1962', in *Cahiers du CDSH*, no. 3 (Oran: Centre de Documentation des Sciences Humaines) pp. 201–23.

Baghriche, Leila and Claudine Chaulet, (1980) 'Le Travail des Algeriennes dans l'Agriculture', in *Cahiers du CDSH* (Oran: Centre de Documentation des Sciences Humaines) pp. 11–150.

Benissad, M.E. (1982) 'Demographie et Problemes Sociaux en Algerie', *Maghreb Review*, 7, no. 3–4, pp. 73–81.

Clark, Alice (1968) *Working Life of Women in the XVIIIth Century*, Reprints of Economics Classics, (New York: Augustus Kelley) preface (unnumbered pages).

Fekkar, Yamina (1979) 'La Femme, Son Corps et l'Islam', *Annuaire de l'Afrique du Nord*, vol. XVIII, pp. 135–46.

Freedman, Ronald (1979) 'Theories of Fertility Decline', *Social Forces*, vol. 6, no. 3.

Hakiki, Fatiha (1980) 'Le Travail Feminin. Emploi Salarie et Travail Domestique', in *Cahiers du CDHS* (Oran: Centre de Documentation des Sciences Humaines) pp. 35–107.

Jansen, Willy (1987) *Women without Men* (Leiden: Brill) pp. 211–22.

Julien, Charles Andre (1964) *Histoire de l'Algerie de la Conquete a Nos Jours* (Paris: Presses Universitaires de France).

Lazreg, Marnia (1988) 'Feminism and Difference: The Perils of Writing as a Woman on Women in Algeria', *Feminist Studies* vol. 14, no. 1.

Lazreg, Marnia (forthcoming) 'Unravelling the Religious Paradigm: Gender and Politics in Algeria' *Signs*.

Mies, Maria (1982) *The Lace Makers of Narsapur* (London: Zed Press).

Ministere de la Planification et de l'Amenagement du Territoire (1977) *Recensement General de la Population et de l'Habitat*, pp. 37, 45, 69–73.

Mussallam, B.F. (1986) *Sex and Society in Islam* (Cambridge University Press).

Oubouzar, Ali (1976) 'Population and Development', in Appelman, Philip (ed.) *Thomas Robert Malthus, An Essay on the Principle of Population* (New York: W.W. Norton).

Office National des Statistiques. (1985) *Annuaire Statistique de l'Algerie, 1983–1984*. no. 12, pp. 15 and 43.

Sen, Gita, and Caren Grown, (1987) *Development, Crisis and Alternative Visions. Third World Women's Perspectives* (New York: Monthly Review Press).

Youssef, Nadia (1974) *Women and Work in Developing Societies* (Westport, Connecticut: Greenwood Press).

7 Patterns of Patriarchy in the Peruvian Working Class

Alison MacEwen Scott

In contrast to the advanced industrial countries where feminist work has concentrated on the family as the main site for women's oppression, in Latin America the focus has been more on the economy. Considerable effort has gone into documenting and analysing the effects of capitalist development on women's economic roles in rural and urban areas. Yet one of the weaknesses in all this work has been the lack of an adequate theory of the family both as a source of gender inequality in the labour market and as an institution itself. It is not that the family is neglected as an explanatory variable, on the contrary, there is a tendency to use it as a catch-all category that explains everything. One particular problem is that much of this work relies too heavily on stereotypical representations of the family and fails to appreciate its fundamentally *contradictory* nature as a specific institution and as an influence on women's employment.

Let me give an example of some of these contradictions. In Lima, as in many other parts of urban Latin America, there is a pronounced gender division in the labour market; there are low rates of female labour force participation, extreme segregation between 'men's jobs' and 'women's jobs', and high income inequality between men and women workers (see Scott 1986a).[2] This pattern is consistent with the dominant gender ideology, often described in terms of *machismo*, that women should be confined to the domestic sphere, preferably not working at all, or at most only in suitable 'female' jobs and only prior to marriage. The temptation, given the correspondence of these two patterns, is to explain one in terms of the other, giving predominance to supply over demand and an ideological determination of supply at that. Yet closer empirical investigation in Lima reveals contradictions with this normative picture. There are many women who declare themselves to be available for work — any work — and men who expect their women to contribute economically to the household. There is increasing investment in education for girls as

198

well as boys and rising labour market participation amongst married women. Within the family there are also a number of instances where men's and women's roles diverge from the dominant *machista* norms, not merely because of some 'deviant' circumstance, such as a female-headed household but because the people concerned do not subscribe to the dominant ideology.

These data present a number of empirical and theoretical problems. How do we deal with situations where actual practices diverge from the norm or where norms conflict? Should such situations be seen as 'deviant' phenomena, temporary maladjustments produced by rapid social change? Or does the whole relationship between family structure and ideology have to be rethought to allow for contradictions of a permanent nature? Where there is divergence between structure and ideology, whether of a temporary or a permanent kind, which factors are decisive in influencing women's economic roles? These questions indicate that the family's influence on women's (and men's) employment has to be examined much more critically and the nature of the family itself may have to be rethought.

The failure to come to grips with these questions has been due to the partial focus of much of the work on the family in Latin America and the tendency to divorce structural and ideological aspects from one another. There are three distinct and separate traditions of scholarship: (a) anthropological analyses of kinship, usually carried out in rural areas; (b) studies of household structure, particularly the survival strategies of poor households; and (c) the literature on gender ideology, especially *machismo*.[3] Each of these traditions brings different elements to the analysis of the family but is limited by a partial focus. Kinship studies, for example, do not generally address the question of power relations between men and women, while those that do, which usually give greater emphasis to gender ideology, pay little attention to the role of kinship and inheritance in underpinning gender roles. The literature on household strategies often ignores both kinship and gender ideology in underpinning the division of labour within the household. There is an urgent need to bring these different approaches together and to examine the interactions between structure and ideology within the family. It is precisely because such interactions have been ignored that the latent contradictions in the family have not been revealed.

Each of these traditions has an implicit emphasis on normative aspects of family relationships which promotes a unitary and coherent representation of the family. The literature on Andean kinship systems has largely focused on principles of equality and complementarity in gender roles (see, for instance, Bolton and Mayer, 1977; Skar, 1979, 1981; Isbell, 1978). Yet although these principles have much normative support in Andean villages and are reflected symbolically in gender ideology, there are also instances of the use and abuse of male power over women which apparently contradict them. The literature on household survival strategies has made great strides in 'unpacking' the notion of the household and revealing its diversity, yet much of this diversity is analysed in terms of deviation from an unstated, ideologically coherent norm (that is the nuclear family). Studies of *machismo* have a similar tendency to assume an internally consistent, strongly normative model of gender roles.

The image of coherence is also perpetuated by the use of ideal-types in the analysis of the family. It is necessary to distinguish here between ideal-types and stereotypes. The latter term refers to subjectively defined models of behaviour held by actors about aspects of their own society; they are usually descriptively thin and exaggerated; they are rooted in actual behaviour but are a caricature of it; they embody shared perceptions and values and hence are strongly consensual. They are not therefore accurate representations of real behaviour. An ideal-type, on the other hand, is an analytical device constructed by social scientists for heuristic purposes, on the basis of objectively observed behaviour. As such, it has a greater capacity for reflecting the complexity and contradictoriness of real social life. The problem is, however, that ideal-types are often badly constructed, relying too heavily on stereotypes and losing much of this complexity and objectivity.

In this paper I shall argue that we need to move away from stereotypical and partial analyses of the family. Structural and ideological considerations must be brought together, but without necessarily assuming coherence. On the contrary, there are likely to be many contradictions, both in terms of the relationship between structure and ideology and in terms of historically-specific phenomena produced by rapid social change. I shall attempt to show that the working-class family in Lima exhibits two levels of contradiction; one is historically determined and derives from the combination of two class-specific patterns of patriarchy brought together by migration (the traditional Andean peasant and the bourgeois *machista* pattern), the other consists of a number of structural contradictions inherent in both patterns. I shall then argue that because of these complexities, the influence of the family on the labour market is much less self-evident than is assumed in many studies and the specific mechanisms of linkage between the two have been obscured.

Note that although this paper is concerned primarily with the relationship between the family and the labour market, it should not be assumed that the family is the only institution that shapes the pattern of women's employment or is the only source of gender inequality. Other institutions such as the state, religion, education and the media are also important (see Scott 1986b) but they are not the subject of specific analysis here.

On Patriarchy

The term 'patriarchy' invokes both identification and aversion amongst feminists, therefore a brief terminological discussion is necessary here. In this paper the term is used in a fairly loose descriptive sense to refer to an institutionalised pattern of gender relations which involves inequalities of power, sexuality and resource allocation favouring men over women. No assumptions are made here about the universality or transhistorical nature of patriarchy[4]; on the contrary, as the title suggests, the intention is to identify different patterns of patriarchy within a specific society and class. Nor are any assumptions made about 'original causes' (such as men's control over women's labour or sexuality) or about the primacy of patriarchy in relation to other systems of inequality such as class and race.[5] Despite its problems, I use the term because in my view it provides a better summary indication of male-female inequality than any other term produced so far.[6] It captures the gender-specific nature of women's oppression and indicates that this is rooted in, although not necessarily confined to, the family. Note that as used here a 'pattern of patriarchy' involves both structural and ideological components (rather than merely the latter as in some interpretations), and within a particular pattern, male dominance is not necessarily absolute — women may have some measure of autonomy and responsibility.

THE WORKING CLASS FAMILY iN LIMA, PERU[7]

In this paper, 'working class' corresponds to the Latin American term *clase popular* rather than to the narrower one, 'proletariat'. It refers to families who rely mainly on manual work in both formal and informal sectors and includes, for example, factory and construction workers, craftsmen and outworkers, street vendors and domestic servants. As will become evident below there is some diversity in family and gender patterns within this class but it is first necessary to sketch the broad features shared by most families.

The striking characteristic of the working class family in Lima is its strength and stability. There is strong nuclearisation of the family as a residence unit, accounting for between half to three-quarters of all households (Caravedo *et al.*, 1963; Matos Mar, 1966; Smith, 1984; Raffo, 1985). Extended family links and ritual co-godparenthood (*compadrazgo*) are also immensely important, giving rise not only to extended family households (between 16 per cent and 23 per cent according to the same sources), but also to wider residential groups, local job recruitment networks and welfare systems based on kinship (Skeldon, 1974, 1977; Isbell, 1978; Lloyd, 1980; Lobo, 1982; Smith, 1984; Altamirano, 1984; Raffo, 1985). Roughly two-thirds of all conjugal pairs are legally married and only a third are in consensual unions. Whether formally married or not, the conjugal unit shows great stability. According to one survey, about 83 per cent of those living in shantytowns had only lived with one person and almost all the rest had only had one previous union. Two-thirds of all couples had been together for more than ten years (Fernández, 1983).

It is difficult to obtain information on marital breakup but the little there is suggests low separation rates. Census data for a number of working-class districts show that the proportion of non-single women who were separated, divorced or widowed was between 10–16 per cent (ONEC, 1974, Vol. 1, pp. 60–7). Of these approximately two-thirds were widowed and the rest were separated, very few were legally divorced. Note that these figures were similar even amongst street sellers — a group often thought of as attracting abandoned women (Mercado, 1978).[8] Data on female-headed households or unmarried mothers are very scarce.[9] According to one early study, female-headed households were 19 per cent of the total, two-thirds of which consisted of mothers living alone with their children and the rest were composite families (Matos Mar, 1966). Other studies have estimated the figure at 10–14 per cent, which is low compared with other parts of Latin America (Buvinić and Youssef, 1978). According to two early neighbourhood studies, unmarried mothers were less than 10 per cent of all adult women (Caravedo *et al.*, 1963; Matos Mar, 1966).

These data reveal the enormous strength of the family in structural terms. It is also manifested at the ideological level, in the strong affective identification with the nuclear family and wider kin group and its capacity to mobilise collective solidarity on a regular basis and in crisis situations (see especially Lobo, 1982; Raffo, 1985). The family is seen as something sacred, the source of comfort and support in a hostile world. This is as true for women as for men, if not more so. 'My children have brought happiness to my life and to my home . . . they enable me to carry on, they have turned out well . . . my greatest happiness is to be together with my family' (Caravedo et al., 1963, p. 174). This situation contrasts strikingly with other parts of Latin America, particularly the Caribbean, where the nuclear family is much weaker structurally and ideologically.

Gender Inequality within the Working-Class Family

If the family is a source of solidarity and support for working-class men and women, it is also a source of inequality. There is a strong segregation between male and female roles, underpinned by an ideology of conjugal co-operation. 'Marriage (or consensual union) is community, you work, I work . . . and we make something together' (Barrig 1982, p. 158). Broadly speaking there is a segregation between production and consumption within the family, with men being more strongly associated with the former and women with the latter. However, neither sex is precluded from either sphere; women are expected to have some role in income-generation and men participate in certain consumption activities. There is an internal division of labour within each sphere, so that as far as production is concerned, men are associated with heavy physical work and women with domestic services and as far as consumption is concerned, women are in charge of child rearing, welfare and food preparation, while the men are responsible for large-scale domestic purchases, housebuilding and neighbourhood improvements. There are also rules of primacy between spheres, so that men's participation in consumption is subordinated to that of production, while for women it is the reverse. These principles of segregation and primacy affect women's access to resources in two ways; first, they tend to be restricted to the less lucrative jobs in the labour market and second, they have less claim on family savings for productive purposes.[10] Although the division of labour within the family may thus be represented as complementary in functional terms, it results in an unequal distribution of resources between men and women.

Despite the fact that women are not precluded from working, indeed may be encouraged to do so, and although they may generate resources of their own and acquire a certain economic independence, they are subject to considerable control by men. Power and authority within the family is organised on the basis of gender and seniority and this is underpinned by the legal system which defines women as men's dependents and, in some instances, as minors. Males have power over females at all levels: husbands over wives, fathers over daughters and brothers over sisters. Even where wives have authority within their own sphere in the family, it is a delegated authority and ultimately they are responsible to their husbands. Seniority refers to the birth order of siblings and parental rights over children. Sometimes seniority can compensate for women's subordination to men, giving them authority over younger siblings and their own children. However, the conflation of gender and seniority considerably augments male power. The male head of household is an important figure, not just because he is the major breadwinner and legal representative of the nuclear family, but because he occupies a strategic position in both systems of authority there.

Power relations in the family are highly authoritarian and are underpinned by an ideology of natural rights and abilities. 'The man should be in charge. He has more "character", he was created to command' (Bunster and Chaney, 1985, p. 140). There is frequent mention of words like 'obedience', 'respect', discipline and command ('mando'). This applies not only to husband-wife relations but also to relations between male and female siblings and extended kin. 'All my uncles watched over me, I had to obey them all, they had tight reign on me. . . . My uncle is very strict, he was the same with my Mum, with me and with my cousin' (Barrig, 1982, p. 75). The emphasis on obedience and respect in both the gender and seniority systems can result in verbal and physical violence against those in subordinate positions. Verbal aggression consists of shouts, swearing and humiliation. *Estupida, imbecil* and *tonto* are frequent words of abuse. Physical aggression consists of slapping, beating or whipping. Many families have a special whip for the purpose (Lobo, 1982). In one study over half of working-class families used physical punishment as a form of 'correction' and the vast majority of these used the whip (Sara-Lafosse, 1983). Men are prone to aggression towards their wives, parents towards children, brothers towards their sisters, elder siblings towards younger ones and so on.

> I don't like my Dad because he beats me, he beats us all . . . I have my sisters, they are nice . . . sometimes they hit me but not too hard, but my older brothers hit me when I don't do what they want. I have another little brother of a year old, he doesn't hit me, I hit him' (Pimentel, 1983, p. 61).

Note that women are as likely to use physical violence as a form of discipline as men: 'When I have to correct them, I shout at them, I yell at them. Well, sometimes I get the whip and I give it to them hard . . . I give them a good beating' (Barrig 1982, p. 103).

Although beating is conceived as a legitimate form of discipline, there seems to be some normative control on its extreme frequency or brutality exercised by the extended kin group (who are often neighbours). However, it is clear that these norms are often broken, especially with respect to male-female relations.[11] An early study of an inner city slum showed that family violence accounted for a third of all reported crime and of this, the largest category was aggression against the wife or *conviviente*. Violence towards spouses was three-quarters of all violence against persons (Caravedo et al., 1963).

Here, then, we have the first set of contradictions in the Peruvian working-class family: an ideology of mutual co-operation, communal solidarity and affective identification juxtaposed with internal inequality and highly authoritarian and at times violent interpersonal relations. Are these contradictions inherent in the structure of the Peruvian working-class family? A reflection of *machismo* perhaps? Are they deviant phenomena, the result of adaptation to urban poverty and marginality?[12] Or are they the result of transitional changes, the historical relics of some pre-migratory past? Let us now consider these questions.

Machismo in the Working-Class Family

Much of the literature on working-class women in Peru, as in other Latin American countries, has assumed that both their low rates of labour force participation and the violence they experience in the family is the result of *machismo*. This term has acquired general currency not only in Latin America but throughout the western world, but its meaning is far from clear. In essence, it refers to a male obsession with dominance and virility, manifested in the sexual conquest of women, possessiveness towards one's own women especially regarding the advances of other men, and acts of aggression and bravery in relations with other men.[13] Structurally it is underpinned by a patrilineal kinship system, a legal system that endorses male power within the household, prostitution and illegitimacy, and a domestic division of labour that restricts women to the private domain. It is thus more than an ideology; it is a system of patriarchy that has structural components as well.

However, its precise meaning and the way in which it is institutionalised varies in different social contexts. *Machismo* has altered over the years, it takes slightly different forms in different Latin American countries, and above all, it varies in different social classes. Historically, *machismo* was introduced into Peru by Spanish-colonialism, where it merged with class and ethnic relations. It was mainly associated with the ruling class (and the middle classes who were dependent on it) and with white and *mestizo* urban culture. The dual sexual morality enabled the family to be used as a mechanism of bourgeois class consolidation, while also legitimating predatory and exploitative relations with the lower classes. Over the centuries, the pattern of patriarchy amongst these classes has changed somewhat, but the stress on male dominance and virility has persisted. It has been sustained institutionally by the state, the Roman Catholic Church and the educational system, and has remained unchallenged as the hegemonic gender ideology (Scott, 1986b).

However, there were certain contradictions within this pattern of patriarchy — created by the difficulty of controlling women in what was for years a frontier society, by the fact that women could inherit property and use it to conduct business on their own (see Wilson 1984), by the influence of foreign gender ideologies and practices, and by some women's struggle to liberate themselves from the constraints of *machismo*. In recent years, there has been evidence of a liberalisation of gender norms amongst the urban middle classes, especially amongst professionals, with rising participation of married women in the labour market and in politics and some renegotiation of the domestic division of labour (Sara-Lafosse, 1978, 1983; Barrig, 1979; Fernández, 1983). Whether these changes have led to a diminution in *machismo* or merely a change in its form is the subject of continuing debate in Peru.

If *machismo* is defined in terms of a dual sexual morality, the domesticity of women and male dominance in relations with women and other men, we can find many examples of *machista* attitudes amongst the working class. This is manifested in predatory attitudes towards women, men's perceived entitlement to multiple affairs and the desirability of women's chastity and fidelity. 'They say I'm a man if I have two or three women: even more so if I have four'. (Barrig, 1982, p. 161). Many women complain that jealousy from their husbands is a major reason for family quarrels and limits their ability to make friendships or work outside the home (Caravedo et al., 1963; Barrig, 1982). In one study 46 per cent of the men surveyed said that they made the basic decision over whether the wife worked and only 22 per cent said it was up to her (Sara-Lafosse, 1978). In another, 41 per cent of the married women had left work after marriage to conform with their husband's wishes (Chueca, 1982). Girls are strongly controlled after puberty. Boggio (1970) noted that some working-class families subscribed to the idea that girls' virginity should be preserved until marriage (previously unheard of in the countryside).

However, although these data provide evidence of the presence of some *machista* attitudes, few studies have actually tried to measure how widespread they are. According to one of these, only about half of working-class men exhibited such attitudes: 49 per cent agreed with the statement that a man who had the opportunity to make a sexual conquest should do so, 59 per cent thought that if a man really wanted to he could get any woman and 57 per cent thought that women were just made for having children. A composite dichotomous variable gave only 40 per cent in the *machista* category and 60 per cent in the non-*machista* one (Fernández, 1983). According to this study then, although *machista* attitudes were reasonably widespread amongst working-class men, there were many who did not support this ideology. Some of these supported the liberal model of gender relations characteristic of the professional middle classes but they were a minority. A much larger group supported a different style of patriarchy that was highly authoritarian but different from *machismo*. In fact, Fernández' study found no significant statistical association between the two in her study of working-class men.

Let us now consider the pattern of patriarchy amongst the traditional peasantry in the Southern Andes as an alternative source of authoritarianism between men and women. The Lima working class has strong links with the countryside; in 1972, 73 per cent af all manual workers were migrants, mostly from rural or semi-rural areas.[14] Even those who came from cities in the interior were often part of a wider kin network that originated in the countryside. Many migrants maintain their links with the place of origin, sending money home, helping more recently arrived relatives and continuing the rituals practised in their former communities. For these reasons many rural based practices and beliefs have survived within Lima, albeit in a modified form (see Isbell, 1978; Lobo, 1982; Altamirano, 1984).

THE TRADITIONAL ANDEAN PEASANT FAMILY

It is important to note that there is a great diversity in rural social structures in Peru, especially with regard to kinship institutions (Bolton and Mayer 1977). It is something of a travesty to reduce this diversity to a single pattern. However, for the sake of brevity I shall concentrate on those features that are common amongst villages in the southern part of the Peruvian Andes. This is the area that has had least contact with urban-based social change and which has best preserved its traditional institutions.[15]

At first sight, traditional patterns of family and gender in this area do not seem promising as an alternative source of authoritarianism amongst migrants. Its main features, according to traditional anthropological analyses[16] are:

(a) The family is the main unit for production and relies on the co-operation of all its members, not merely the head of household. Women are highly participant in the peasant economy, although there is a marked segregation between male and female roles.
(b) There is a bilateral rather than a patrilineal kinship system. Women therefore have independent access to certain economic resources (crucially land) through inheritance rather than merely marriage.
(c) At the ideological level there is an emphasis on parallelism and complementarity of male and female roles throughout life and on the unity of the sexes in the spiritual world.
(d) There is no dual sexual morality within the peasant family; there is little preoccupation with girls' virginity prior to marriage and fidelity is expected of both spouses after marriage. Sexuality plays a relatively minor role in the definition of masculinity and femininity: bravery, strength and industriousness are more important.

These gender roles appear to contrast greatly with the *machista* ones in the city — women are not restricted exclusively to the domestic sphere, they are not perceived as the dependent property of men, the symbols of men's honour or their play things. The survival of these traditions in the city might thus explain the presence of non-*machista* support for women's participation in the labour market and access to economic resources, although such egalitarianism would hardly lead us to expect authoritarianism.

However, all is not sweetness and light in these peasant families. There is evidence of highly authoritarian attitudes towards women and children. There is an emphasis on obedience and respect for authority and physical coercion appears to play an integral part in the socialisation process.

> When we were little, if we lost a sheep my Dad would beat us hard . . . also, when we were looking after the sheep, Mum gave us wool to spin, and if we didn't finish this wool, she would hit us with the spindle in her hand (Sindicato de Trabajadores del Hogar, 1982, p. 51)

> My Dad was easy-going some of the time and at other times very strict. He had a violent temperament, we had to pay attention to whatever he said, and do what he said as quickly as possible (Caravedo et al., 1963, p. 249)

> At home they used to punish us a lot if we were lazy . . . there was a lot of punishment, a lot of respect in the *sierra* (Caravedo et al., 1963, p. 250)

There is considerable evidence of violence against wives[17]; wife beating has been especially linked to men's drinking, although life history data suggests that it is not confined to this. Boyden (1983) reports complaints of physical abuse being filed by peasant women with the local police in the central *sierra*, many of which were linked to disputes over property. It would appear that wife beating is part of a system of violence that is practised at many levels; by parents against children, husbands against wives and by older siblings against younger ones (Bolton 1972, 1974; Sindicato de Trabajadores, 1982). The large number of children who came to Lima to escape from their homes bears witness to this (own case study data). Also, let us not forget that peasants are immersed in a system of class relations that have traditionally been characterised by unequal power, the summary exercise of authority and violence.[18]

Unfortunately since this subject has been largely ignored in conventional anthropological studies, there is no way of knowing how common these experiences of violence are, nor how the structure of authority is actually constituted and controlled within the peasant family. Nor is it possible to assess whether these reports of authority and violence within peasant families form part of a stable structure or whether they reflect social changes that have modified family structure. Certainly there is evidence of the latter — in terms of a weakening of marriage institutions as a result of male emigration and a degree of assimilation of *machista* ideology amongst migrants themselves.[19] However, arguments can also be made to support the hypothesis that this situation is not merely the result of social change, but reflects an inherent contradiction in the traditional peasant family.[20] For one thing, notions of complementarity are usually based on analyses of kinship systems and symbolism, both of which are strongly normative and may be expected to stress harmony and balance; but this does not preclude the possibility of a divergence between norms and practices. For another, an unequal structure of authority within the family is not necessarily incompatible with an ideology of complementarity. The mistake may be to equate complementarity with equality and economic participation with political power.[21] Possibly a system of subordination within the family is necessary to maintain the very balance and stability so emphasised by peasants, especially considering the centrality of kinship to their social organisation. Whatever the case, it is clear that even within the most traditional of Andean villages, there is a juxtaposition of complementarity and male power and some divergence between the ideology of family relations and actual day-to-day behaviour. These contradictions are likely to be both structural and historical, that is both inherent and a product of social change.

PATTERNS OF PATRIARCHY IN THE URBAN WORKING CLASS

Returning now to Lima, it is clear that many of these rural patterns are present in working-class families, especially those from the countryside. Various studies have shown that while *machismo* is negatively associated with migration, rural origin and the kinds of jobs occupied, recent migrants are positively associated with strict discipline and physical violence (La Jara, 1983; Sara-Lafosse, 1978, 1983). This means that while women of rural origin may have more tolerant husbands as far as labour market participation is concerned, their independence is held in check by the structure of male power within the family. On the other hand, women of urban origin or who grew up in the city may be less vulnerable to male authoritarianism but more confined to the domestic sphere by the ideology of *machismo*. A third group are able to benefit from the more liberal norms percolating down from the professional middle class.

Thus, within the working class there are various patterns of patriarchy and these have different consequences for different women. Moreover, these patterns combine in various ways creating further complexities. Sometimes the traditional peasant and the *machista* patterns merge to compound women's subordination, producing extreme forms of violence but in other cases, the influence of liberal bourgeois attitudes makes for greater independence and less authoritarianism. In a situation of social change, these shades of variation can be manipulated by women in their attempts to renegotiate gender roles within the family. One should not always assume that women accept their subordination passively (Kandiyoti, 1988); on the contrary there is a long history of women's struggles in both the countryside and urban areas (see Andreas 1985). We can see then how misleading it is to represent the situation of all working class women in terms of the dominant stereotypical ideology of *machismo*.

PATRIARCHY AND LABOUR MARKET PARTICIPATION

Conventionally, labour market theory explains the pattern of female employment in terms of supply rather than demand, and it is here that the family is assumed to exert its influence. It is said that the domestic division of labour results in women becoming secondary wage-earners and gender ideology leads them to accept it. It is possible to see *machismo* as an extreme variant of this pattern, which might thus explain working-class women's very limited participation and high segregation in the Peruvian labour market. Yet, I hope to have shown that because of the contradictions discussed above, the supply of female labour to the Lima labour market is much more complex than this.

There are undoubtedly some women who conform to the dominant stereotype: they have few educational ambitions, they regard themselves as secondary wage-earners, and voluntarily or involuntarily they withdraw from the labour market after marriage. However, there are many others who are highly committed to educational achievement, occupational mobility and some measure of economic independence within marriage. Some of the women I interviewed had a completely unbroken work history, even in middle age and with numerous children. Others had taken only a short break and had returned to work as soon as possible. Within the sample of working women as a whole, there was no clear correlation between labour market participation and marital status, number of children or stage in the life cycle. Although surveys which include inactive women do show a clearer association between these variables (see Scott 1986a), these data confirm that within the larger pattern, there is a group of women whose employment careers do not conform to the dominant stereotype.

Yet, the aggregate structure of female employment reflects very little of this more complex pattern of supply to the labour market. Even where women do manage to acquire the relevant skills and exhibit a continuous commitment to employment, they are still confined to 'women's jobs' at relatively low wages. For an adequate explanation of this we need to look more closely at demand-related questions. Two important points need to be made here. First, by focusing on demand rather than supply, we are *not* abandoning the family as an explanatory variable as is often assumed. Second, in an economy such as Peru's, which has a large informal sector (amounting to almost half of total metropolitan employment), conventional demand explanations which hinge on employer discrimination or advanced technology are relatively unhelpful.

There is no space here to provide a complete analysis of the ways in which demand structures female employment in Peru, but merely to make a few suggestions. Within the *formal* sector, there is extensive sex-typing of jobs which is derived in part from implicit or explicit sex-discrimination. These include: (a) employer discrimination influenced by the *machista* pattern of patriarchy in the Peruvian upper and middle classes; (b) employer discrimination structured by the gender ideology of foreign entrepreneurs operating in Peru; (c) technological change which embodies gender assumptions about the appropriateness or inappropriateness of women for certain manual jobs.[22]

Different types of discrimination are built into the structure of demand historically in ways that would require detailed specification. The point is however, that they contain gender assumptions that can be traced to *employers'* perceptions of women's role in the family and these are normative, class-based perceptions. We have seen that in Peru, the pattern of patriarchy amongst the urban bourgeoisie was historically quite different from that in traditional peasant areas and from that of urban working-class families influenced by rural traditions. This produced a disjuncture between the gender assumptions incorporated in the demand for female manual labour, which was based on *machista* stereotypes, and its supply, which was not. Working-class women thus found themselves constrained by a narrow range of job choices, even when they were willing and able to work.

As far as the *informal* sector is concerned, the pattern of gender segregation is related to the way in which men rather than women gain access to the means of production and markets required for informal sector work, that is, apprenticeships, capital, tools and clients. Since production is heavily structured by the family in this sector, gender ideology, patterns of role segregation and authority within the family play an important part in determining women's access to such resources. Thus the sex-typing of activities within the *domestic* sphere, the structure of domestic budgeting, and the historical exclusion of women from the public sphere where urban crafts were defended by guilds, all had implications for women's ability to set themselves up in small-scale businesses (see Scott, forthcoming). Once again, these obstacles existed notwithstanding some women's willingness to work and their greater availability for work given that many informal sector activities were conducted in the home.

These are only some of the mechanisms through which patterns of patriarchy affect the structure of women's employment from the demand side; there are others. Some will be industry or occupation-specific, some may have their roots in specific historical circumstances (such as the state of the labour market when a particular industry expanded or when a particular technological innovation was introduced), conflicts between employers and unions or between municipal councils and the guilds, and so forth. The point is that attention needs to be paid to the *particular mechanisms* through which the family is linked to the labour market, rather than relying on a broad correspondence between the general pattern of female employment and the dominant, stereotypical pattern of patriarchy.

In this paper, I have tried to show that such stereotypes can be very misleading as factual representations of the family; they gloss over a number of contradictions that can have important consequences for the labour market. These include historically-determined contradictions produced by social change, and structural contradictions that have to do with the disjuncture between ideology and practice, economic participation and domestic subordination and between complementarity and inequality. These contradictions mean that a class that has experienced dramatic social change, involving migration between radically different cultures, may exhibit a variety of patterns of patriarchy that diverge from the hegemonic one. Moreover, within each of these patterns, norms and values may not be good predictors of behaviour on their own.

Without examining these contradictions then, we cannot say whether the pattern of employment of working-class women in Peru is the effect of: (a) societal norms which restrict them to the domestic sphere; or (b) patterns of role-segregation within the family which while endorsing their participation in the labour market limit their access to the relevant resources; or (c) patterns of authority which constrain women's capacity to exercise their own preferences; or (d) demand constraints imposed by another social class with different gender assumptions altogether. Finally, we need to understand these contradictions not only to achieve a more adequate analysis of women's changing position in the economy but also to improve the level of theorisation of the family as a site for women's oppression in Latin America.

Notes

1. A version of this paper was presented in 1988 at the Institute for Latin American Studies, University of Liverpool and the 46th Congress of Americanists in Amsterdam. I am grateful to the Fuller Bequest to the Essex University Sociology Department for funds to attend the latter conference and to participants on both occasions for their comments.
2. In 1974, the female participation rate in Lima was 31 per cent (based on a population of 14 years and over) and women were 29 per cent of the total labour force. The figures were similar amongst both manual and non-manual women. Manual women's earnings were 45 per cent that of manual men (Scott, 1986a). According to Anker and Hein, Lima showed the highest degree of gender segregation of all the Third World countries surveyed in their volume (Anker and Hein, 1986).
3. For a recent survey of the literature on women and the family in Latin America see Lavrin, 1987; for references to anthropological kinship studies see note 16; for a review of the literature on household strategies see Schmink, 1984; systematic analyses of *machismo* are rarer, but see

Youssef, 1974; some of the essays in Pescatello, 1973; Nash and Safa, 1980; and various Peruvian writings for example Barrig, 1979.
4. After a period in which patriarchy was claimed as a single system of female oppression and then rejected because of its inability to cope with historical variation and change (see the review of these issues by Barrett, 1980) there now seems to be a trend towards reconsidering the concept through its deconstruction, see for example Kandiyoti 1988.
5. In early debates within feminism the issue of primacy was important, that is whether patriarchy took precedence over class as the cause of women's oppression or vice versa (classic contributions can be found in Delphy, 1977; Eisenstein, 1979; and Sargent, 1981). Nowadays, there is general acceptance of the view that the two are so inter-related that it is impossible to establish primacy. The current debate revolves around whether it is more useful analytically to conceive of the two as separate but linked systems or as a single unified one.
6. Alternative terms include the 'sex-gender system' (Rubin, 1975) 'gender subordination' (for example the articles in Young et al., 1981) and 'viriarchy'. The first of these indicates nothing specific about the nature of power and inequality between men and women, the second is vague about the roots of women's oppression and the third is not yet a generally accepted term.
7. Data sources in this section are eclectic. They range from personal data gathered in Lima in the early 1970s, which consisted of 192 case study interviews plus data tapes from Ministry of Labour employment surveys and more recent publications coming out of Peru in the last decade. All the sources cited here are based on working-class samples, usually drawn from slums or shanty-towns. Since much of this information is fragmented and incomplete, the sources cited cover a relatively long period, that is since the mid-1960s. I therefore use the 'ethnographic present' to describe the situation during the last twenty years. Although there have been important social and economic changes during this period, there are remarkable continuities in the structure of the family and I am therefore confident that the generalisations made here are valid.
8. There may be some underestimation of the amount of family breakup because of an under-reporting of absent husbands or a self-declaration as 'widows'. Women may be declaring themselves to be married even though their spouse has departed or else abandoned wives are establishing new unions fairly quickly. Note also that we cannot assume that all those separated, widowed or divorced are living on their own, or that all those who are formally married are living with their husbands.
9. It is extremely difficult to obtain data on unmarried mothers because they are usually absorbed into the households of their own kin (Boggio, 1970).
10. Women are restricted to the less lucrative (usually unskilled) jobs because they tend to be confined to jobs that reflect their domestic roles or because their access to capital or credit via the family for establishing small businesses has to take second place after the men.
11. As usual, it is difficult to obtain data on domestic violence. The information

cited here comes from social workers, a psychiatric clinic which deals with disturbed children in the shantytowns, police records and personal observations of anthropologists who have lived in the shantytowns.

12. Early studies of urbanisation often assumed that social disorganisation and family breakup were common in the shantytowns and were due to the abandonment of rural traditions or lack of adaptation to the city, for example, Lewis, 1966; Mangin, 1965.

13. Since we are dealing with male-female relations in this paper, I shall exclude reference to male-male relations from the discussion here.

14. Peruvian government statistics have a generous definition of 'urban', that is communities of around 2000 in population, therefore the literature on migration tends to emphasise its urban nature. However, since most of these communities are small and based on agriculture I prefer to call them 'semi-rural'.

15. The mountainous Andean region known as the *sierra*, which historically housed the majority of the Peruvian population, is usually divided into three regions, the northern, central and southern *sierra*. In the northern and central *sierra* Quechuan and Aymaran culture have been much less important and peasants have been less protected by linguistic and cultural separatism from Spanish influence. There has also been much greater contact with the areas of capitalist development, in the north because of temporary migrations to the canefields on the coast, and in the centre because of commercial links with Lima. The southern *sierra* has not been totally protected from external change, as is witnessed by the heavy migration to Lima but there has been less of it than in other areas.

16. See Nuñez del Prado, 1975a, 1975b; Bolton and Mayer, 1977; Isbell, 1978; Skar, 1979, 1981; Radcliffe 1986a, 1986b.

17. Again this evidence is fragmentary but see Bolton, 1972, 1974; Stein, 1974; Escobar, 1973; Nuñez del Prado, 1982; La Jara, 1983. Most information has become available through life history data. It appears that people are more prepared to talk about their experiences once they have left the countryside, see Caravedo et al., 1963; Sindicato de Trabajadores del Hogar, 1982; and own case study data.

18. There has been a long history in Peru of violent relations between peasants on the one hand and landowners, mineowners, municipal and national governments and the army, on the other. This is reflected in equally violent political responses by peasants, see for example, Allpanchis, 1978; Gonzales, 1987.

19. There is evidence of wives being abandoned in the *sierra* as their men migrated and of casual liaisons between migrants and urban women in the towns. References to increasing *machismo* amongst peasants are made by Escobar, 1973; Bourque and Warren, 1981; and Babb, 1985. Note, however, that all of these are based on peasant villages in or around the central *sierra*. In most studies, *machismo* is particularly associated with *mestizos*, who have more contact with urban culture and yet are important agents of change in the countryside. This process has been reported in the southern part of the Andes as well as in the central valleys.

20. Recently, anthropologists have been increasingly questioning the validity of the model of equilibrium and balance formerly stressed in Andean ethnographies, see for example Sanchez, 1982. In a recent publication based on a different society, Bloch (1987) has raised the question of contradictions *within* gender ideology.
21. Despite the stress on complementarity of gender roles in all other aspects of peasant society, women were usually excluded from participation in the political organisation of the community. Although they were sometimes present at assemblies they were not consulted directly, rarely spoke and did not hold office (Nuñez del Prado, 1982; Bronstein, 1982; Radcliffe, 1986b).
22. Interestingly, there has been a shift from the heavy-technology phase which favoured male skills (for example in the textile industry) to the light-technology phase which has shown a preference for women (for example electronics), see Chaney and Schmink, 1980; Elson and Pearson, 1981.

References

Allpanchis (1978) Special number on peasant movements, vol. XI (11/12), (Cusco).
Altamirano, T. (1984) *Presencia andina en Lima Metropolitana* (Lima: Fondo Editorial, Pontificia Universidad Catolica del Peru).
Andreas, C. (1985) *When Women Rebel* (Westport: Lawrence Hill).
Anker, R. and C. Hein (eds) (1986) *Sex Inequalities in Urban Employment in the Third World* (Basingstoke: Macmillan).
Babb, F.E. (1985) 'Men and Women in Vicos, Peru: A Case of Unequal Development', in W. Stein (ed.), *Peruvian Contexts of Change* (New Brunswick: Transaction Books) pp. 163–210.
Barrett, M. (1980) *Women's Oppression Today* (London: Verso).
Barrig, M. (1979) *Cinturon de Castidad* (Lima: Mosca Azul).
Barrig, M. (1982) *Convivir: La pareja en la pobreza* (Lima: Mosca Azul).
Bloch, M. (1987) 'Descent and Sources of Contradiction in Representations of Women and Kinship', in J.F. Collier and S.J. Yanagisako (eds), *Gender and Kinship: Essays Toward a Unified Analysis* (Stanford University Press) pp. 324–37.
Boggio, K. (1970) *Estudio del ciclo vital en Pamplona Alta*, Cuadernos Desco, Lima, Peru, mimeo.
Bolton, R. (1972) *Aggression in Qolla Society*, PhD dissertation, Cornell University.
Bolton, R. (1974) 'El abusivo y el humilde', *Allpanchis* vol. VI, pp. 42–78.
Bolton, R. and E. Mayer (eds) (1977) *Andean Kinship and Marriage* (Washington: American Anthropological Association).
Bourque, S.C. and K.B. Warren (1981) *Women of the Andes* (Ann Arbor: University of Michigan Press).
Boyden, J. (1983) *The Transformation of Production in and the Economic*

Development of, a District in the Central Peruvian Andes: 1700–1979, PhD dissertation, London School of Economics.

Bronstein, A. (1982) *The Triple Struggle: Latin American Peasant Women* (London: World on Want Campaigns).

Bunster, X. and E. Chaney (1985) *Sellers and Servants* (New York: Praeger).

Buvinić, M. and N.H. Youssef (1978) 'Women-headed Households: the Ignored Factor in Development Planning', report submitted to AID/WID, Grant AID/otr-G-1593, Washington, DC.

Caravedo, B., H. Rotondo and J. Mariategui (1963) *Estudios de Psiquiatría Social en el Peru* (Lima: Ediciones del Sol).

Chaney, E. and M. Schmink (1980) 'Women and Modernization: Access to Tools', in J. Nash and H. Safa (eds), 1980, pp. 160–82.

Chueca, M. (1982), 'Mujer, Familia y Trabajo en Villa El Salvador'. *Mimeo*. Paper presented to the seminar, Analisis y Promoción de la Participación de la Mujer en la Actividad Economica, Lima, 2–5 March.

Delphy, C. (1977) *The Main Enemy* (London: Women's Research and Resource Centre).

Eisenstein, Z. (ed.) (1979) *Capitalist Patriarchy and the Case for Socialist Feminism* (New York: Monthly Review Press).

Elson, D. and D. Pearson (1981) 'The Subordination of Women and the Internationalisation of Factory Production', in K. Young et al., 1981, pp. 144–66.

Escobar, G. (1973) *Sicaya* (Lima: Instituto de Estudios Peruanos).

Fernández, B. (1983) 'Unión y estabilidad conyugales', Pontificia Universidad Catolica del Peru, Departamento de Ciencias Sociales, Lima, mimeo.

Gonzales, M.J. (1987) 'Neo-colonialism and Indian Unrest in Southern Peru, 1867–1898', *Bulletin of Latin American Research*, vol. 6 (1), pp. 1–26.

Isbell, B.J. (1978) *To Defend Ourselves: Ecology and Ritual in an Andean Village* (Austin: University of Texas Press).

Kandiyoti, D. (1988) 'Bargaining with Patriarchy', *Gender and Society*, September.

La Jara, E. (1983) 'Socialización de los hijos del migrante de la sierra', Pontificia Universidad Catolica del Peru, Departamento de Ciencias Sociales, Lima, mimeo.

Lavrin, A. (1987) 'Women, the Family and Social Change in Latin America', *World Affairs*, vol. 150, no. 2, pp. 109–28.

Lewis, O. (1966) 'The Culture of Poverty', *Scientific American*, vol. 215, no. 4, pp. 19–25.

Lloyd, P. (1980) *The 'Young Towns' of Lima: Aspects of Urbanization in Peru* (Cambridge University Press).

Lobo, S. (1982) *A House of My Own: Social Organization in the Squatter Settlements of Lima, Peru* (Tucson: University of Arizona Press).

Mangin, W.P. (1965), 'Mental Health and Migration to Cities', in R.N. Adams and D.B. Heath (eds), *Contemporary Cultures and Societies of Latin America* (New York: Random House).

Matos Mar, J. (1966) *Estudio de las barriadas limeñas (1955)* (Lima: Department of Anthropology, Universidad Nacional Mayor de San Marcos, Lima, Peru).

Alison M. Scott 219

Mercado, H. (1978) *La Madre Trabajadora* (Estudios de Poblacion y Desarrollo) serie C, no. 2.
Nash, J. and H. Safa (eds) (1980) *Sex and Class in Latin America* (New York: Bergin and Garvey).
Nuñez del Prado, D. (1975a) 'El rol de la mujer campesina Quechua', *America Indigena* (Mexico) 35 (2), pp. 391–401.
Nuñez del Prado, D. (1975b) 'El poder de decisión de la mujer Quechua Andina', *America Indigena* (Mexico) 35 (3), pp. 623–30.
Nuñez del Prado, D. (1982) 'El papel de la mujer campesina en los Andes y su contribución a la economia familiar', paper presented to the Congreso de Investigacion de la Mujer en la Region Andina, Lima, 7–10 June 1982, mimeo.
ONEC (Oficina Nacional de Estadística y Censos) (1974) 'Censos Nacionales de Población y Vivienda, 1972', (Lima).
Pescatello, A. (ed.) (1973) *Female and Male in Latin America* (University of Pittsburgh).
Pimentel, C. (1983) 'Problemas Psicológicos de los niños y represión familiar y escolar en la barriada', in Pimentel, C. et al., *Peru: la población diversa*, Serie Investigación I, (Lima: Ediciones Amidep), pp. 15–78.
Radcliffe, S.A. (1986a) 'Gender Relations, Peasant Livelihood Strategies and Migration: A Case study from Cuzco, Peru', *Bulletin of Latin American Research*, vol. 5, no. 2, pp. 29–47.
Radcliffe, S.A. (1986b) 'Female Migration and Peasant Livelihood Strategies in Highland Peru', PhD dissertation, University of Liverpool.
Raffo, E. (1985) *Vivir en Huascar* (Lima: Fundacion Friedrich Ebert).
Rubin, G. (1975) 'The Traffic in Women: Notes on the "Political Economy" of Sex', in R. Reiter (ed.), *Toward an Anthropology of Women* (New York: Monthly Review Press) pp. 157–210.
Sanchez, R. (1982) 'The Andean Economic System and Capitalism', in D. Lehmann (ed.), *Ecology and Exchange in the Andes* (Cambridge University Press) pp. 157–90.
Sara-Lafosse, V. (1978) 'La famila y la mujer en contextos sociales diferentes', Pontificia Universidad Catolica del Peru, Departamento de Ciencias Sociales, Lima, mimeo.
Sara-Lafosse, V. (1983) 'La socialización de los hijos en contextos sociales diferentes', Pontificia Universidad Catolica del Peru, Departamento de Ciencias Sociales, Lima, mimeo.
Sargent, L. (ed.) (1981) *Women and Revolution* (London: Pluto).
Schmink, M. (1984) 'Household Economic Strategies: Review and Research Agenda', *Latin American Research Review* vol. XIX, no. 3, pp. 87–101.
Scott, A. MacEwen (1986a) 'Economic Development and Urban Women's Work: the Case of Lima, Peru', in R. Anker and C. Hein (eds), 1986, pp. 313–69.
Scott, A. MacEwen (1986b) 'Industrialization, Gender Segregation and Stratification Theory', in R. Crompton and M. Mann (eds), *Gender and Stratification* (Cambridge: Polity Press) pp. 154–89.
Scott, A. MacEwen (forthcoming), 'Informal Sector or Female Sector? Gender Bias in Urban Labour Market Models', in D. Elson (ed.), *Male*

Bias in the Development Process (Manchester University Press).

Sindicato de Trabajadores del Hogar (1982) *Basta: testimonios* (Cusco: Centro de Estudios Rurales Andinos).

Skar, S.L. (1979) 'The Use of the Public/Private Framework in the Analysis of Egalitarian societies: The Case of a Quechua Community in Highland Peru', *Women's Studies International Quarterly*, vol. 2, no. 4, pp. 449–60.

Skar, S.L. (1981) 'Andean Women and the Concept of Space/Time', in S. Ardener (ed.), *Women and Space* (London: Croom Helm) pp. 35–49.

Skeldon, R. (1974) 'Migration in a Peasant Society: the example of Cuzco, Peru', PhD dissertation, University of Toronto.

Skeldon, R. (1977) 'The Evolution of Migration Patterns during Urbanization in Peru, *The Geographical Review* vol. 67, no. 4, pp. 394–411.

Smith, G.A. (1984) 'Confederations of Households: Extended Domestic Enterprises in City and Country', in N. Long and B. Roberts, *Miners, Peasants and Entrepreneurs* (Cambridge University Press) pp. 217–234.

Stein, W.W. (1974) 'El peon que se negaba', *Allpanchis*, vol. VI, pp. 79–142.

Wilson, F. (1984) 'Marriage, Property and the Position of Women in the Peruvian Central Andes', in R.T. Smith (ed.), *Kinship Ideology and Practice in Latin America* (Chapel Hill: University of North Carolina Press) pp. 297–325.

Young, K., Wolkowitz, C. and McCullagh, R. (eds) (1981) *Of Marriage and the Market* (London: CSE Books).

Youssef, N.H. (1974) *Women and Work in Developing Societies* (Westport: Greenwood Press).

8 Socio-economic Determinants of the Outcomes of Women's Income-Generation in Developing Countries
Constantina Safilios-Rothschild

It has been often claimed that if women are helped to earn a relatively substantial income on a steady basis, they will be able to gain a higher status in the family in terms of greater decision-making power and control over their lives. And while there are many difficulties in setting up programmes and projects that facilitate women's access to a substantial and steady income, there are even more nagging questions as to the outcomes of women's access to such income. These questions arise from evidence showing that not all women earning a substantial income are able to translate this income into decision-making power and autonomy. Furthermore, some of the difficulties encountered in setting up and in maintaining profitable projects for women result from the same combination of socio-economic factors responsible for women's inability to turn economic profits into higher status for themselves.

The powerful sex stratification system existing in all developing countries is based upon and justified by women's economic dependence on men. Programmes and activities, therefore, aiming to enable women to earn more than a meagre income on a steady basis represent a clear threat to the established social order. Here it is important to distinguish clearly between firstly programmes and projects that involve women in labour intensive and little profitable 'sex-appropriate' income-generating activities and secondly programmes and projects that help women obtain marketable skills and enter into clearly profitable activities with an assured market (which are most often non-traditional activities for women). The experience from a number of developing countries shows that the former types of programmes and projects are acceptable in practically all countries and areas and receive the wholehearted support of men, husbands, local leaders and policy makers. The reason for this widely based acceptance is that the income that women are usually able to gain is very small and rarely steady or long-lived. The second types of programmes and projects, however, often encounter considerable resistance on the part of husbands, local leaders and policy makers and if these projects promise to be successful, they are usually taken over by men. Even when this take-over is not feasible in the public domain, it takes place in the private domain by husbands who control the income of their wives or by husbands who begin to cultivate the profitable food crops which were previously 'women's crops'. Among the Tiv of Nigeria, for example, when the market value of rice, a crop traditionally cultivated by women, increased significantly, men began to dominate the cultivation and earnings of the crop (Burfisher and Horenstein, 1985). Similarly, at present in the Cameroon because food crops have a steady local demand and are often sold at higher prices than export cash crops which are affected by international market conditions, men are beginning to grow food crops.

The only exception to the fears about and the resistance toward women's economic autonomy is encountered in the case of legal women heads of household who are recognised as having to support themselves and their families. But when husbands are present, within the context of a traditional society, wives' earning capacity is often seen as questioning the breadwinning ability of husbands and, therefore, their superiority and authority over women. As it can be expected, this threat of income-earning wives is more often felt by husbands who, because of their own shortcomings or because of high unemployment, have great difficulty being good breadwinners. Also it can be expected that the more powerful is the prevailing traditional sex-role ideology according to which men must be able to provide well for their families, the more threatening will be the wives' ability to earn as much as, or more than, their husbands.

Research evidence available from a number of different countries, such as Greece, Honduras and Kenya, when examined within the context of prevailing cultural ideology regarding men's and women's roles and the husband's socio-economic status, shows that the wife's earned income does not necessarily become a valuable and powerful resource that wins her decision-making power and equality in the division of labour (Safilios-Rothschild, 1982). It is only when husbands feel quite secure in their superior male position because they successfully fulfill their breadwinning role that they are willing to allow women who work and earn a substantial income, more family power and equality in the family.

The evidence from Greece is from the middle 1960s when intensive rural-urban migration was responsible for the uprooting of rural people with a very traditional sex role ideology to Athens where they swelled the ranks of the low-income population. According to this traditional sex role ideology, husbands ought to occupy the unchallenged superior position in the family in terms of income, authority, knowledge and prestige. But it was also in this group that, due to a number of structural reasons, husbands often had trouble successfully fulfilling their breadwinning role and often had to decide that it was necessary for their wives to work outside the home. In fact, in many cases it was the husband's decision that the wife had to work because he needed the money rather than her own decision. Within this context, it is clear why the wife's ability to earn an income, which was often higher than the husband's or the only income in the family, was very threatening to husbands' ability to maintain the superior position in the family as the breadwinner and protector. Different types of mechanisms had, therefore, to be devised that would minimise the importance of the wife's economic contribution and help restore social order. Indeed, the data showed that in these couples it was the husband who managed the wife's income or all income was pooled so that the income earned by the wife lost its distinguishing label. In this way, the wife's income did not become a visible resource that could be translated into decision-making power. Furthermore, husbands asserted their superiority through sheer bossiness and control by becoming more domineering and restrictive of their wife's behaviour and participated less in family tasks and responsibilities than husbands whose wives did not work at all (Safilios-Rothschild and Dijkers, 1978).

Husbands, however, in the middle and upper classes who were successful breadwinners did not seem to be threatened by their wives' income earning ability even when they managed to earn more than themselves. Their breadwinning confidence established the fact that they had lived up to the expectations of male achievement and that their wives' income could in no way shake this confidence. Also it is possible that their higher level of education was responsible for their relative emancipation from traditional sex role stereotypes. Thus, they allowed their wives more freedom including that of managing their own money and took an active part in the household division of labour. Wives were also able to translate their economic role into greater autonomy since they were also able to refuse having sexual relations when for a variety of reasons they did not feel like it (Safilios-Rothschild and Dijkers, 1978).

Similar and even more detailed and striking findings come from rural Honduras where the traditional sex role ideology is equally shared by men and women and men have often a great difficulty playing successfully the breadwinner role. The data show that men who earn incomes well above subsistence are not threatened by their wives' ability to earn an income. They acknowledge their wives' level of income by not underestimating it and they let their wives control the income they earn and in most cases their own income as well. Husbands, on the other hand, whose income cannot guarantee family survival and who are not, therefore, secure in their breadwinning role seem to be quite threatened by their wives' income, especially when this income is almost as large as theirs. In these cases, it is clear that the wife is a co-breadwinner since her income is at least as important for family survival as the husband's income and in some ways even more important since a greater percentage of her income than his is spent for food and household needs. Because of this reality that can shatter the very basis of male superiority and authority over women, men resort to a variety of mechanisms that either minimise women's income or assert their control and authority. The one mechanism often used is the underestimation of women's income which is greatly facilitated by the nature of women's income and by women's own efforts to minimise the importance of their economic contributions. Women tend to earn small sums of money from a variety of sources and at irregular times, and they often use these small sums as soon as they receive them to buy food needed for the family. In this way, the concept of 'earning an income' is not well delineated even in their own minds so that some of the women report that they do not earn an income or that they spend it all on food. Most of the wives in this category, therefore, tend to mask their income and thus, through its invisibility, help decrease the potential tensions between themselves and their husbands by making it easier for the husbands to underestimate their level of economic contributions. In addition to these mechanisms, husbands also attempt to assert their control, even in areas traditionally considered women's domain such as decisions about shopping for food, while men who are secure as breadwinners relegate these responsibilities to their wives. It is even more important to note that low-income husbands, with wives who earn almost as much as themselves, ignore the fact that their wives also shop and spend most of their income on food so that the family can survive. It is, therefore, at the expense of reality that these threatened husbands manage to tolerate the fact that their wives are co-breadwinners (Safilios-Rothschild, 1988).

In the Honduras case, it must be noted that women's income was in all cases quite small. This explains why even when husbands were secure breadwinners and women could retain the visibility of their economic contributions, they were not able to translate these small economic contributions into much power except that they were able to control their money and that of their husband, to make decisions about food and to have their opinion heard about agricultural decisions (Safilios-Rothschild and Mejia, forthcoming). Their low level incomes also explain why there was no decline in fertility since the available evidence indicates that women's income must be high before they begin investing substantially in each child and reducing their total numbers of children (Safilios-Rothschild and Mburugu, forthcoming).

The third set of evidence comes from Kenya where a detailed study of women's groups enterprises in Mombasa shows similar trends. Although it has been hypothesised that within the context of a very traditional milieu women's involvement in a group would help safeguard their access to income (as has been found to be true in the case of women's milk co-operatives in India, Somjee and Somjee, 1978; and Sundar, 1981), the Kenya data show that even group membership does not necessarily guarantee such access. This was due to the fact that in most of the areas of women groups' operation, husbands had poorly-paid, marginal occupations and could not in a sense afford to let women's group income-generating activities out of their control. Women's incomes, therefore, were controlled by the men and the women were not able to acquire prestige or decision-making power as a function of the income they earned. It was only in one community in which husbands had a stable and sufficient economic base that women were able to translate their economic contributions into a valuable resource that earned them more decision-making power and more equality in the division of labour (McCormack, Walsh and Nelson, 1986).

Another example from Kenya clearly delineates the conditions under which women are able to translate their income into decision-making power and autonomy. Research undertaken in Mbogoini, a village in Nyeri District of Central Province, showed that because men had access to profitable occupations other than agriculture, in 90 per cent of the cases the women cultivated the entire family holdings. Women's agricultural and non-farm income was substantial and in about one-third (32 per cent) of the households, they earned as much as half or more of the husband's income and their total income (from all sources including contributions from relatives and husband) constituted 51 per cent of the husband's total income. The majority of these women also made all key agricultural decisions, except those relating to credit and their decision-making power was even greater when the husband worked and lived away from home. Also women in this village used their income proportionately to its size to pay for their children's clothing and school fees and have the highest contraceptive prevalence recorded in Kenya (Safilios-Rothschild and Mburugu, forthcoming).

In Hamisi 'A', on the other hand, a village in Kakamega District, Western Province, men have less profitable non-farm occupations than in Mbogoini, earning less than half of men's non-farm income in Mbogoini and although women's earned income is quite low (two and a half times smaller than the women's earned income in Mbogoini), their earned income constitutes 42 per cent of men's earned income and their total income 79 per cent of men's total income. Under these conditions, even women's low levels of income which are essential to family welfare constitute a considerable threat to male superiority. As a result of this threat posed by women's income, men are quite reluctant to allow their wives to make all agricultural decisions and to have control over income from export cash crops grown in the family plot even when the women are entirely responsible for the cultivation of these plots. In addition, women try to diminish the threat posed by their income to their husbands' sense of masculine superiority by giving the income to their husbands. In almost half of the cases 10 per cent of their income is given to their husbands in the form of cash or presents and 18 per cent of them give most or all of their money to their husbands while only 3 per cent of the women in Mbogoini turn their money to their husbands. In this context, it is not surprising to find that women who are not able to control economic resources on their own, greatly value children for their labour and financial contributions and do not engage in family planning (Safilios-Rothschild and Mburugu, forthcoming).

While all these research findings are quite consistent, data collected in one rural area of Ethiopia (among the Gurage) show that husbands' inability to be adequate breadwinners and their having to migrate for a few months a year in search of an additional income have undermined their authoritarian role in daily interactions with their wives and children. 'Women and children are relatively free to openly disagree with, and take independent positions from, the male head of household' (Kebede, 1978). The only clue to an explanation of these different trends is that the situation in which men are not adequate breadwinners has lasted for a long time. It seems, therefore, that when male breadwinning inadequacy becomes chronic and women become co-breadwinners on a permanent basis, men are no longer able to maintain their superior and authoritarian position vis-a-vis their wives. We do not know, however, what the 'turning' point is, in terms of duration of male breadwinning inadequacy that is necessary and sufficient, at which women are able to translate their economic contributions into power and autonomy.

The above findings have very important and clear-cut policy implications. First, they show that special projects for women aiming to increase women's access to income in areas in which men have a great difficulty in being adequate breadwinners cannot help improve the status of women. This is due to men's response to the threat presented by women's potential relative economic independence which is translated either in taking over promising women's project activities or by controlling women's income and by increasing their authority and control within the family. Second, they indicate that in order to improve the status of women, it is necessary to integrate women in large development projects that target equally men and women with respect to access to profitable skills training, credit and other services. Because of the threat that women's income presents when men are not secure as breadwinners and because men and women use their income according to different priorities, only development interventions that help increase both men's and women's income can be successful in alleviating poverty, improving the status of women, and increasing productivity as well as family welfare.

References

Burfisher, Mary E. and Nadine R. Horenstein (1985) *Sex Roles in the Nigerian Tiv Farm Household* (West Hartford: Kumarian Press).
Kebede, Hanna (1978) *Improving Village Water Supplies in Ethiopia: A Case-Study of Socio-Economic Implications* (Economic Commission for Africa, ECA/SDD/ATRCW).
McCormack, Jeanne, Martin Walsh and Candace Nelson (1986) 'Womens'

Group Enterprises: A Study of the Structure of Opportunity on the Kenya Coast' (Boston Massachusetts: World Education).

Safilios-Rothschild, Constantina (1982) 'Female Power, Autonomy and Demographic Change in the Third World', in R. Anker, M. Buvinic and N. Youssef (eds), *Women's Roles and Population Trends in the Third World* (London: ILO).

Safilios-Rothschild, Constantina (1988) 'Men's and Women's Incomes in Rural Honduras', in Daisy Dwyer and Judith Bruce (eds), *A Home Divided: Women and Income in the Third World* (Stanford University Press).

Safilios-Rothschild, Constantina and M. Dijkers (1978) 'Handling Unconventional Asymmetries', in Rhona and Robert N. Rapoport (eds), *Working Couples* (London: Routledge and Kegan Paul) pp. 62–73.

Safilios-Rothschild, Constantina and Edward K. Mburugu (forthcoming) *Men's and Women's Agricultural Production and Incomes in Rural Kenya* (New York: The Population Council).

Safilios-Rothschild, Constantina and Luis Mejia (forthcoming) *The Impact of Agrarian Reform on Men, Women and Children in Honduras* (New York: The Population Council).

Somjee, K.S. and Geeta Somjee (1978) 'Cooperative Dairying and the Profiles of Social Change in India', *Economic Development and Cultural Change*, vol. 26, pp. 577–90.

Sundar, Pushpa (1981) 'Khadgodhra: A Case Study of a Women's Milk Cooperative', *Social Action*, vol. 31, pp. 79–88.

9 Public Employment and Private Relations: Women and Work in India

Ursula Sharma

It is Friedrich Engels who is generally credited with having first proposed a causal connection between women's employment and their liberation. In the context of a discussion of women's inferior legal position he points out that this legal inequality is 'not the cause but the effect of economic oppression'. Economic subordination stems from the dependence of the wife on her husband's earnings and the privatisation of the services she renders in the household. 'Then it will be plain', Engels says, 'that the first condition for the liberation of the wife is to bring the whole female sex back into public industry, and that this in turn demands that the characteristic of the monogamous family as the economic unit of society be abolished' (Engels, 1972, pp. 137–8).

This has proved a most influential statement and the effects of mass entry into employment outside the home is a theme which has received much attention from the women's movement in the west and from feminist social scientists in particular. Indeed, the whole relationship between the 'public' and the 'private' spheres is a subject which continues to inspire feminist debate and controversy. Probably most would agree that the three-way connection Engels proposes between women's emancipation, women's employment outside the home and the social form of the family is a valid one in general terms, even if the widespread entry of women into the labour market in modern times has not brought about instant liberation. (Remember, however, that Engels only said that entry into public labour markets was the *first* condition for liberation, not that it was the *only* condition).

Social scientists conducting research in the Third World have been much more sceptical of the emancipatory potential of women's participation in public industry. Typically, working-class women in the Third World are absorbed into highly segregated labour markets

229

and allocated to low paid industrial and service tasks. Often little credit is given to the skills they possess and few opportunities are provided for them to learn new ones. The fact that in some Third World countries elite women are very visible in professions such as medicine, law and administration compared with their sisters in the west is highly encouraging but should not blind us to the fact that the reality of employment for most women is quite different. The low wages of working-class women ensure that they remain dependent on male wage earners in the household and that independent survival is precarious for a woman. Haleh Afshar, introducing a collection of studies of Third World women, points out that the position of women in the labour market has to be seen as an *effect* and not a cause of their subordinate position in general. 'Women are cheap, work hard and stay long; capital only reflects existing social relations in this respect' (Afshar, 1985, p. xiii). Should the kind of employment which most women are forced to accept perhaps be seen as a symptom of subordination rather than the herald of liberation?

Yet the very language of cause and effect may be inappropriate. In the South Asian context it is particularly difficult to separate and oppose the social relations of gender which women experience at work and in the home. There is a striking interpenetration of the public and the private; the high courtyard walls which bound the women's quarters turn out to be more permeable than we thought.

Such is the line of argument I would like to develop in this paper. However, it may be helpful to the reader who is not familiar with recent writing on women and work in South Asia if I first identify some dominant themes emerging from this literature which are relevant to the discussion in hand, especially those concerning North West India which is where my own research has been conducted.

INSIDERS AND OUTSIDERS: RESEARCH ON WOMEN IN SOUTH ASIA

The western interest in South Asian women's social position has been very largely informed by a perspective which (implicitly or explicitly) stresses the differences between Asian and western family forms and emphasises the effect of cultural norms of seclusion and segregation. Much (some might argue disproportionate) attention has been given to the purdah 'complex' — most marked and explicit among Muslims but found in Hindu communities also — which demands that women restrict their public visibility in the interests of maintaining the *izzat* (honour) of their families. *Izzat* is held to be especially vulnerable to women's sexual misdemeanours but can be tarnished by any immodest behaviour. Immodesty can be so defined as to include the performance of work which brings them into contact with unrelated men. (See Jacobson, 1970; Papanek and Minault, 1982; and Mandelbaum, 1988; for ethnographic accounts of purdah morality in India and Pakistan). Only in its extreme form (often associated with 'orthodox' interpretations of Islam) does this discretion mean veiling of the whole body or rigid seclusion, but even weaker forms may affect women's activities outside the home. Purdah is not equally strong in all parts of South Asia and there is some regional co-variation between the vigour of purdah morality and certain other phenomena, such as a strong preference for sons, high mortality rates for girl children and low female labour market participation (see Miller, 1981).

The very influential ideas of Ester Boserup have encouraged some scholars to make a firmer linkage between norms governing women's roles and the organisation of production. Boserup, it will be remembered, distinguished between the 'female' farming systems of sub-Saharan Africa and the 'male' farming systems of Eurasia, relating gender roles in production to agricultural technology and forms of land tenure and inheritance (Boserup, 1970). Goody and Tambiah develop a related line of argument with regard to South Asia but see seclusion and control over women as part of an institutional 'package' in which dowry, monogamy, status hierarchy and the form of inheritance which they call 'divergent devolution' are more important features than the organisation of farming as such. Women bring inherited property to their marriages in the form of dowry, but precisely because marriage involves the transfer of property, the sexual relations of women are subject to stringent control (Goody and Tambiah, 1973). This strand of research sees norms of seclusion as part of a culture that typically accompanies or is generated by a certain form of social structure and is less concerned with the experiential details of how norms of seclusion affect women in everyday life.

To South Asian researchers, the purdah 'complex', if such a thing exists, is no exotic cultural explicandum, simply the constant background to women's endeavours to improve their situation and contribute to public life. For them, Boserup's concern that women may be losing out to men in the course of 'economic development' has been a more urgent and practical issue than explaining purdah. Research on South Asian women conducted by South Asian scholars themselves has more frequently focused on problems such as how poor and low caste women manage to gain a livelihood (Gulati, 1981), how women can organise themselves to better their condition, how discrimination against women operates in the labour market. Some interesting studies have been carried out on particular economic or occupational groups of women, for instance that of Chitra Ghosh on construction workers (Ghosh, 1984) or Zarina Bhatty's work on *bidi* (cigarette) workers (Bhatty, 1980), Bina Agarwal's various studies of women in agriculture (for example Agarwal, 1984). Such studies emphasise the discrimination which women face in the labour market, their low wages and often insecure employment, their frequent economic marginalisation and underemployment. The implications of such conditions for policy is another major theme in the research of South Asian feminists. (Many of the papers in Raunaq Jahan and Hanna Papanek's collection treat this theme [see Jahan and Papanek, 1979]. Some western scholars, especially those who have adopted a Marxist or political economy approach, have shared this practical concern for the nature and organisation of women's work and employment [Mies, 1982; Omvedt, 1980; Arens and van Beurden, 1977]).

This is not to say that the feminists and activists who have developed this strand of research have ignored the effect of cultural constructs such as purdah and *izzat*; rather they do not adopt a problematic which presents them as something requiring *special* explanation or over-emphasises the cultural peculiarity of specifically South Asian notions of female respectability. In terms of methodology this more focused research had tended to concentrate on particular *economic* categories of women (poor women, occupational groups) using a variety of data collection techniques. Western scholars have more frequently (though not exclusively) been informed by the methodological predispositions of social anthropology. They have tended to study South Asian women as members of *local* or *cultural* communities (villages, urban quarters, caste groups) and have preferred ethnographic description to surveys. Sometimes, it has to be said, such field studies show little awareness of the dimension of historic change other than a general sense of the novel effect of 'modern influences', 'western education' or 'new opportunities for employment'.

These observations are intended only as the broadest characteris-

ation of recent research directions relevant to the theme of this
paper; there is no space for a more detailed review here. The
divergence of emphasis between western and South Asian scholars is
probably becoming less marked as the growth of an international
women's movement encourages scholarly conversation and the exchange of political ideas and experience between western and South
Asian feminists. One of the things this recent and 'convergent'
literature is revealing, I believe, is that if we take the strong division
between the public and the private sphere (acknowledged by both
western and South Asian scholars) and the cultural designation of
women to the private domestic sphere as our starting point for the
study of gender in South Asia, we are in danger of obscuring some
important linkages between the two. In practice it is very difficult, for
reasons I shall discuss, to define women's work participation outside
the home and their activities within the domestic sphere and then to
oppose them to each other as mutually interacting variables. I shall try to
demonstrate this, using recent literature on women in South Asia,
more especially North West India, the area with which I am most
familiar.

PUBLIC WORK AND PRIVATE WORK: PERMEABLE
BOUNDARIES

Let us take first of all the vexed question of the actual extent of
women's economic participation. India is said to be an area characterised by 'male' farming systems. Yet everywhere one travels, even
in those parts of North West India where women are supposedly most
constrained by purdah ideals, one sees women in the fields — women
weeding, women planting and sowing, women harvesting crops,
women manuring land and grazing cattle. In the towns, female
sweepers and maidservants can be seen going about their business in
any residential area and conspicuous in the week-day rush hour are
busloads of girls and young women travelling to school and college.
Whatever the norms may be, women are *not* publicly invisible in
many areas, though they may be absent from certain important
labour markets and there may be some public space effectively
defined as 'no go' areas for women. How can their public busyness be
squared with the low work participation rates (low that is when
compared with areas like South East Asia, North America) reported
for this region? (According to the 1981 Census of India, the national

female work participation rate, that is, the percentage of the adult female population in paid work or otherwise economically active as defined by the Census Office, was 14.4 per cent.)

Much has been made of the problems of defining economic participation in such a way as to enable the collection of relevant and comparable statistics. Census officers in India have wrestled with the difficulties of finding an operational definition of gainful work which is appropriate to the Indian situation, which allows for the enumeration of both waged employment and productive family labour, and permits comparisons between regions. Women's work may be under-reported by those family members responsible for answering census and other questionnaires. This may happen because women's work outside the home is regarded as shameful, something not to be admitted to, or just because (as in the case of much family labour) it is not *perceived* as work. And then there is the problem of disaggregating the various kinds of productive activities in which women may be engaged (labour on land owned or rented by the family, agricultural wage labour, skilled craft work in some artisan families, industrial outwork, as well as activities like processing dairy products for home use or the market). 'How they allocate their time among these activities depends on the situation of the whole household' and it may therefore be unrealistic to analyse the time allocation of an individual woman in isolation from the household pattern of time distribution (Jain, Singh and Chand 1979, p. 141. These authors provide a good discussion of many of the methodological problems involved in quantifying women's work participation). The assessment of female participation in rural labour markets is especially difficult when many women are marginal or seasonal workers. Quantifying their unpaid family work is even harder. And all the obstacles attending the quantification of women's work participation must equally complicate attempts to estimate the true extent of female unemployment.

I have noted that the under-reporting of women's work may be related to norms about the unsuitability of field labour or waged work for women of status, but this may also be related to the invisibility and unrecognised nature of family labour in general. In one rural area where I worked, my attempts to get some idea of work patterns of men and women were confused by the tendency of villagers to state that such and such a person (either male or female) 'does not work but stays at home', meaning that the person in question was not employed by anyone, but worked on their own land and not someone else's (Sharma, 1980, p. 123). In such a case, the distinction which is crucial for the researcher is whether or not the person is engaged in productive activity, while for the villager it may be whether that productive activity takes place in relation to one's own land or that of non-kin.

To some extent of course these problems attend attempts to gauge work patterns in any society where the self-provisioning peasant household has been a recent reality. But in North India we have to take into account an ideology which gives considerable moral force to the division between those who are and those who are not kin to each other. In Punjabi the term for non-kin is *opra* which carries a far stronger moral meaning than the merely negative 'non-kin'. In practice, the boundaries between kin and non-kin are not so easily drawn as this cultural vocabulary suggests; between 'kin' and 'strangers' there are distant kin and fictive kin — honorary aunties and brothers. However where women's work is concerned, the same services performed for kin and non-kin may have to be quite differently evaluated. Nursing, for instance used to be (and in many parts of India still is) regarded as a demeaning profession for women because it requires them to clean up the blood and faeces of strangers and to perform intimate services for unrelated men. A woman might however be expected to do the same work for her own children or other household members as a matter of duty and without censure.

A further distinction which is important to women themselves is that which they make between work inside or near the house and work outside the house or in the fields. The former category includes cooking, milking cows, processing dairy products, child care, cleaning the house, washing clothes, etc. The latter includes weeding, harvesting, sowing and other agricultural jobs carried out in the fields themselves, also collecting cowdung or sticks for fuel and marketing produce. (See Sharma, 1980, p. 131; Behal, 1984). This distinction does not correspond very precisely to the kind of division western researchers would conventionally make between housework and other kinds of (productive) work. The distinction between inside work and outside work did have normative force for the Punjabi women I knew; work in the fields was held to be more demeaning for women, to be avoided if the household could afford to pay others to do it, whereas work in the house was a normal and honourable activity for a woman; she might like to pay a servant to cook or tend cattle if she could afford to but no one would think ill of her if she was seen doing these tasks herself.

We may, if we choose, see this distinction as an example of purdah norms in operation. Outside work is certainly more visible to the neighbours and the world at large. But women who shun outside work are nevertheless seen in public. The landowner's wives in the Punjab village I studied in 1977 would avoid certain 'male' areas of the village and the nearby town and would avoid being seen gossiping or idling in public (see Sharma, 1980a for a fuller discussion of purdah and the use of public space). However it could hardly be said that their social lives were restricted solely to the house and its courtyard; they would not eschew visits to neighbours and kin, rituals in the houses of friends, religious meetings or other kinds of purposeful outing. Studies of women who claim to observe purdah quite strictly also indicate that it does not by any means equal social isolation from neighbours (for example, Wiser and Wiser, 1963, p. 73).

The purpose of this discussion is not to engage in cultural quibbling or argue niceties about the genuine meaning of 'work', nor simply to reiterate the anthropological truism that different cultures define work variously. What I want to show is that if we take into account the meanings which Indian women give to their own activities and the spatial and conceptual boundaries which are important to them, then the distinction between the public and the private spheres starts to appear rather fuzzy. So far we have referred to the following distinctions (and interstitial categories) which have moral and practical relevance to evaluations of women's work;

own kin	(fictive kin)	non-kin
inside work,		outside work
family labour	(work performed for kin outside the household)	employment by others
domestic space	(space near the house)	public space, such as the bazaar

These do not yield a congruent and tidy division of activities. One may work for others inside domestic space, invisible to the public gaze (as a servant or children's nursemaid, for instance). To help one's own kin by 'lending' them one's labour or attending their rituals may involve excursions into public space. A woman who works on her family's land may be publicly visible as she does so, cutting crops beside the road or carrying straw through the village high street. In India, and probably in other areas of South Asia also, the frontiers of the 'public' and the 'private' spheres are not so self-evident as might appear at first. The assumptions behind Engels's proclamation therefore may be difficult to apply in this area, an idea which I shall explore further in the next section.

As far as purdah norms are concerned it is clear from this brief review, that they are morally operative and do inform women's activities or at least the ways in which they evaluate their own and other women's activities. But they do not operate in a rigidly predictable way. They may certainly inhibit certain kinds of work participation on the part of women, but only exceptionally do they really render women totally inactive or invisible in public.

Sarah White, writing of a village in Bangladesh, an area in which norms of seclusion and public invisibility may be said to be as stringent as in any part of South Asia, recounts a telling incident. The well in front of the house of Hasan Mullah, a prosperous peasant, had dried up and his womenfolk were obliged to walk to the hand pump in front of another house, 150 metres away. The women asked Hasan Mullah to install a tube well since, as his daughter-in-law affirmed 'Bear in mind, we don't go out much, or see people. And then we were having to go out all the time and see people. We really didn't like it. We feel if we can stay in the house, *that* is good' (White, 1988, p. 354). White concludes that the 'conventional phrasing made acceptable an appeal for expenditure to her economical but religiously strict father-in-law. Rather than bowing to the ideology, she was making it work for her'. To me, this (and other instances which could be multiplied from the ethnography of purdah regions) do not deny the force of purdah morality. But they do indicate that the work women do is, in practice, the result of an interaction between household need, personal inclination and perceived public morality which is negotiated by household members, and that (as White shows) women are far from passive in this negotiation.

THE EFFECTS OF CAPITALISM: PUBLIC INDUSTRY CO-OPTS PRIVATE RELATIONSHIPS

So far I have discussed the interpenetration of the public and the private spheres evident through women's systems of moral classification. But it is also evident in the structure of economic production. Engels opposes the household to the world of 'public' industry, but the kind of industry he had in mind was 'modern large-scale industry'. Yet if capitalism was set to dissolve all traditional kin ties through turning all things into commodities, turning marriage into loveless prostitution so far as women were concerned, both he and Marx were in practice well aware that in its early forms, capitalism re-affirms, even exploits existing family relationships, to the great advantage of capital. Proto-industrial production in Britain took the form of domestic industry in which women and children worked alongside men in their own homes, selling to agents which linked them with a wider market. In the extraction industries, the early organisation of mining often took the form of contracts offered to individual men, or to groups of men based on neighbourhood or kinship, to mine a certain area or extract a certain quantity of ore/slate/coal. The contractor owned his own equipment, absorbed most of the risk involved and was responsible for his own safety. Capitalist industry in Britain still exploits kin structures and pre-existing social relationships today where individuals are encouraged to recruit workers from among their own family or acquaintances. In the pottery industry in Staffordshire, for instance, mothers still 'speak for' their daughters or sisters, that is obtain jobs for them in the factories where they work themselves.

I cite these examples to demonstrate that whilst, as many historians have rightly stressed, capitalism did in the end effect the most stringent separation of the (private) home and the (public) work-place, it has equally been capable of actually co-opting the kin relationships of the domestic sphere. The boundary between the private household and public industry then becomes blurred, es-pecially so far as individual women workers are concerned. Some of these organisational forms are still to be found in advanced capitalist countries. Outwork in particular, appears not to be an evanescent form, but one which enables maximum exploitation in conditions of labour surplus (see various contributions to Redclift and Mingione, 1984).

This blurring or running together of the public and the private spheres is equally characteristic of the organisation of many forms of work where capitalist relations of production have established them-selves in South Asia. In the area of Punjab I worked in, it was not uncommon for low caste women labourers to be members of contract gangs, hired to do a particular task, especially harvesting. These gangs were usually kin groups and the pay for the group was handed to the leader, invariably a senior male. The relationship of women and children to the labour market was thus indirect, mediated by relationships of dependence and subordination to husbands or other male kin. Domestic relations and public employment are in such a case not separate and opposable categories.

Outwork and domestic handicraft production is a form of work on which many women in South Asia depend and in which this blurring of the public and private is particularly evident. Maria Mies's description of the lace-making industry of Narsapur provides an excellent example. Women from the poorest agricultural classes in Narsapur (mainly untouchables and Christians) manufacture lace in their homes to designs ordered and collected by middlemen who sell to the export market. The agents are usually male, but are not generally the lace producers' husbands; the latter are mainly 'small farmers or agricultural labourers who lost their land and have no work' (Mies, 1982, p. 113). However, working inside their homes the female lace makers are *invisible* as workers. They appear as housewives, using their 'leisure time' profitably to help maintain their families. Making lace does indeed take place alongside a multitude of other domestic activities, yet a woman may spend six or seven hours a day on this work and her family may depend heavily on her earnings. The appeal of lace making to women is that it is an income generating activity which nonetheless permits this illusion of the respectable life of the housewife to pauperised women. Incidentally, Mies attributes the ideological dominance of the model of the home-based housewife as much to foreign missionary influence as to indigenous concepts of family honour (Mies, 1982, p. 33).

If we turn from the organisation of production and labour markets to commodity markets, we see the same entanglement of public and private relationships so far as women are concerned. A few lace makers also become agents, but the market in finished lace is characteristically dominated by men. In Punjab I noted (Sharma, 1980a, p. 235) that it was possible for a mature widow to supervise the cultivation of her own land but that where the marketing of her produce or banking of the proceeds were concerned she was heavily dependent on her sons. This particular widow was excluded for reasons of propriety — she did not think the *mandi* (wholesale market) was a place where women should be seen. Even if this were not the case many women from farming households would be excluded by reason of inferior education and illiteracy from conducting major commercial and legal transactions independently. Women who rear and tend cattle depend on male kin to negotiate sales for them unless these can be arranged in the immediate vicinity of their own village. As Sarah White reminds us, it is important to bear in mind the many local markets in which women are *not* dependent on their menfolk to negotiate deals; intra-village money lending and petty businesses are carried out by women for and among women even in areas like Bangladesh where Islamic ideals of seclusion have considerable force. Also, of course, personal relationships sometimes play an important part in the market transactions of men. Yet it is still true to say that personal linkage affects remuneration more in female markets for labour and petty goods than is the case in male markets (White, 1988, p. 305; Abdullah and Zeidenstein, 1982, pp. 45ff.).

WOMEN'S WAGED WORK AND THE HOUSEHOLD

In India, women are at present more likely than men to work in an environment where contractual and personal obligations are difficult to disentangle; the private sphere of kinship and personal commitment is impossible to separate from the public sphere of the market. It is difficult to say whether we should see this situation as symptomatic of a certain phase in the expansion of capitalism in the South Asian area or as likely to become a permanent feature of economic relations. It is even harder to say whether this situation is better or worse for women than a more impersonal and unmediated form of proletarianisation. In advanced capitalist countries where kin and contract are relatively distinct spheres, labour markets tend to remain highly segregated along gender lines and women's wages tend to lag well behind those of men; women's economic independence from men is far from assured. What we can certainly assert is that when women still depend on their kin to negotiate employment or other economic transactions outside the household on their behalf, then we cannot treat employment outside the home and family relations inside it as totally separate factors where women are concerned. The public and the private, the industrial and the familial are inextricably tangled and Engels's proposition, though by no means irrelevant, is difficult to test.

But what can we say of the situation where women obtain waged employment in well organised and fairly impersonal labour markets? What of the increasing numbers of (mainly urban) women in white collar work, the professions, government service and the formal industrial sector? Does employment have an effect on the influence of these women in their households, or increase their personal autonomy?

I do not think that this question can ever really be answered definitively; it is difficult to think of ways of measuring autonomy or status accurately and so as to be applicable to women of all classes. For a working class woman, to be able to withdraw from waged work, to be no longer under the supervision of unrelated strangers, no longer to have to expose herself to the male gaze in public places as she travels the crowded urban commuter routes to work may be the chief freedom she desires. For another woman of the same class the same waged work may enable her to envisage the end of dependence on a cruel or tight-fisted husband or a lazy son for her very food and clothing, and the possibility of building some kind of security for herself. For an educated middle-class daughter, obtaining professional work might encourage her to claim a greater voice in her own future or obtain for her a better choice of husband. Equally, waged employment for a daughter could mean having to take up tedious office work so as to provide for younger siblings on the death or retirement of her father while her friends and contemporaries are enjoying the last delights of girlhood before marriage. (See Sharma, 1985, for a discussion of the implications of the employment of unmarried women in an urban area).

One strand of research in India suggests that women's waged work does not in itself increase their autonomy, if by this we mean their power to act independently of other members of the household (especially in the disposal of their own wages). Hilary Standing's work on working women in Calcutta suggests that the situation is very complicated. Some women have very little claim to their own wages, being expected to yield them to the control of the husband or mother-in-law. Gender, age and generation may be as important in determining an individual household member's say in the disposal of funds as employment or lack of employment. On the other hand, where earning members of the household contribute to a common fund from which household expenses are drawn, this fund is very likely to be managed by a senior woman (Standing, 1985, p. 37). My own research in Shimla suggests similar conclusions. Of fifty-nine women in the sample who were living in a household with at least one male wage earner, only nine (mostly economically inactive) said that they played no part in the management of family moneys or property.

On the other hand, *management* is not the same as autonomous *control*, and a woman who manages the payment of bills, banking of savings and shopping for provisions, usually does so with reference to the views of her husband or other senior members of the household. Yet women did appear to be well-informed about their families' resources (apart from the wives of a few traders who claimed to know little about their husbands' property or profits). In a city like Shimla, where most men are employed in government departments with known pay scales, secrecy about wages is not easy to maintain. Women's employment outside the home further increases their opportunity to become knowledgeable about wages and 'it would be hard therefore for husbands to throw a veil of mystery around the family finances in order to exercise control over their wives' (Sharma, 1986, p. 101).

This all suggests that it is difficult to trace a direct causal link between women's waged work and their personal autonomy as there are so many other factors which may determine the say which an individual woman has in household decision making. It may be, of course, that in posing the problem in terms of personal autonomy we are asking a question that is not very relevant in the Indian context. If neither men nor women are expected to operate as though they had distinct and individual interests separate from those of the household and if household survival generally presupposes a high degree of financial and practical co-operation among its members, then perhaps we must formulate the problem differently. Instead of asking whether wages permit personal emancipation we should perhaps ask how they alter the nature of the individual's commitment to the household. Waged work could allow a young husband to establish a household separate from that of his parents. For a young wife, waged work might mean first and foremost an increased burden of work, given that women's employment is seldom accompanied by any increase in the amount of housework and child care done by husbands. A woman's employment may give her a greater say in or familiarity with the management of household finances, but she may well see this in terms of extra work and demands on her time rather than as an opportunity for greater power or discretion for herself as an individual.

What seems fairly clear from both Standing's findings and my own is that a woman's relationship to her own earnings is not the same as that of a man, irrespective of social class. As in Europe we find a public ideology which proposes that only men are really 'breadwinners' whilst women work to 'supplement' the family budget or as a desperate measure when their menfolk die, fall sick or are unemployed. This ideology need not, of course, preclude a quite positive evaluation of certain prestigious occupations for women, such as teaching or medicine. What it does imply is that women do not have a *right* to claim a place in the labour market. At the level of the domestic, this goes with the private reality that women do not feel free to spend their earnings on themselves even when household circumstances are relatively comfortable. A woman's relationship to her own wage is typically different from that of a man. More than ever can be said of men, women work 'for their families' and not 'for themselves'.

In this respect they only resemble women in industrialised countries (see, for instance, Pauline Hunt's account of gender and the household in a British town. Hunt, 1980). But the precise degree to which women experience this moral appropriation of their wages depends to some extent on the cultural environment in which the household finds itself and the kind of reference household members make to this environment. Bhachu's paper on Asian women working in Britain, for instance, suggests that some younger women are able to renegotiate matters such as the division of housework with their husbands as a result of their wage earning role (Westwood and Bhachu, 1988, p. 96). A study of Cypriot women in the same volume also indicates that women migrants from a culture which stressed the dishonour of women's work outside the home were nonetheless able to obtain more personal autonomy as a result of waged work when situated in 'a society which can accept them as independent beings' (Josephides, 1988, p. 55). Warrier (1988, p. 147) and Westwood (1988, p. 126), however, having studied Gujerati women in Britain, both conclude that waged work does not give migrant women any greater autonomy; it may even be seen simply as a multiplication of her burdens in terms of work and responsibility.

The entry of an Indian woman into the labour market does more than simply introduce another wage into the household, although this may well be the prime motivation for her to go out to work. It may increase her dependence on others (on mother-in-law or sister-in-law to mind her children, on husband or other male kin to accompany her there or help her find a suitable job). It will almost certainly increase her total workload since it is unlikely that much of the housework she formerly did will be done by others. She will retain a great deal of responsibility for the health, education and welfare of her children even if other relatives take responsibility for their immediate supervision while she is out. The proportion of household income represented by her personal earnings may be great or small — though usually it will be small in relation to the earnings of her husband or other males in the household. The work she does outside the home may be esteemed in terms of the dominant culture (if she is a lawyer or a hospital consultant) or may represent the ultimate degradation (if she is a sweeper or maidservant). The household is not a bounded and discrete microcosm, although it may appear so. A woman's status in the household is not divorced from the status of the work she does outside it.

These issues should not however distract our attention from the problem which, as Indian feminists have constantly reminded us, is urgent — namely, how to increase employment opportunities for women. Many households depend heavily, some solely, on women's earnings. Women may remain dependent on men because of their low earning capacity, but this assymetry does not do away with the fact that poor households still rely on the earnings of female members for survival. At the bottom end of the class system, where women do not really regard themselves as having any kind of cultural choice as to whether to work or not, the availability of work to them can make the difference as to whether their children starve or survive. Even in the higher reaches of the system women's earnings can make a substantial difference to the economic fate of the household. In my own study of a very mixed group of urban women, the modal percentage of household income represented by the employed respondent's earnings was 40–49 per cent. In female headed households, the respondents' earnings never represented less than 50 per cent of the total household income (Sharma, 1986, pp. 122ff.) In some landless rural households, the earnings of women may typically represent a *higher* percentage of the total household income than those of men (Mencher and Saradamoni, 1982). At any class level, women's earnings are seldom marginal to the family budget. Whatever the consequences of waged work to individual women and however it may be evaluated by either sex, it is generally crucial to the welfare, even survival, of their households.

References

Abdullah, Tahrunnessa A. and Sondra A. Zeidenstein (1982) *Village Women of Bangla Desh. Prospects for Change* (Oxford: Pergamon Press).
Afshar, Haleh (ed.) (1985) *Women, Work and Ideology in the Third World* (London: Tavistock).
Agarwal, Bina (1984) 'Rural Women and High Yielding Variety Rice Technology', *Economic and Political Weekly* 19, 13, pp. 39–51.

Arens, Jenneke and Jos Van Beurden (1977) *Jhagrapur. Poor Peasants and Women in a Village in Bangla Desh* (Amsterdam: Arens and Van Beurden).

Behal, Monisha (1984) 'Within the outside, the courtyard — glimpses into women's perceptions', *Economic and Political Weekly* 19, 41, pp. 1775–77.

Bhatty, Zarina (1980) *Economic Role and Status of Women in the Beedi Industry in Allahabad* (Geneva: ILO).

Boserup, Ester (1970) *Woman's Role in Economic Development* (London: Allen and Unwin).

Engels, F. (1972) *The Origin of the Family, Private Property and the State* (with an introduction and notes by Eleanor Burke Leacock) (London: Lawrence and Wishart).

Ghosh, Chitra (1984) 'Construction Workers', in J. Lebra, J. Paulson and J. Everett (eds), *Women and Work in India. Continuity and Change* (New Delhi: Promilla) pp. 201–11.

Goody, Jack and S. Tambiah (1973) *Bridewealth and Dowry* (Cambridge University Press).

Gulati, Leela (1981) *Profiles in Female Poverty* (Delhi: Hindustan).

Hunt, Pauline (1980) *Gender and Class Consciousness* (London: Macmillan).

Jacobson, Doranne (1970) 'Hidden Faces: Hindu and Muslim Purdah in a Central Indian Village', PhD dissertation for the University of Columbia.

Jahan, Raunaq and Hanna Papanek (eds) (1979) *Women and Development. Perspectives from South and South East Asia* (Dhaka: Bangla Desh Institute of Law and International Affairs).

Jain, D. Singh, Nalini, and Chand, Malini (1977) 'Women's Work: Methodological Issues', in Jahan and Papanek, 1979, pp. 128–70.

Josephides, Sasha (1988) 'Honour, Family and Work: Greek Cypriot Women before and after Migration', in Westwood and Bhachu, 1988, pp. 34–57.

Mandelbaum, David (1988) *Women's Seclusion and Men's Honor. Sex Roles in North India* (Tucson: University of Arizona Press).

Mencher, Joan and K. Saradamoni (1982) 'Muddy Feet and Dirty Hands: Rice Production and Female Agricultural Labour', *Economic and Political Weekly* 17, 52, pp. 149–69.

Mies, Maria (1982) *The Lace Makers of Narsapur. Indian Housewives Produce for the World Market* (London: Zed Press).

Miller, Barbara (1981) *The Endangered Sex. Neglect of Female Children in Rural Northern India* (Ithaca and London: Cornell University Press).

Omvedt, Gail (1980) *We Will Smash this Prison* (London: Zed Press).

Papanek, Hanna and Gail Minault (eds) (1982), *Separate Worlds: Studies of Purdah in South Asia* (Delhi: Chanakya Publications).

Redclift, Nanneke and Enzo Mingione (eds) (1984) *Beyond Employment. Household, Gender and Subsistence* (Oxford: Blackwell).

Sharma, Ursula (1980) *Women, Work and Property in North West India* (London: Tavistock).

—— (1980a) 'Purdah and Public Space', in Alfred de Souza (ed.), *Women in Contemporary India and South Asia* (Delhi: Manohar), pp. 213–39.

—— (1985) 'Unmarried Women and the Household Economy. A Research

Note', *Journal of Social Sciences* (Dhaka) no. 30, pp. 1–12.
—— (1986) *Women's Work, Class and the Urban Household. A Study of Shimla, North India* (London: Tavistock).
Standing, Hilary (1985) 'Women's Employment and the Household', *Economic and Political Weekly* 20, 17, pp. 23–38.
Warrier, Shrikala (1988) 'Marriage, Maternity and Female Economic Activity; Gujerati Women in Britain', in Westwood and Bhachu, 1988, pp. 132–52.
Westwood, Sallie (1988) 'Workers and Wives. Continuities and Discontinuities in the lives of Gujerati Women', in Westwood and Bhachu, 1988, pp. 103–31.
Westwood, Sallie and Parminder Bhachu (eds) (1988) *Enterprising Women. Ethnicity, Economy and Gender Relations* (London and New York: Routledge).
White, Sarah (1988) 'In the Teeth of the Crocodile. Class and Gender in Rural Bangla Desh', dissertation for the University of Bath.
Wiser, William and Wiser, Charlotte (1963) *Behind Mud Walls, 1930–60* (Berkeley and Los Angeles: University of California Press).

Index